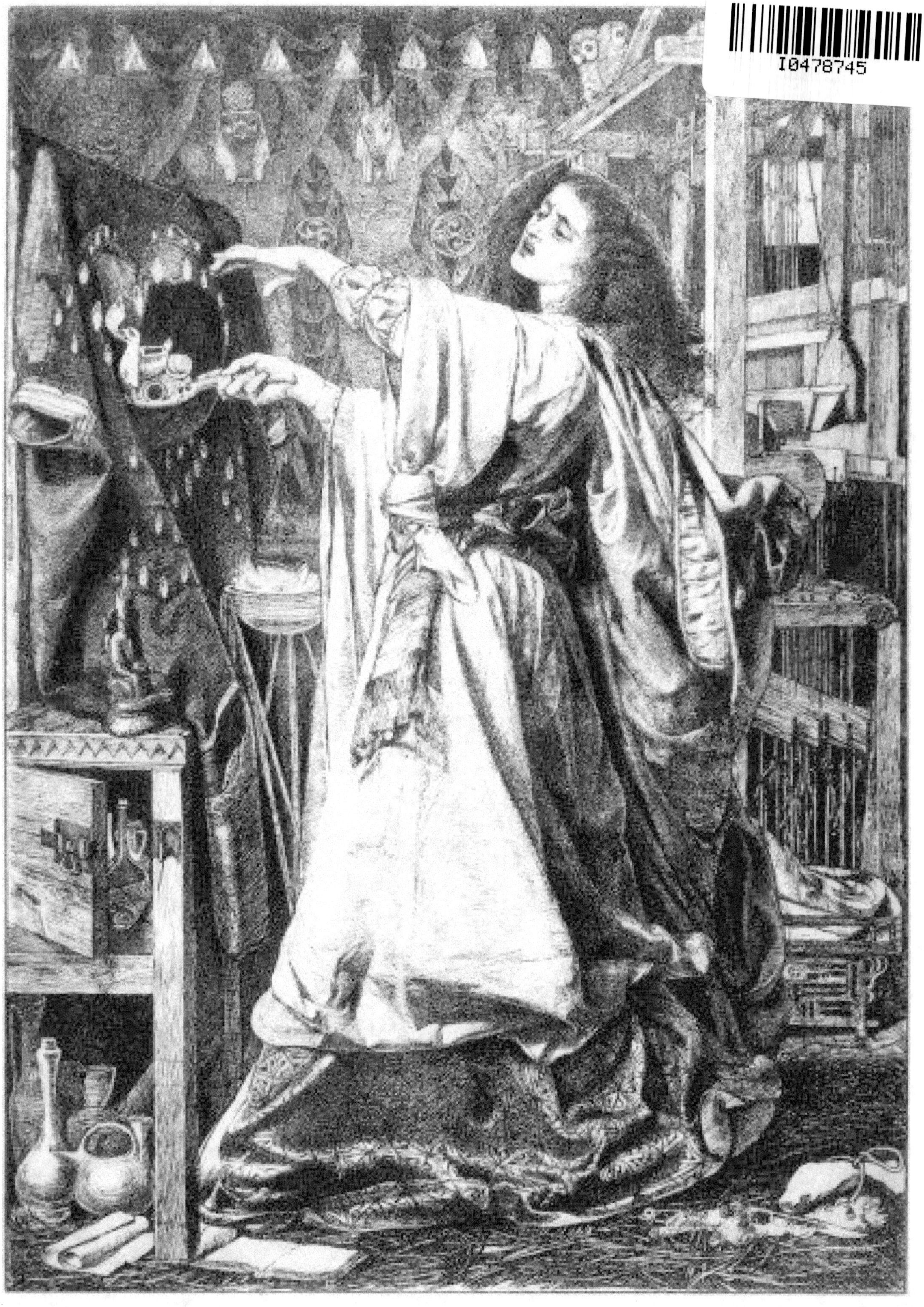

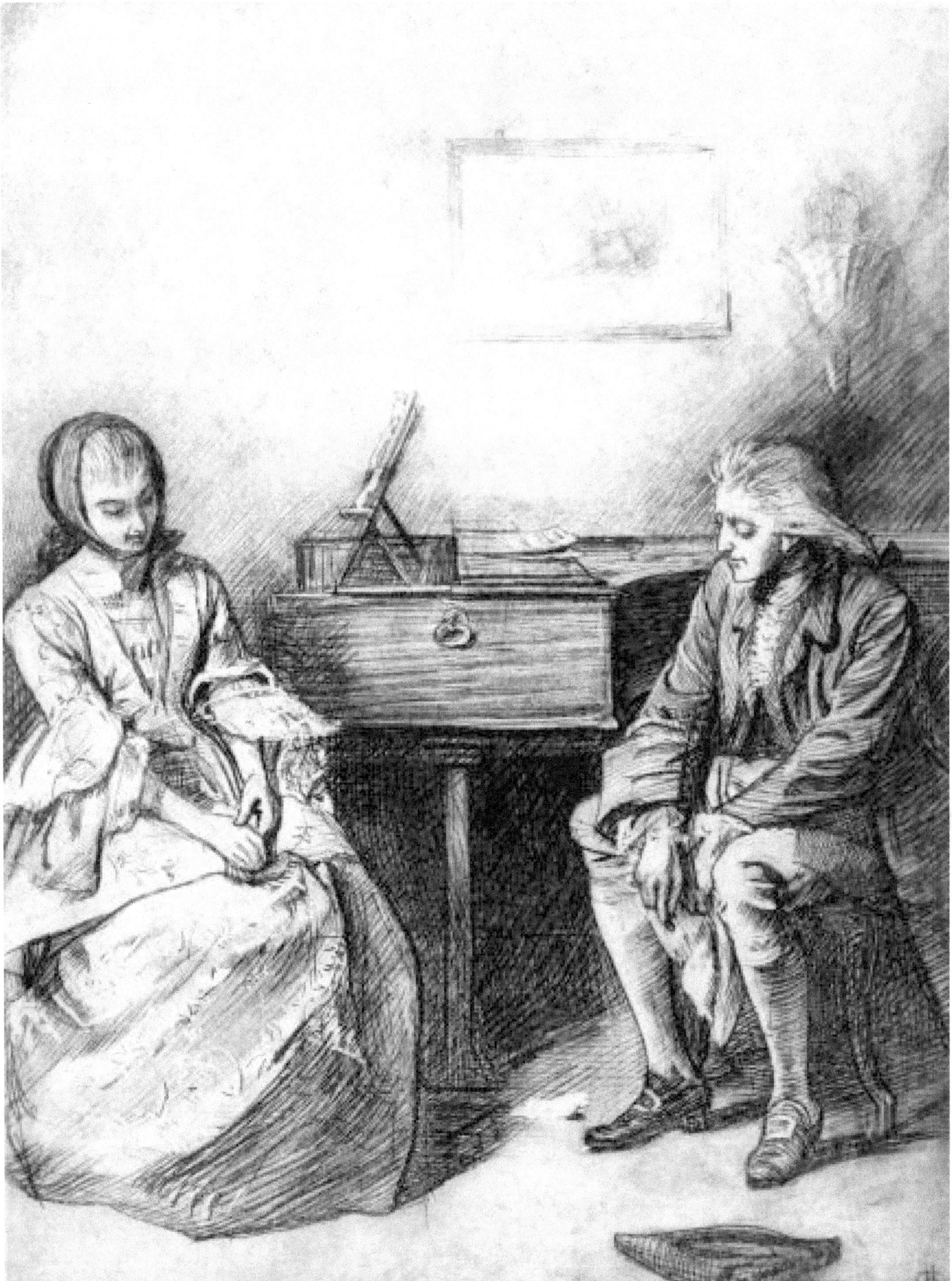

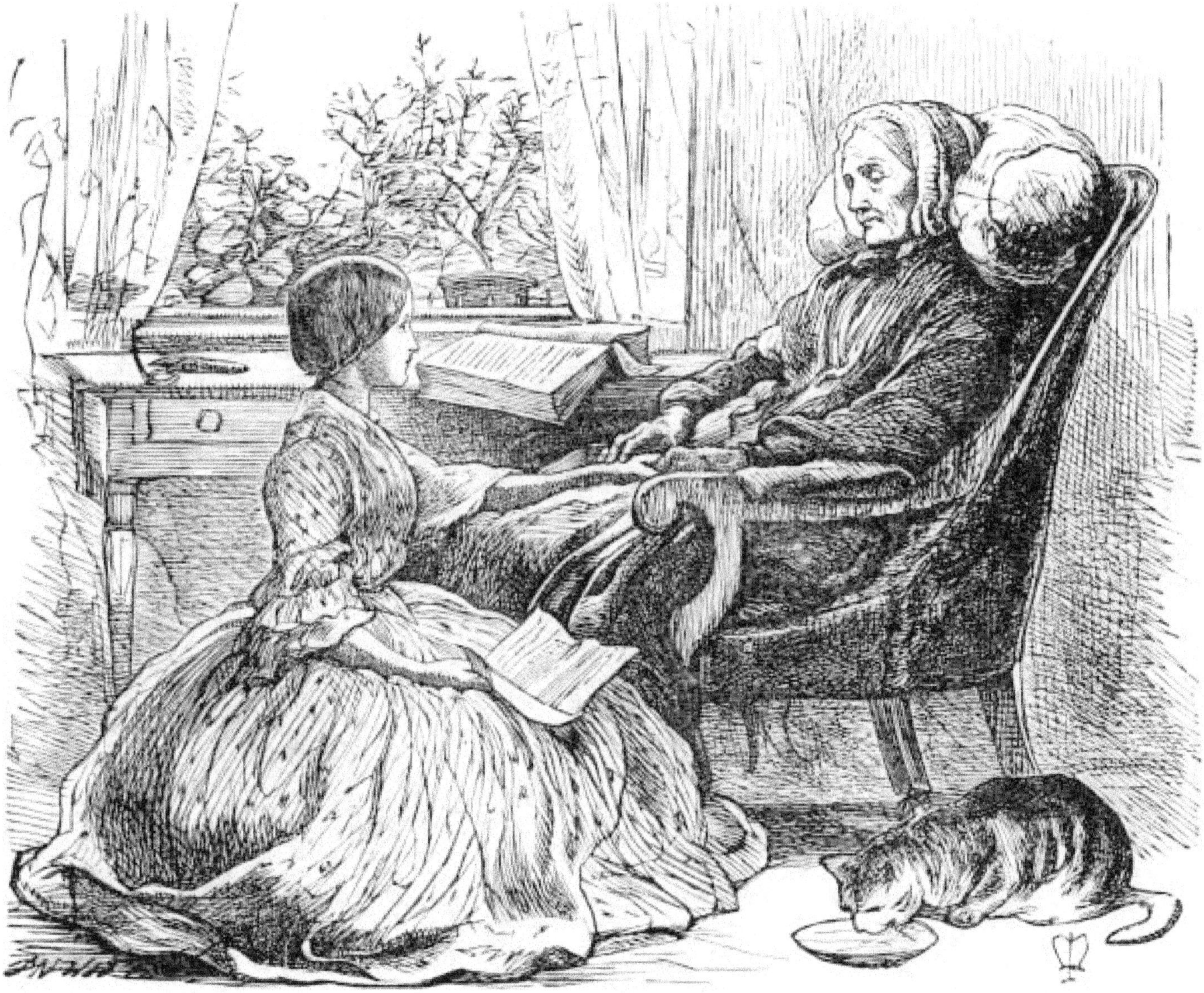

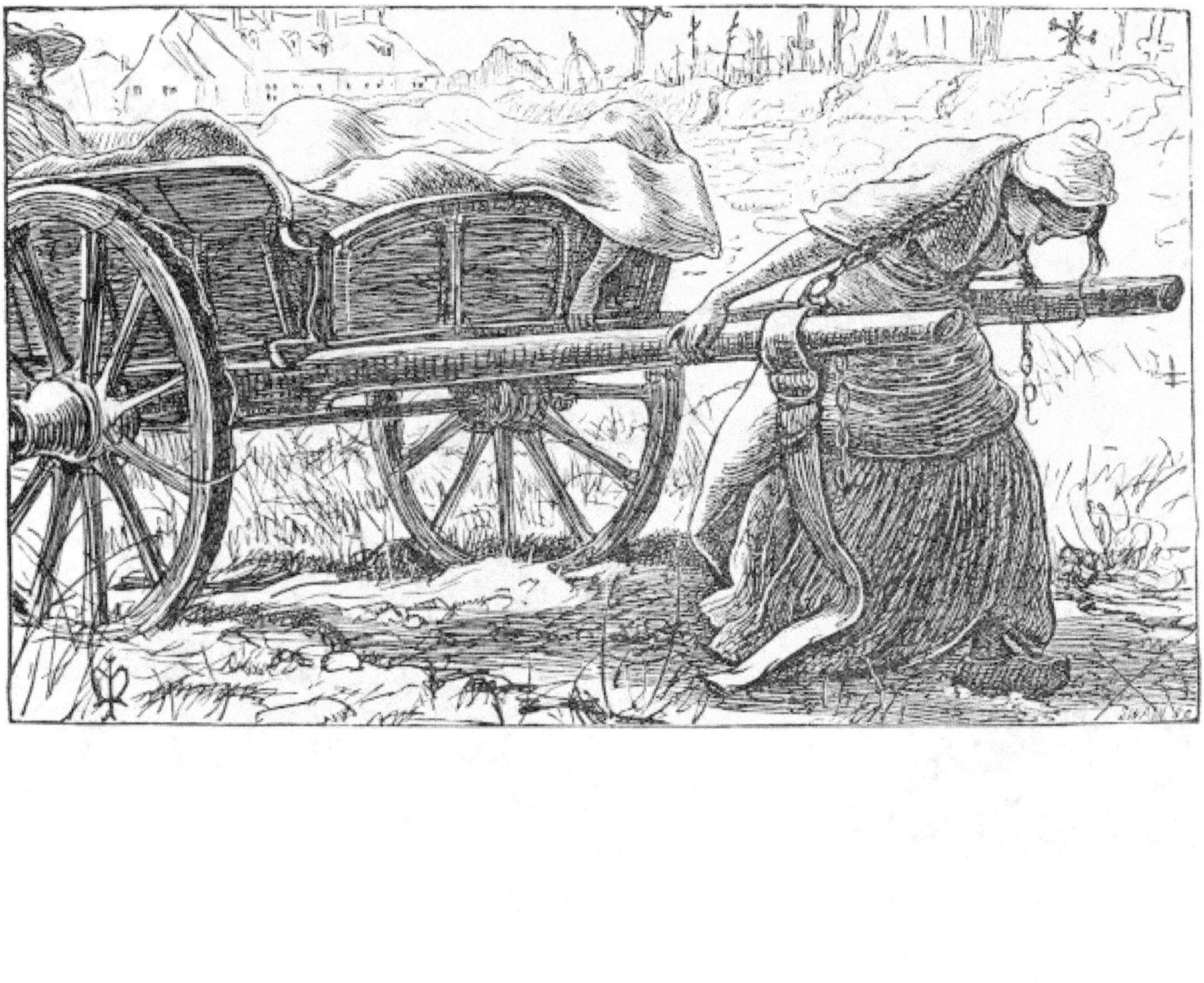

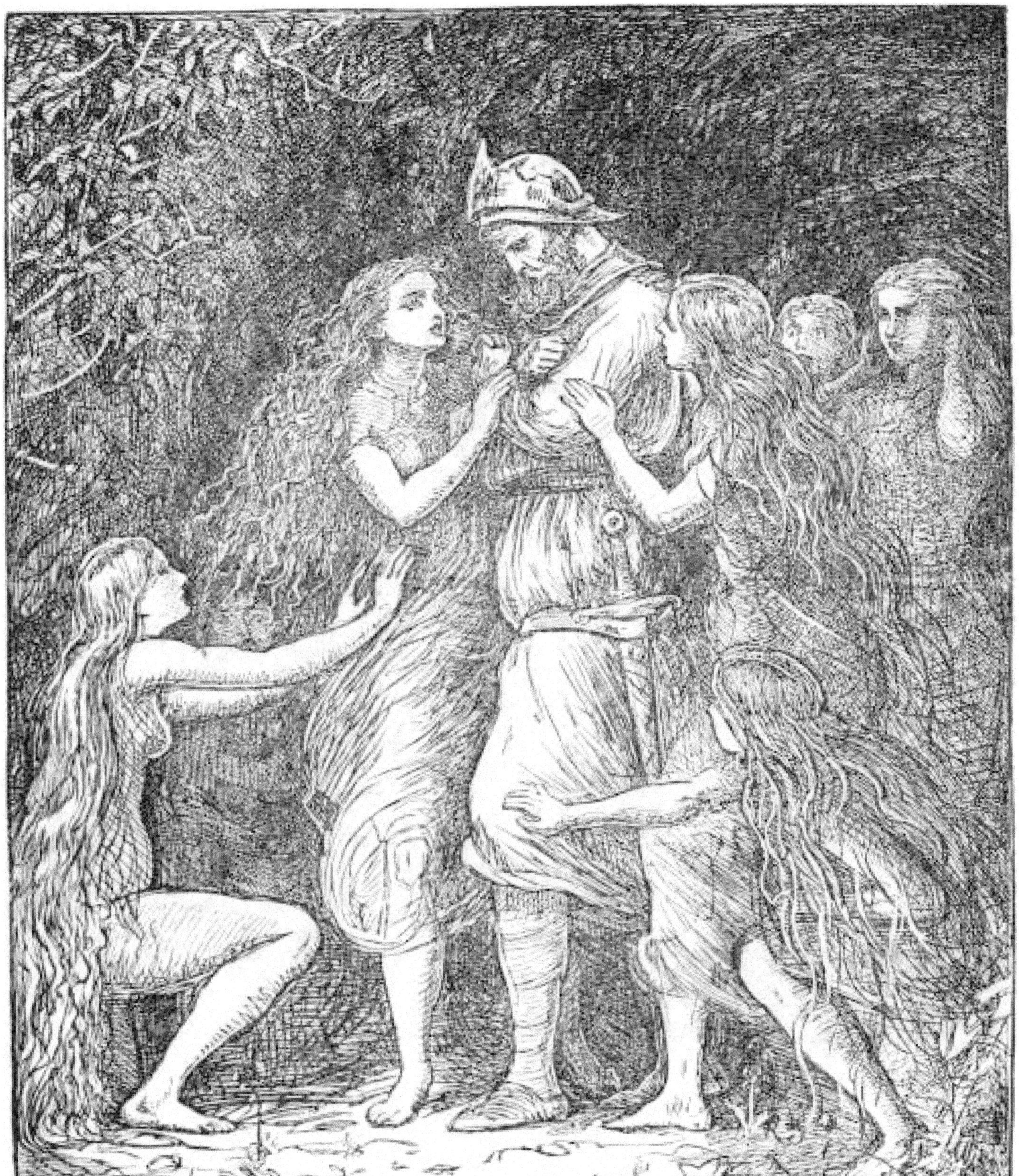

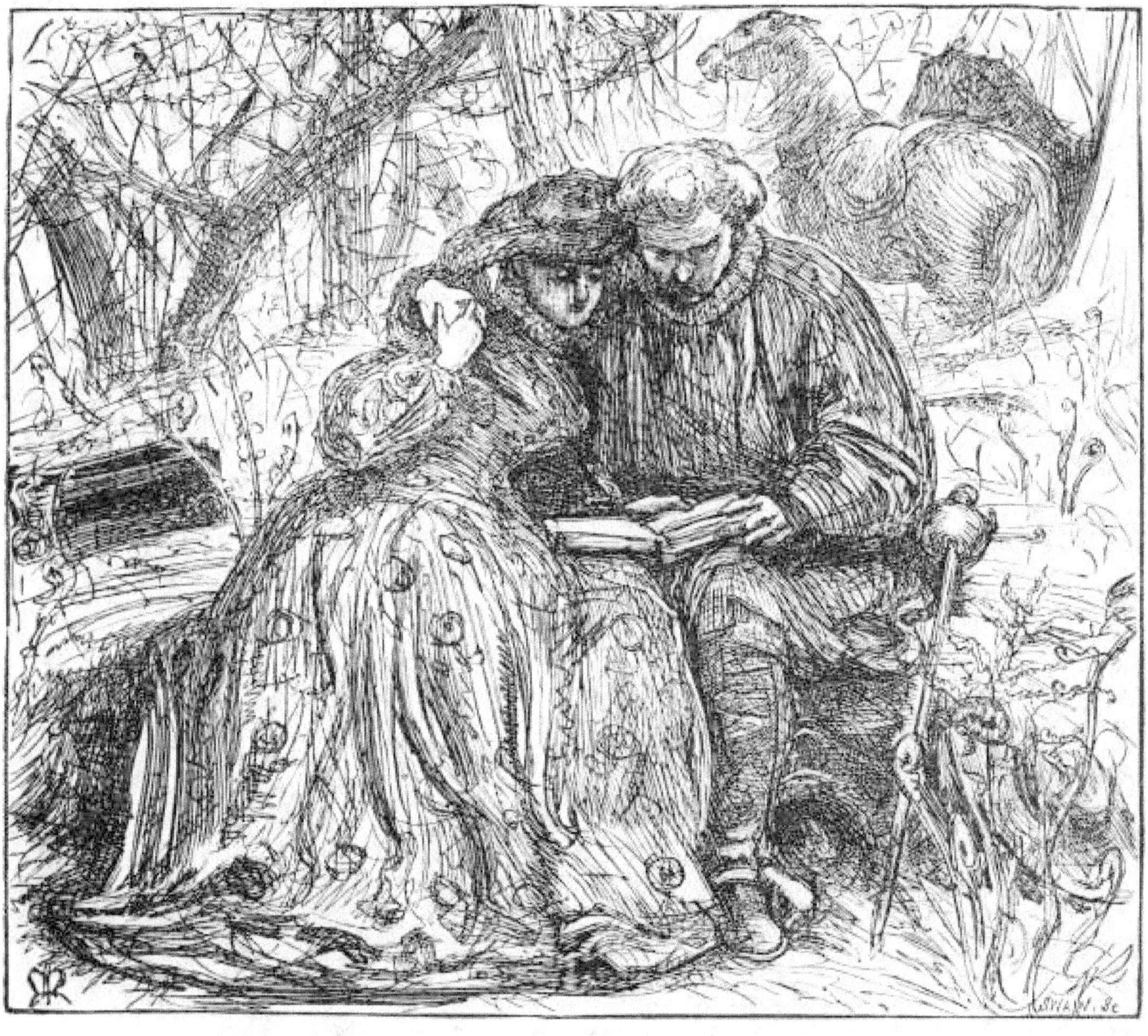

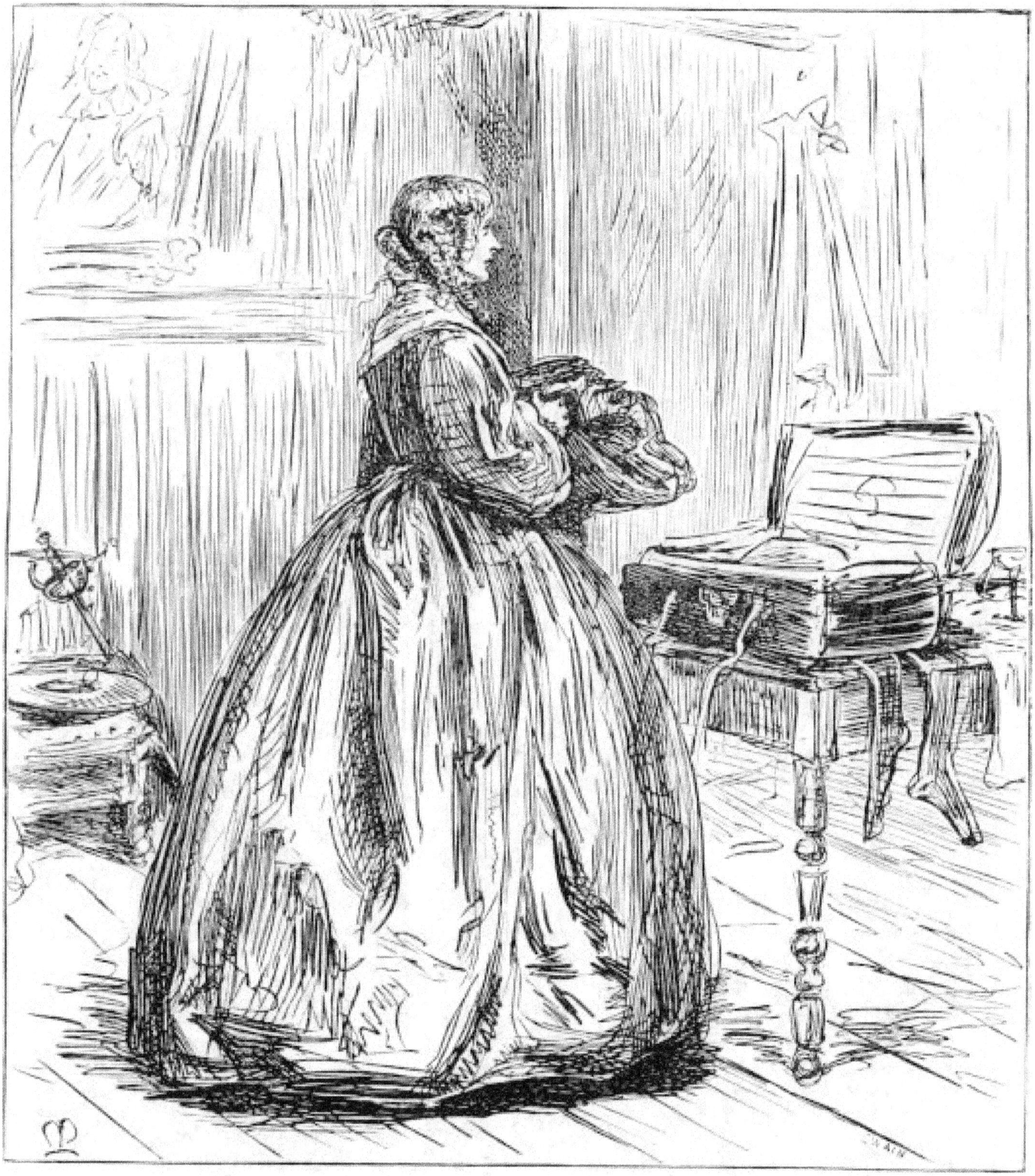

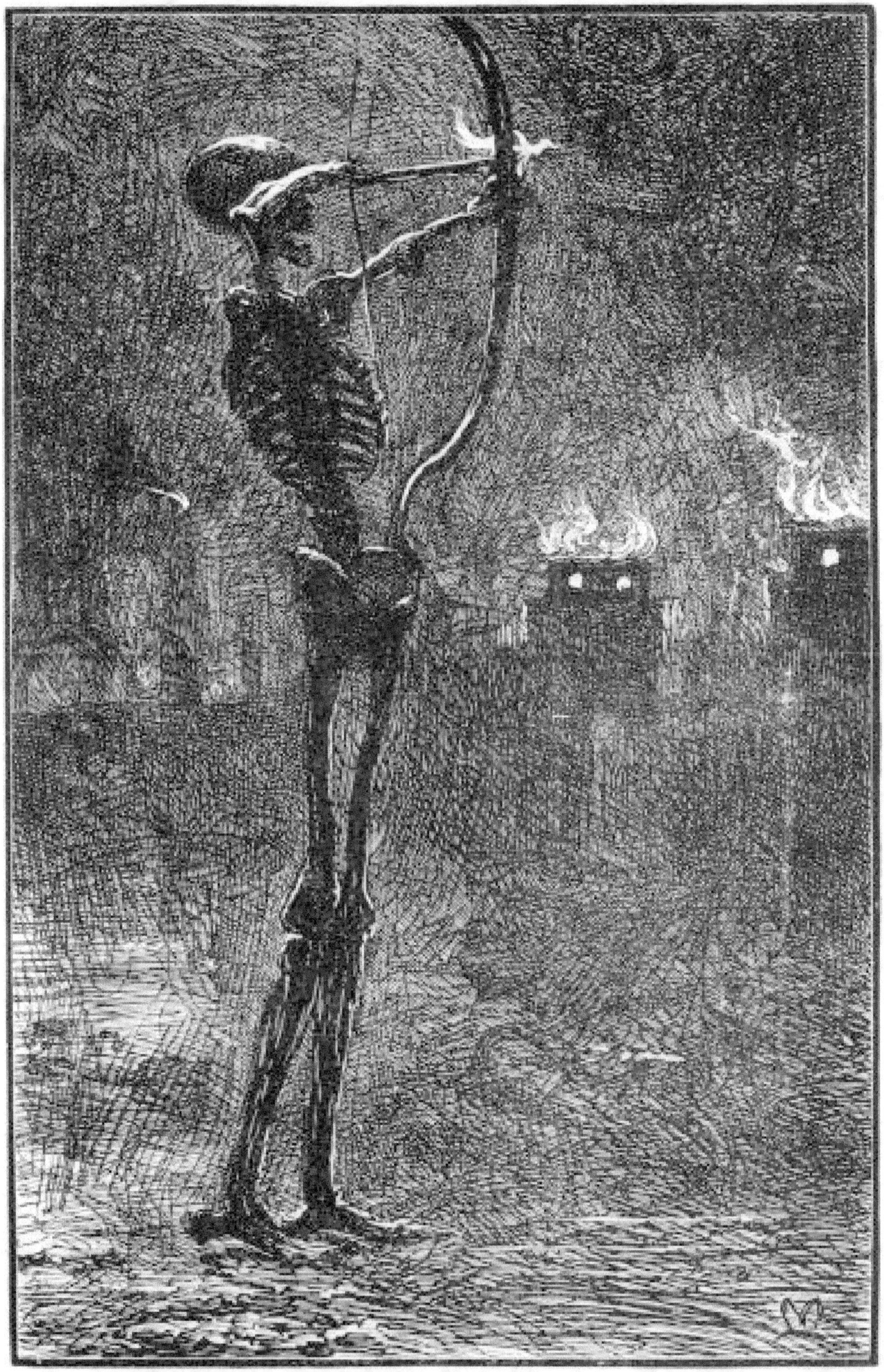

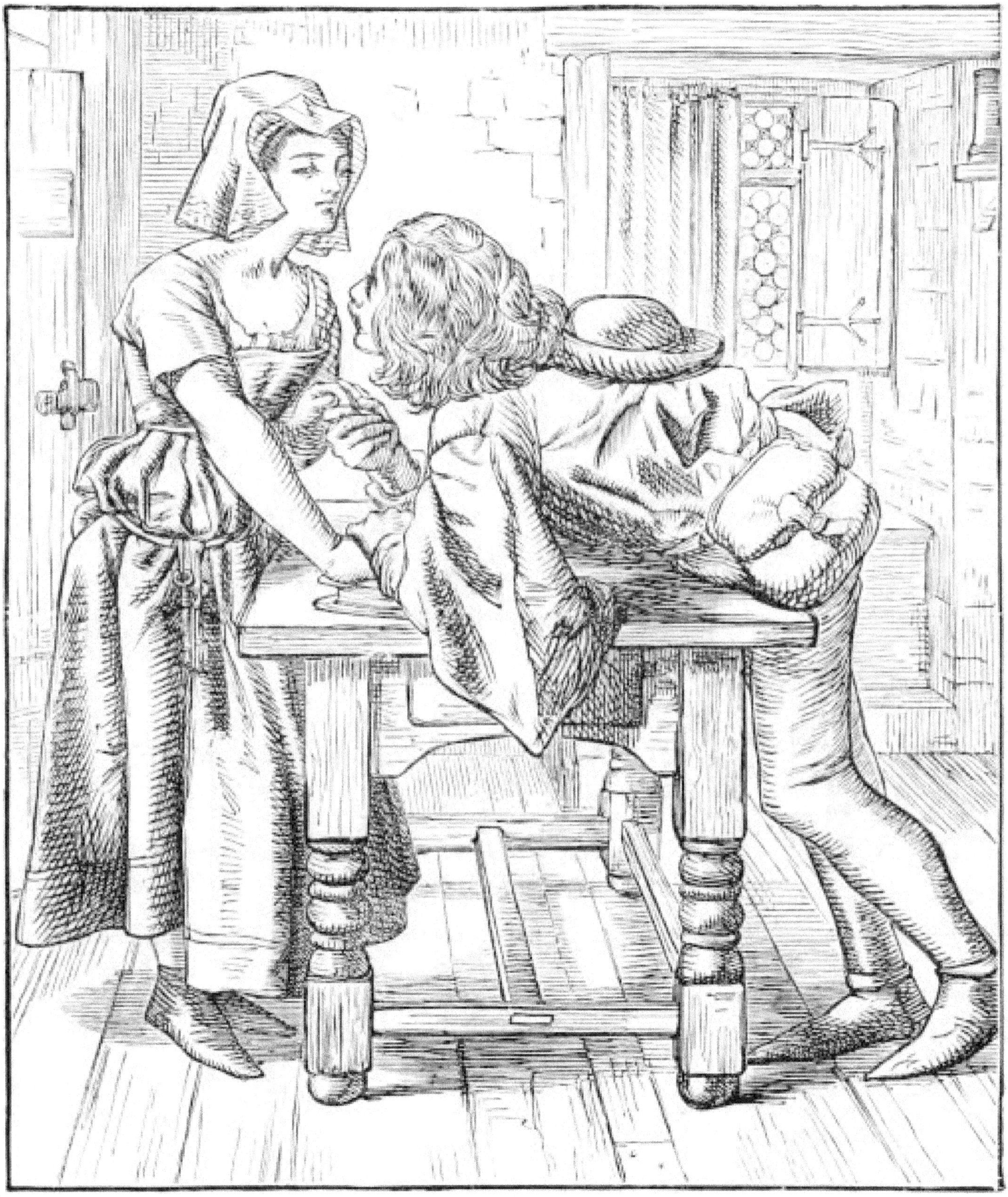

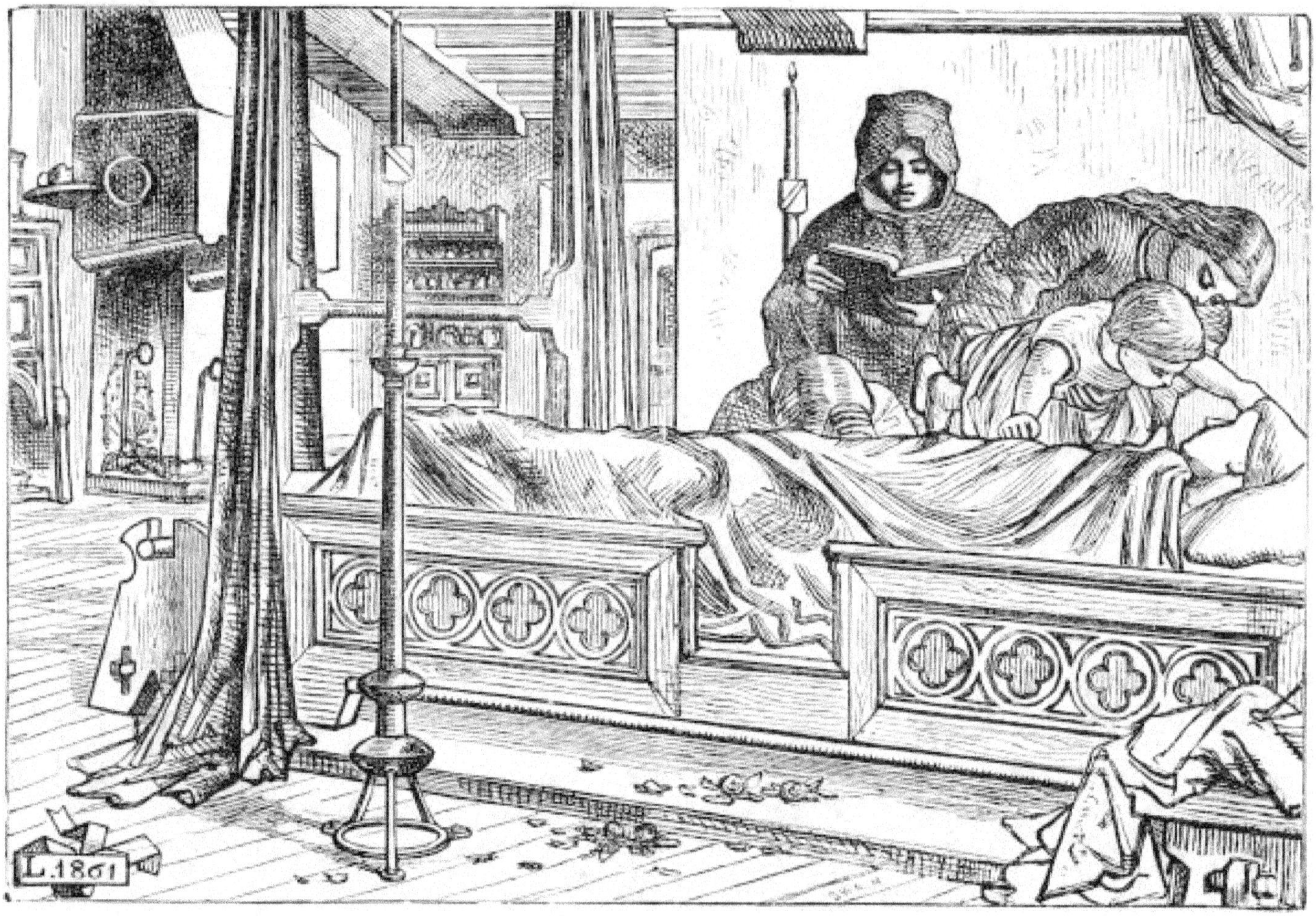
L.1861

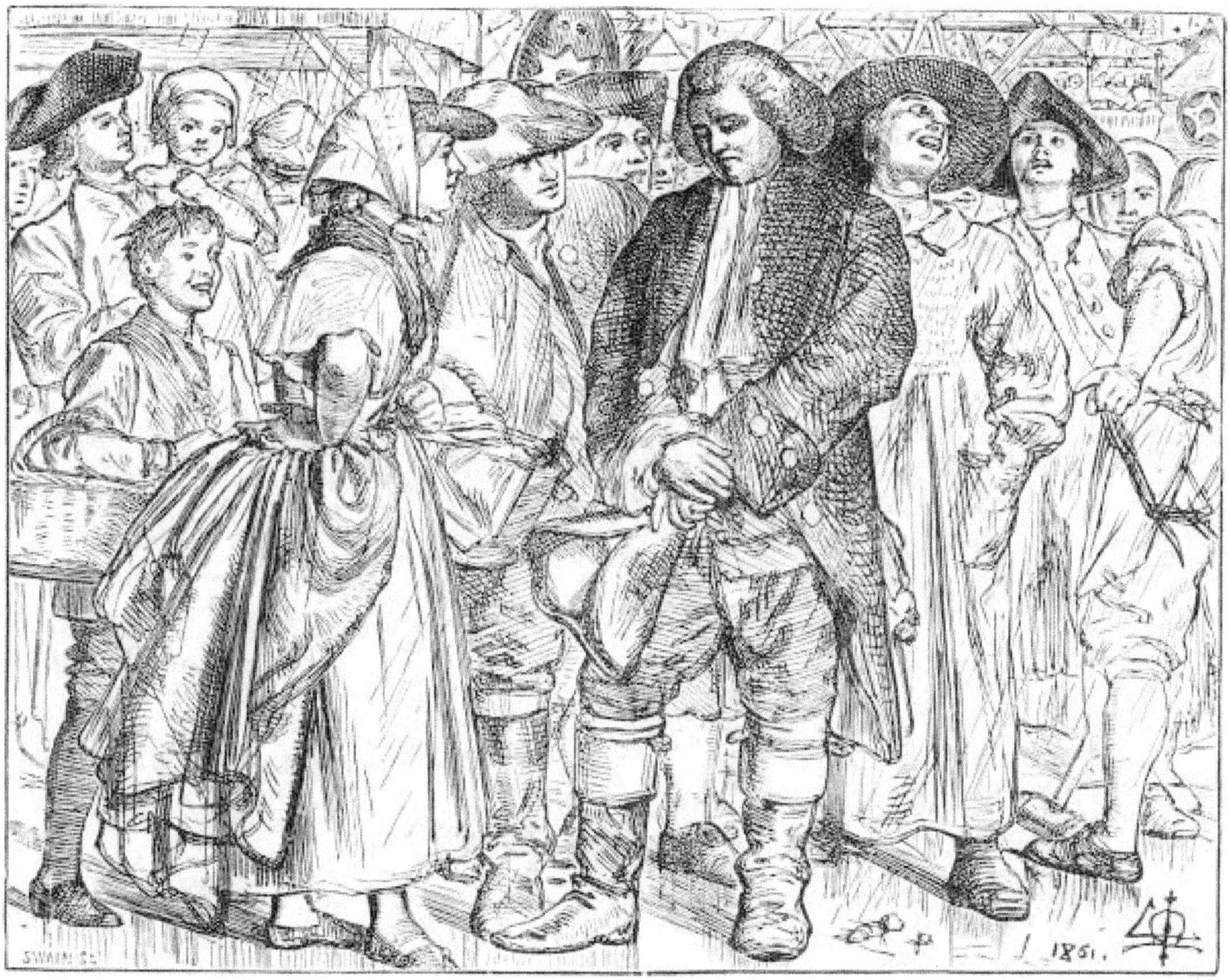
SWAIN SC
1861.

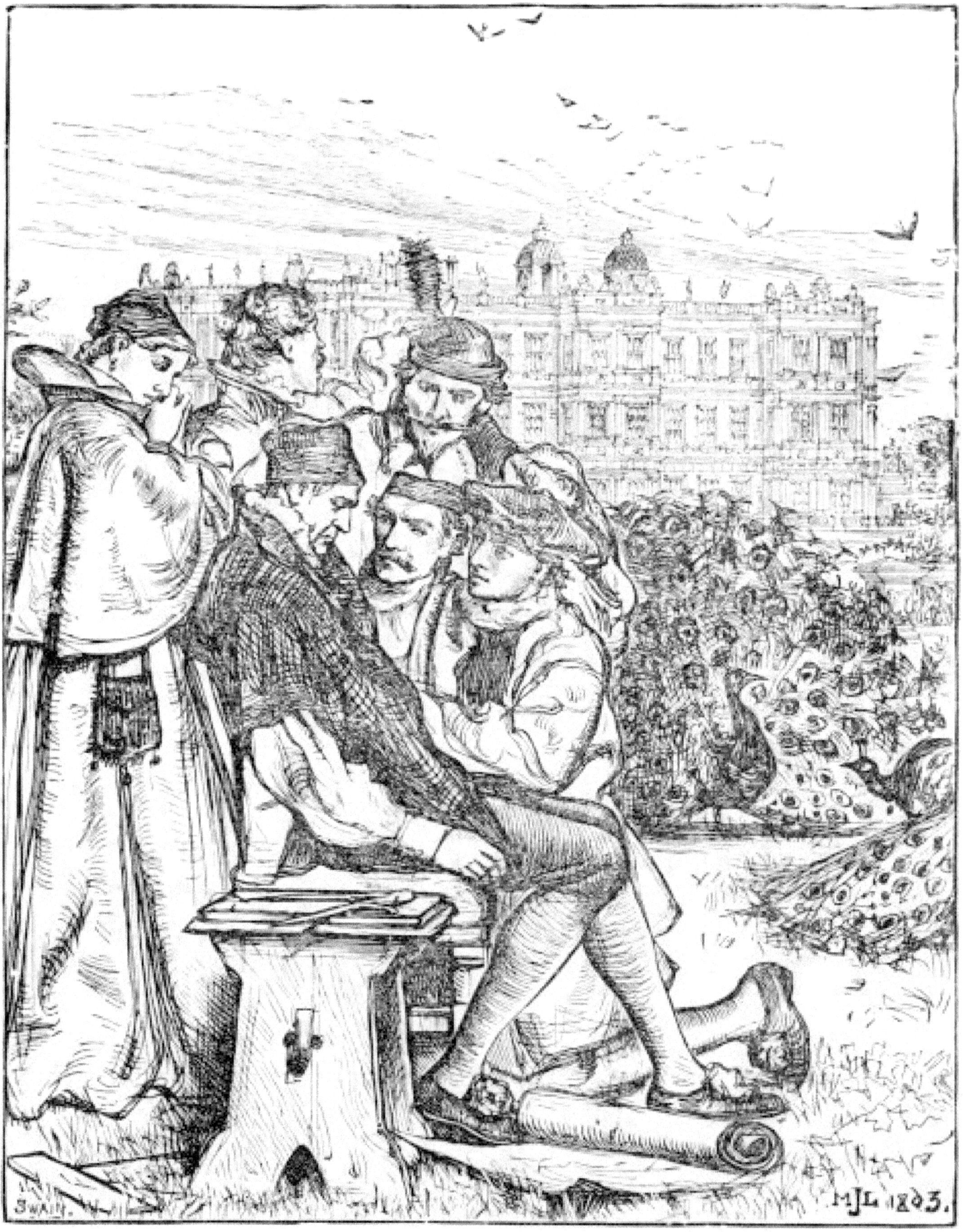
SWAIN
MJL 1863.

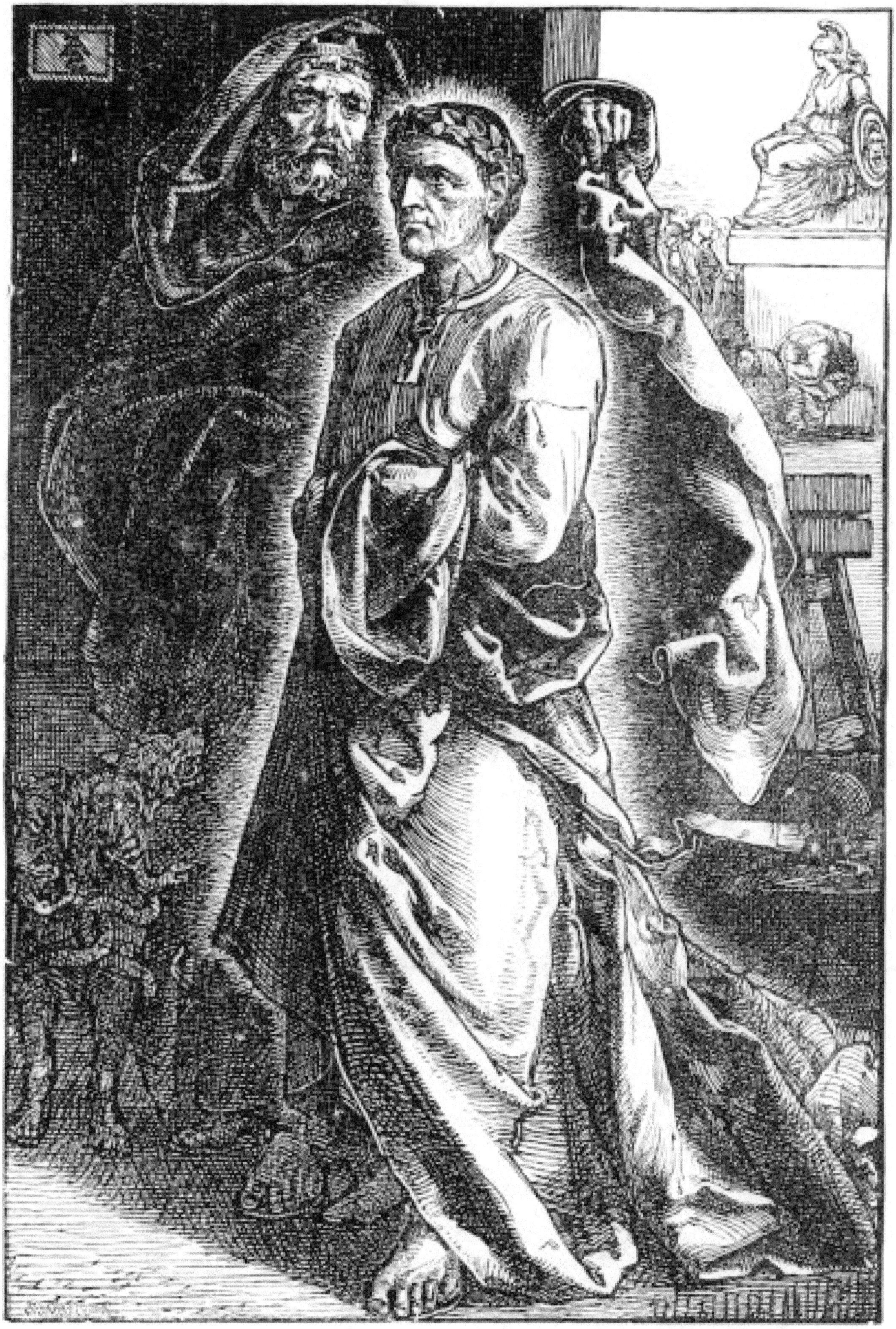

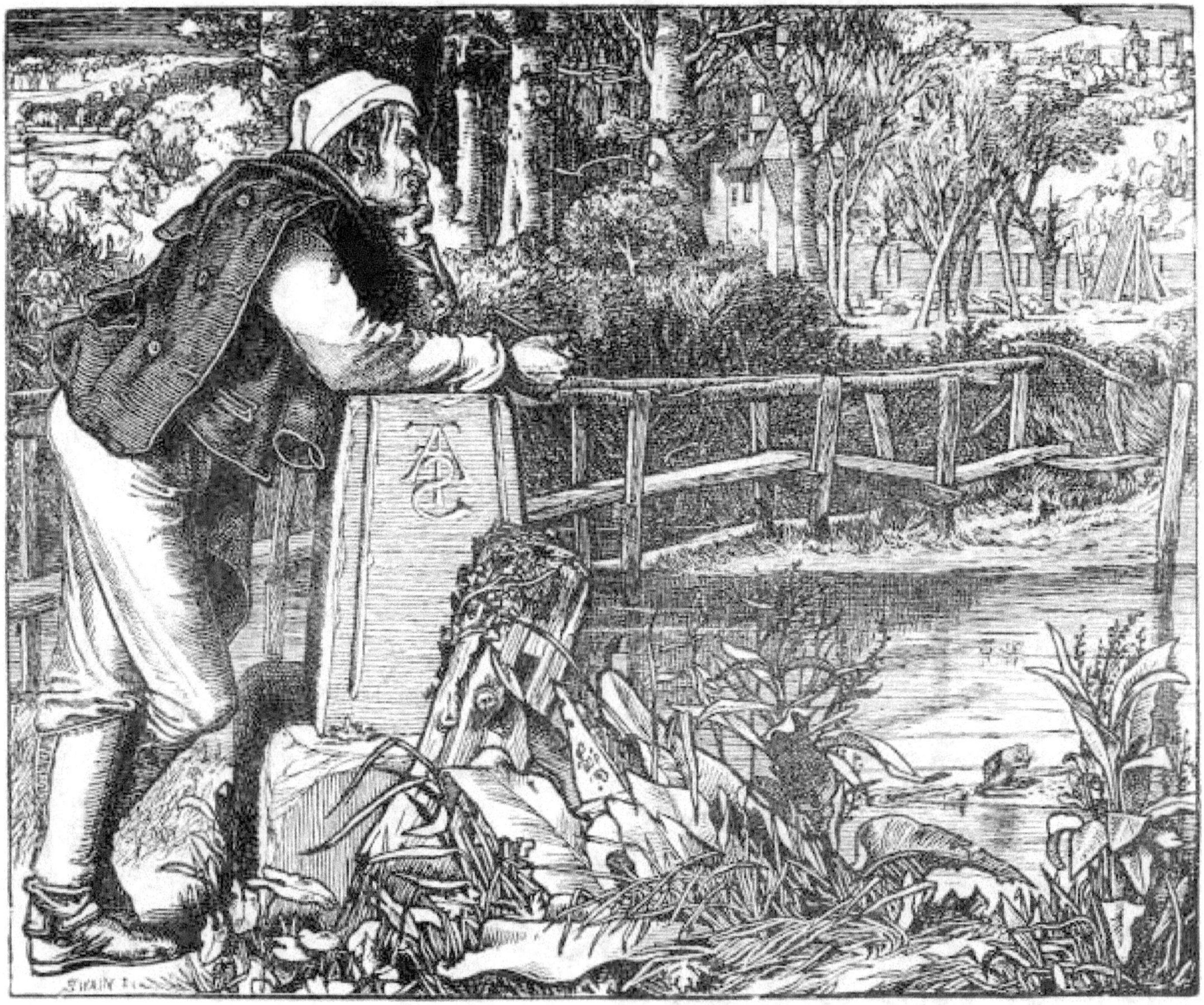

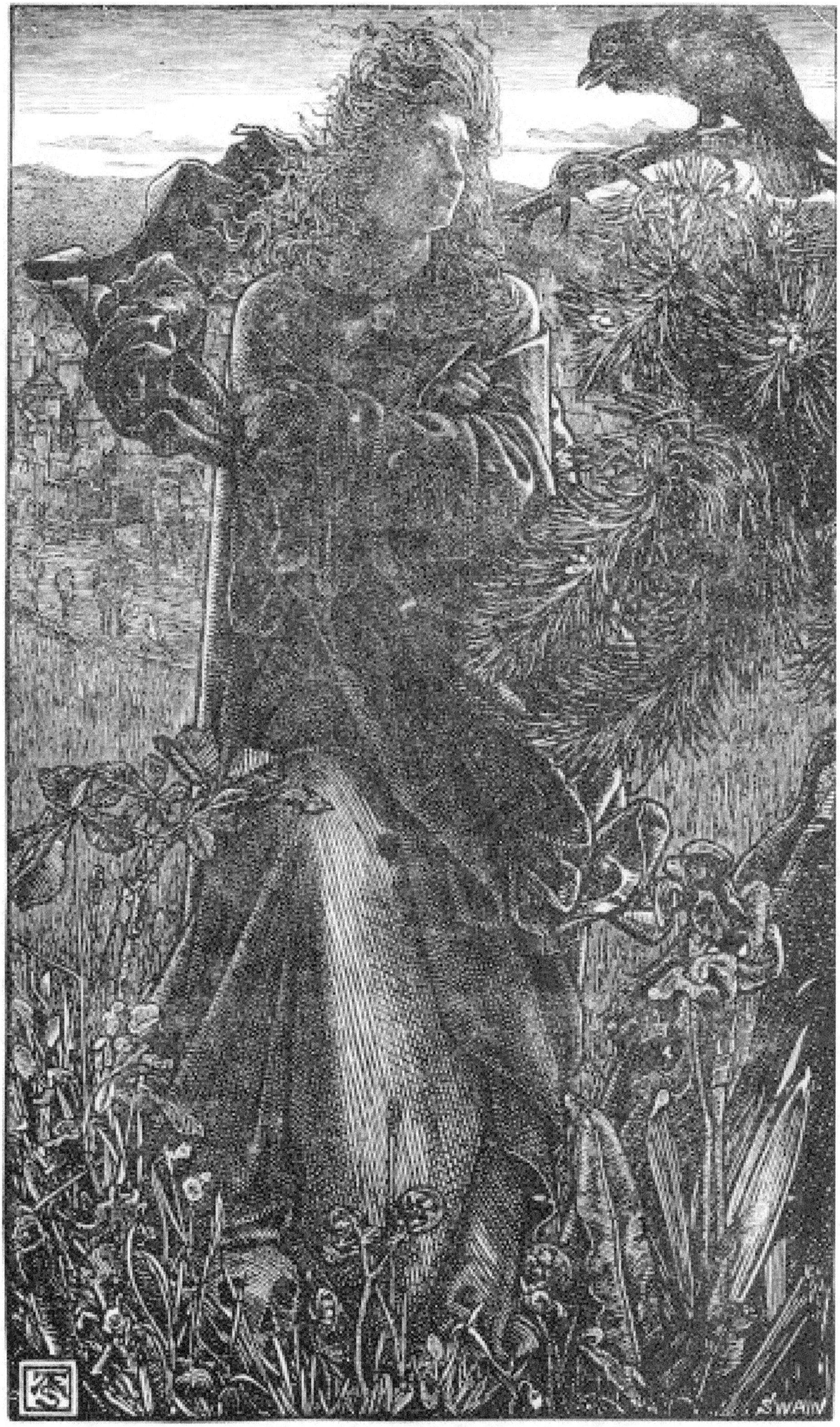
SWAIN

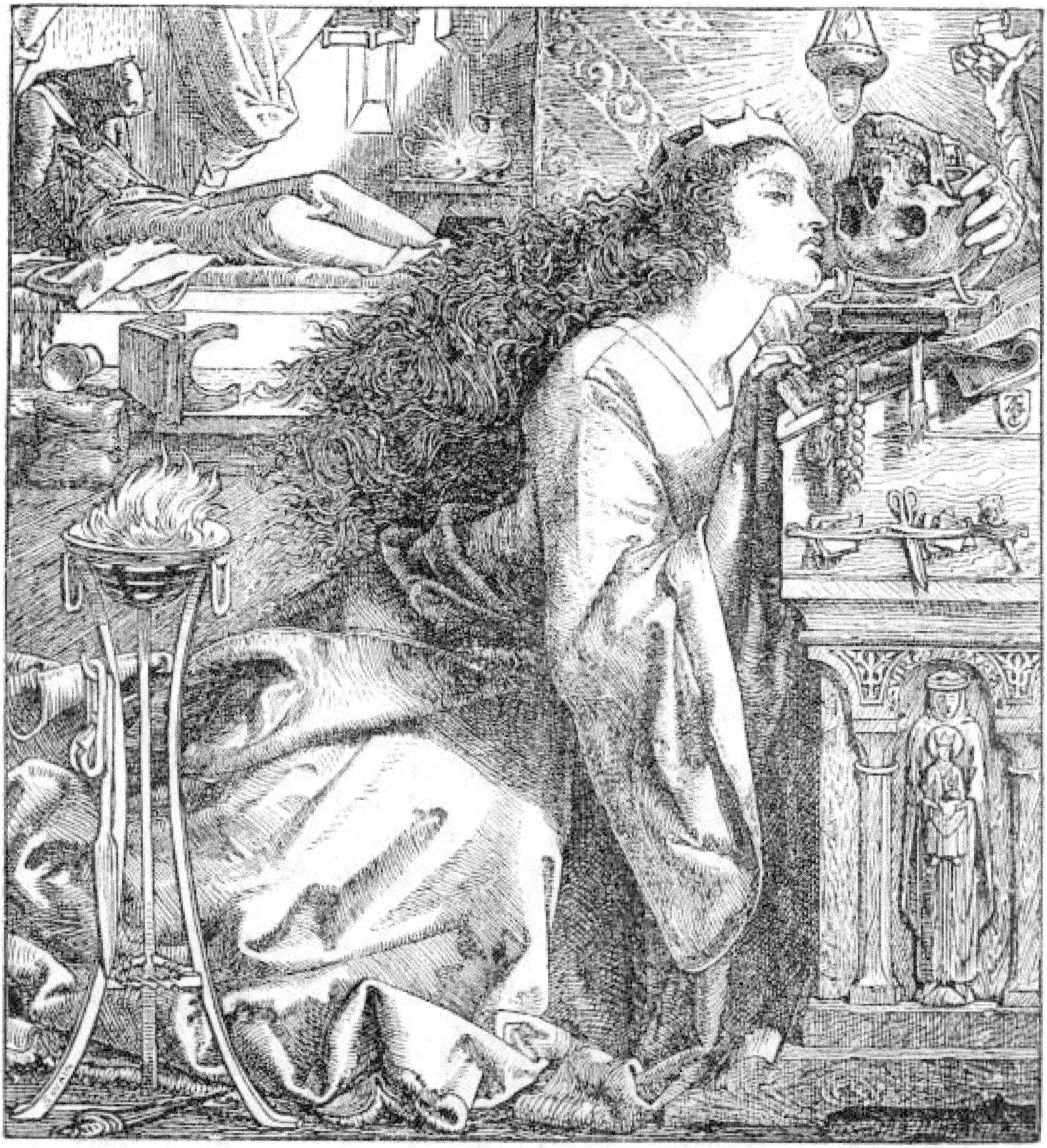

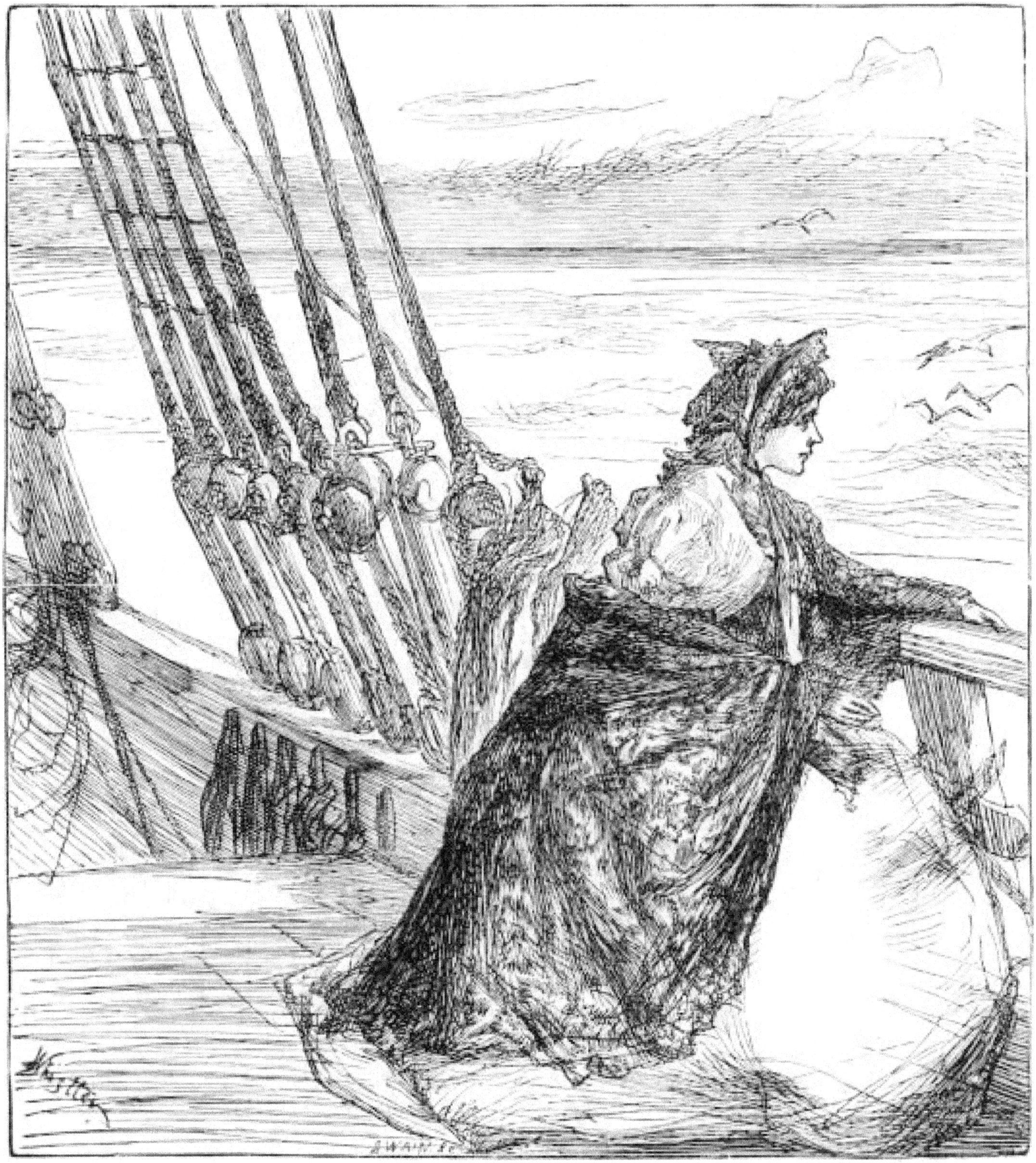

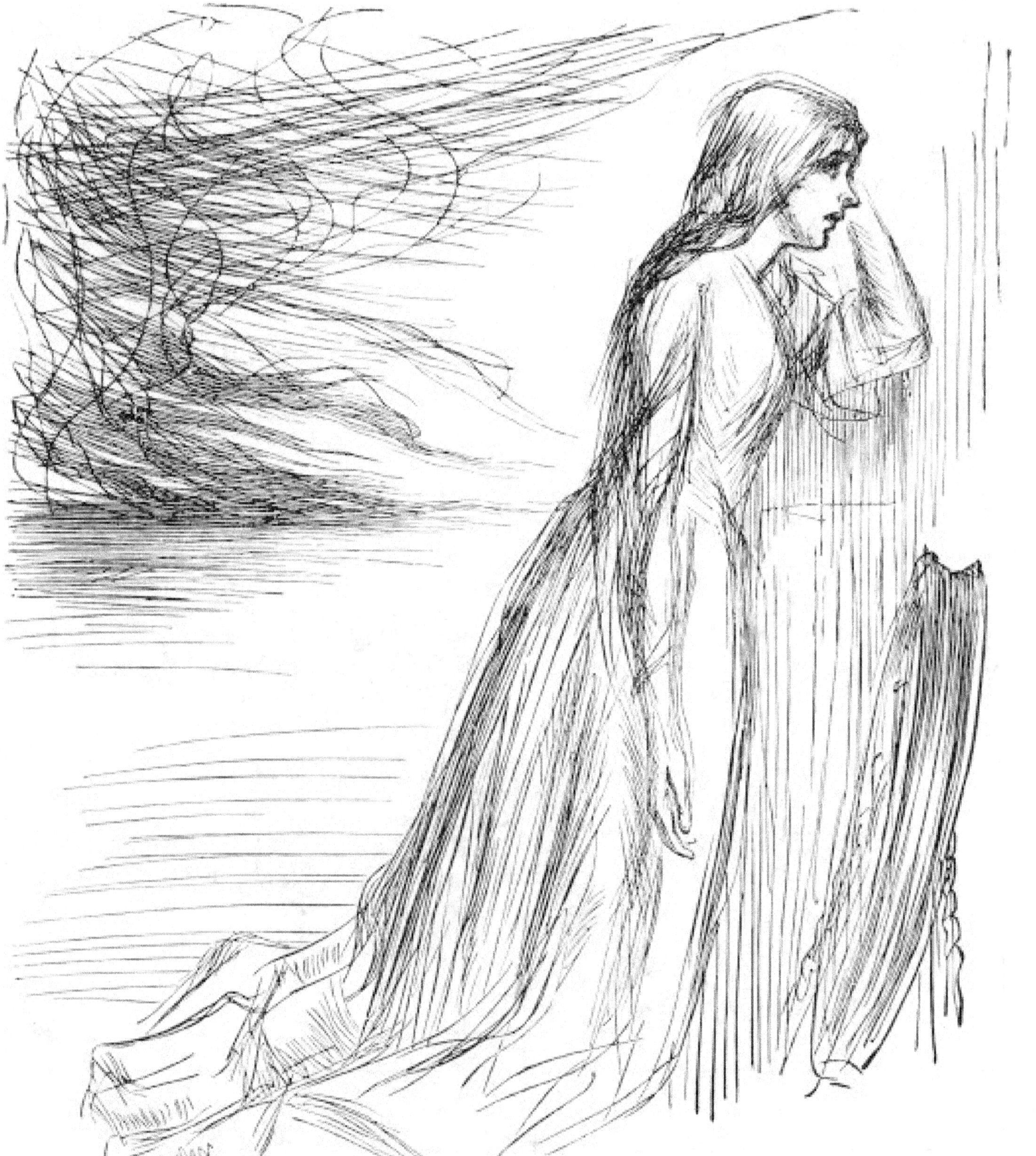

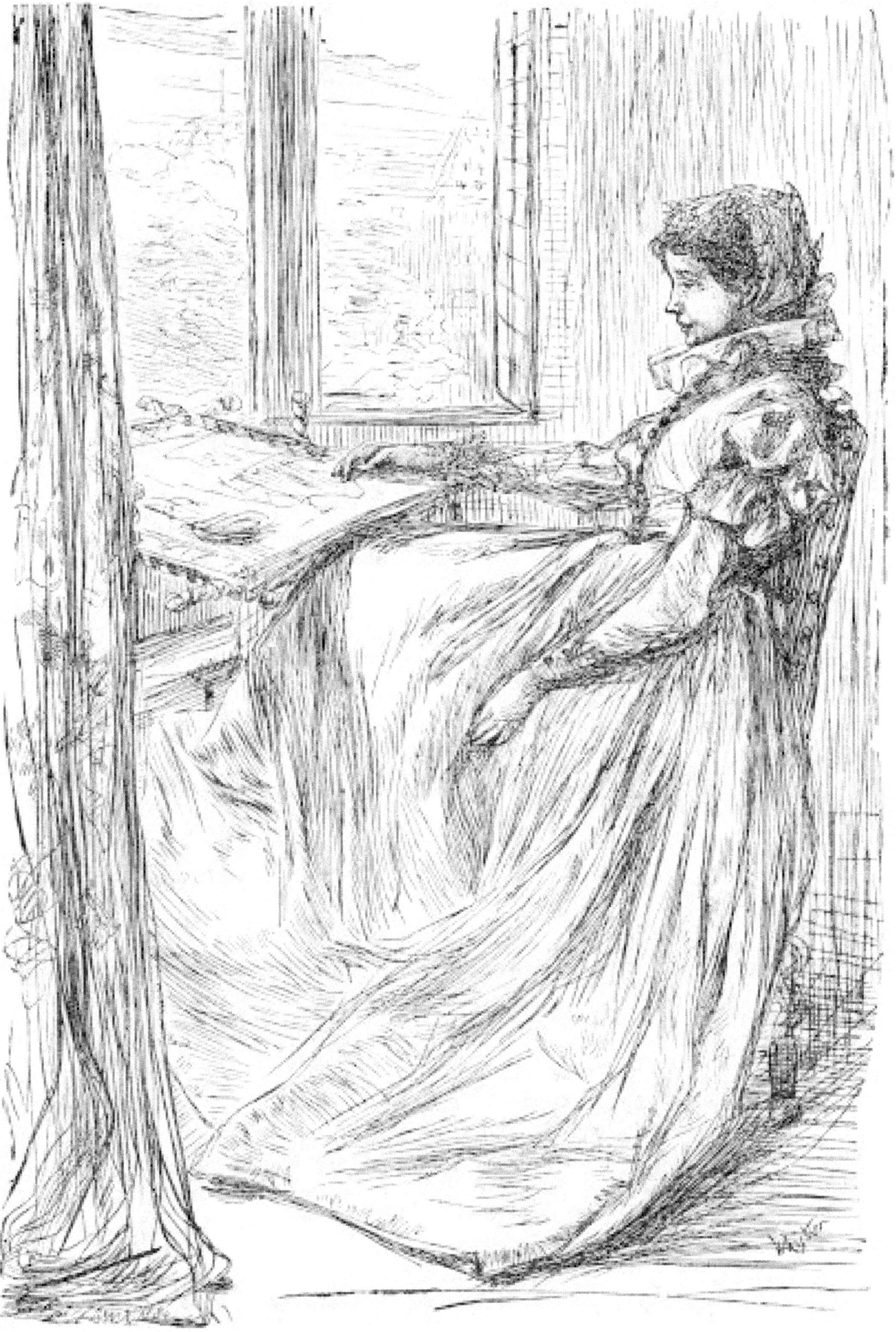

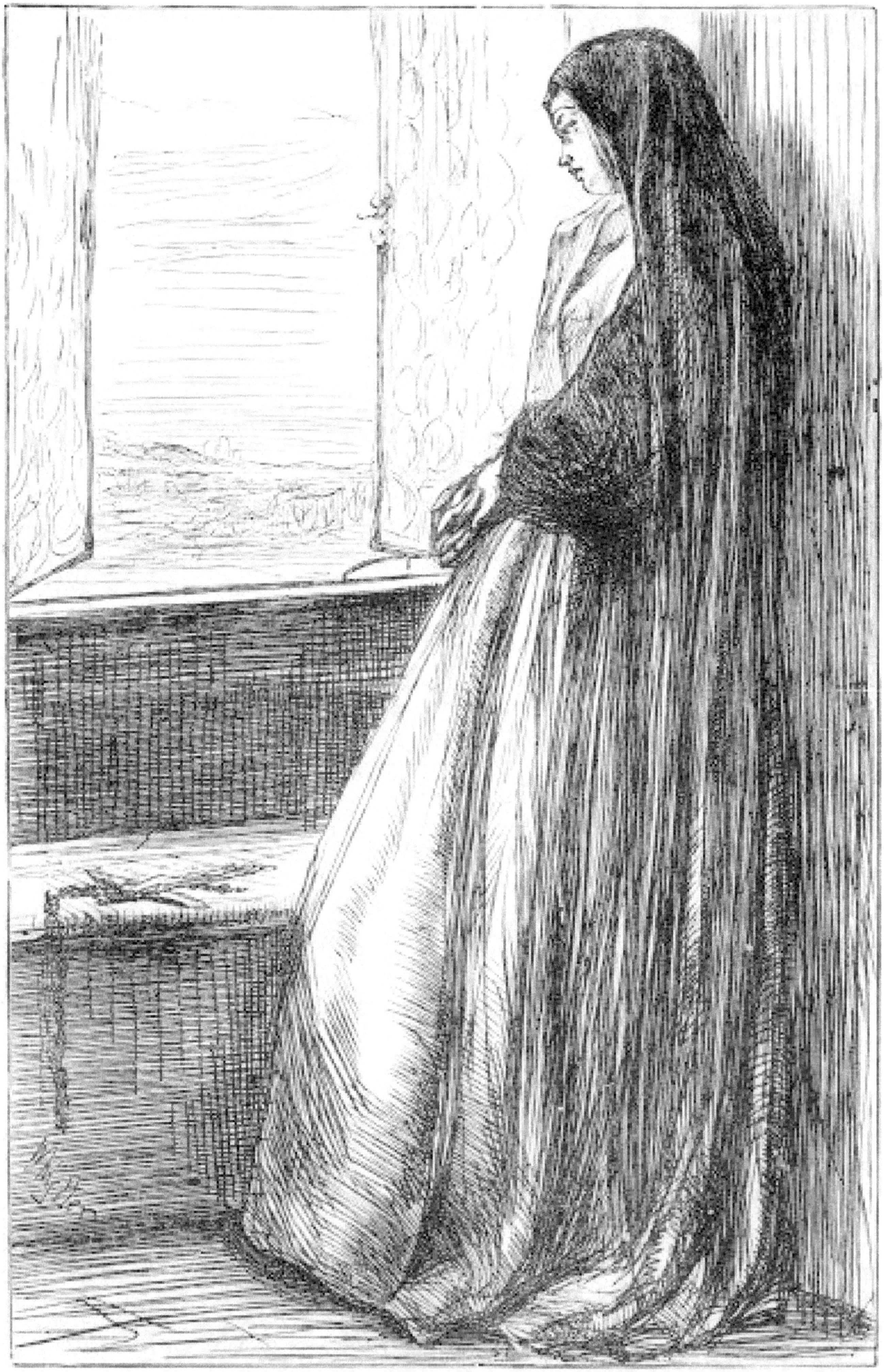

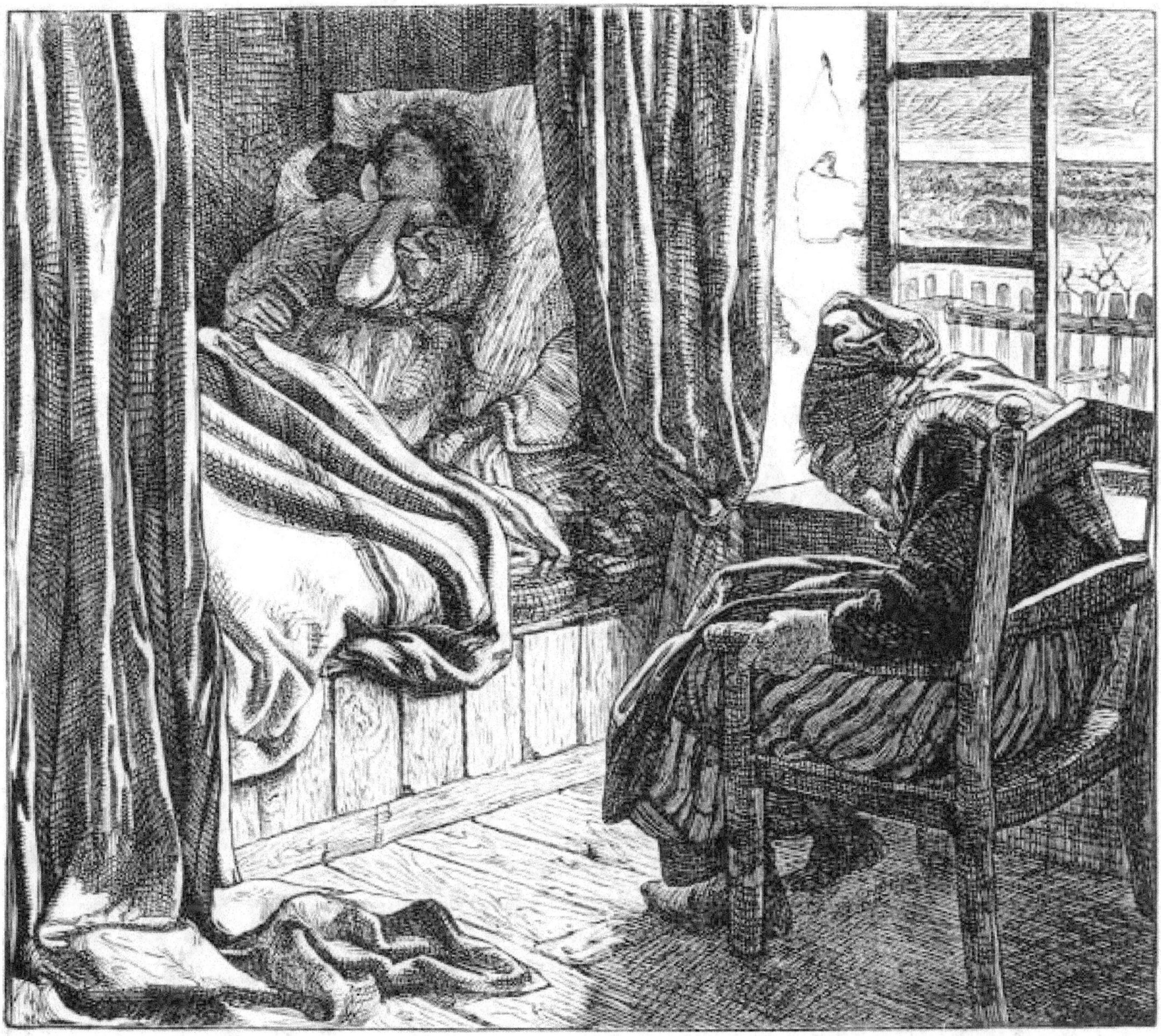

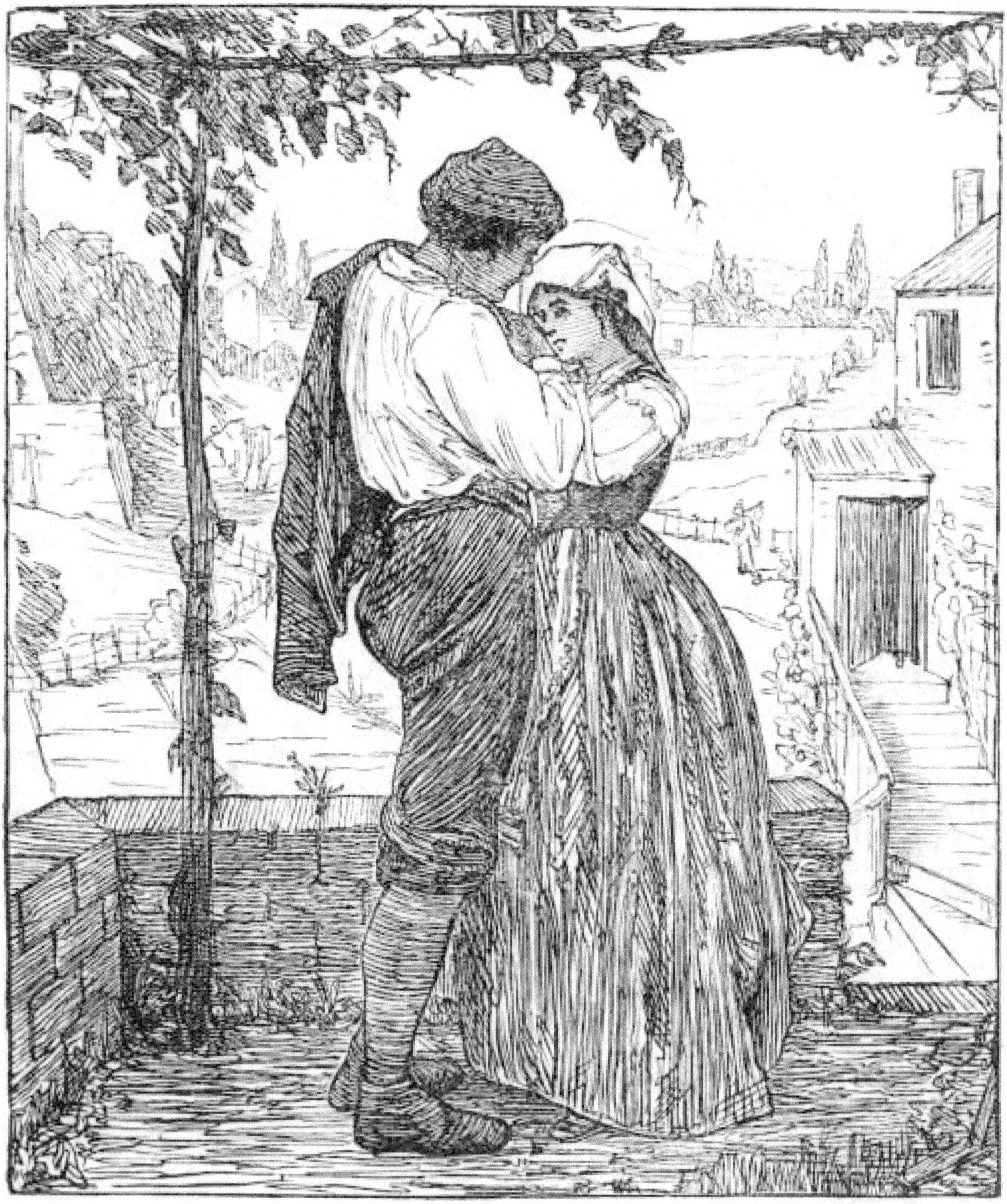

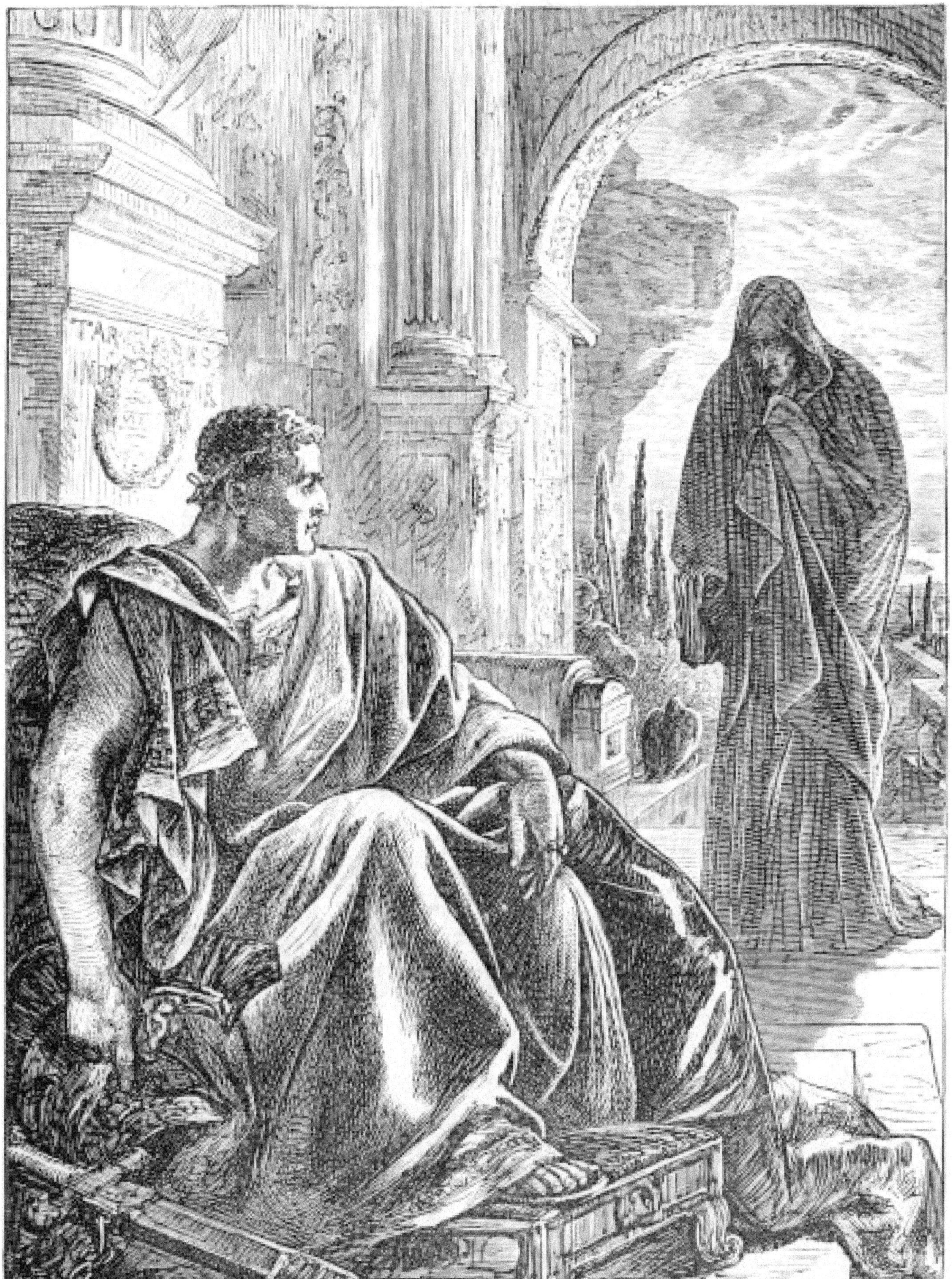

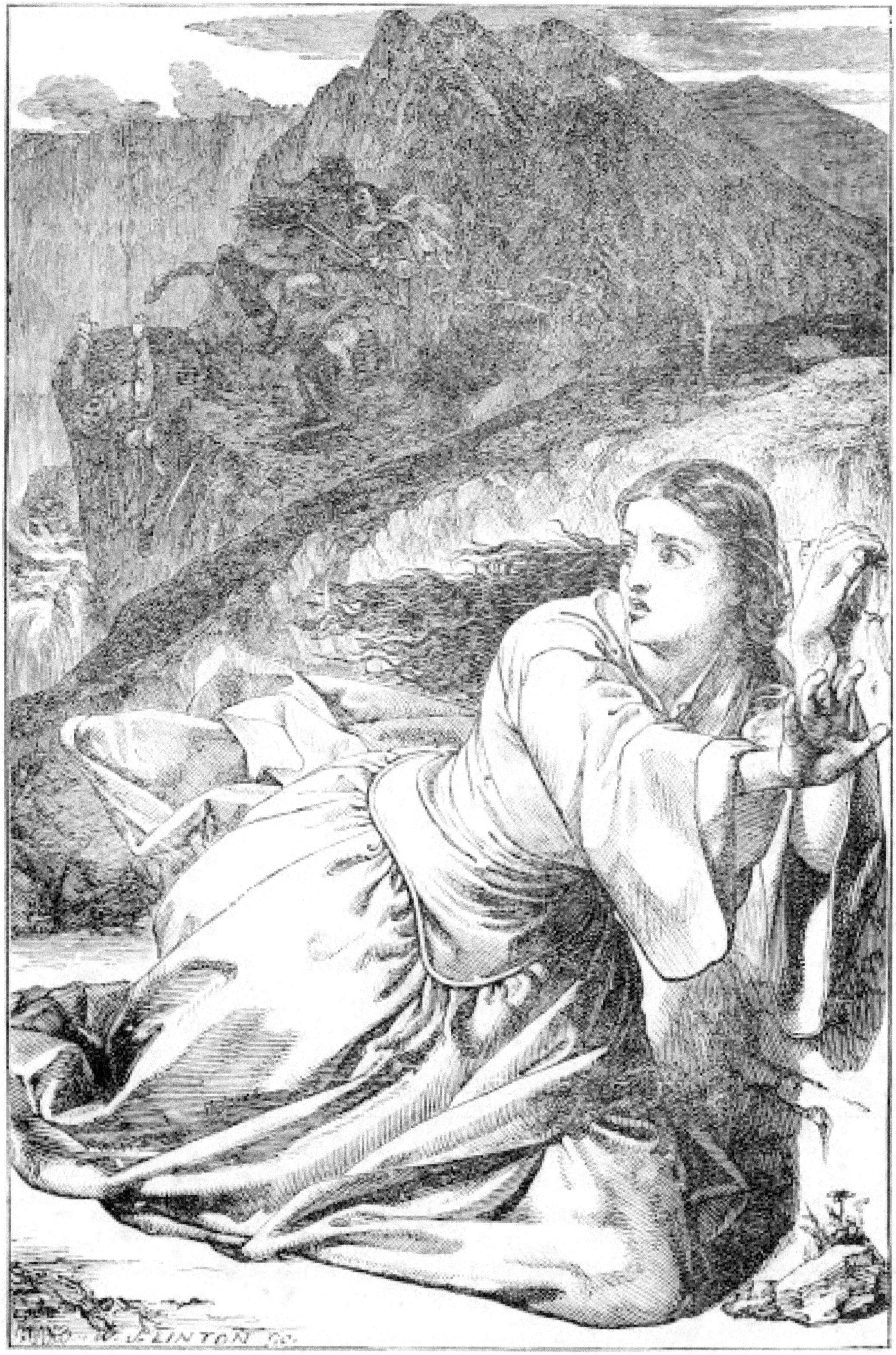
LINTON Sc.

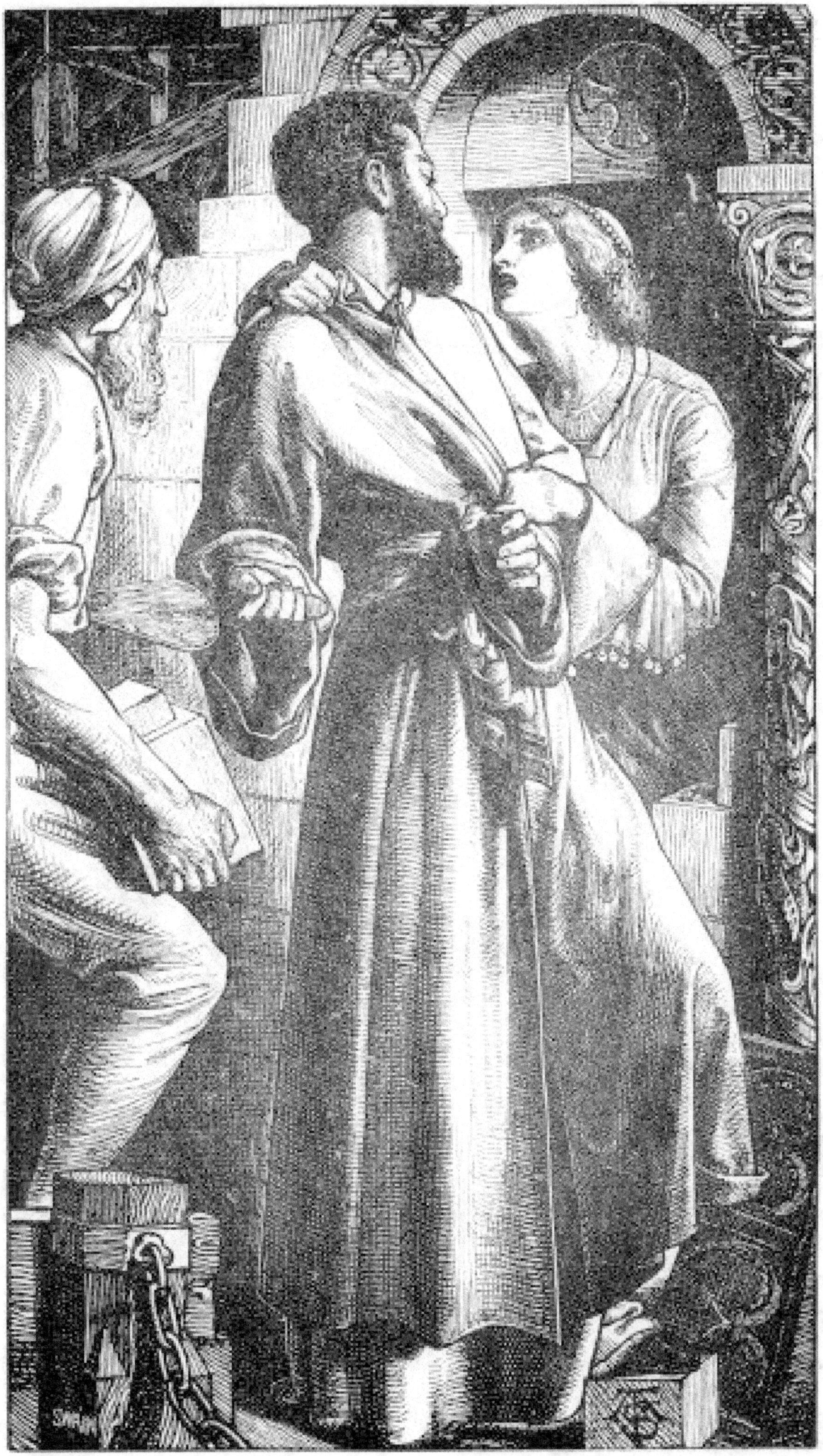
SWAIN

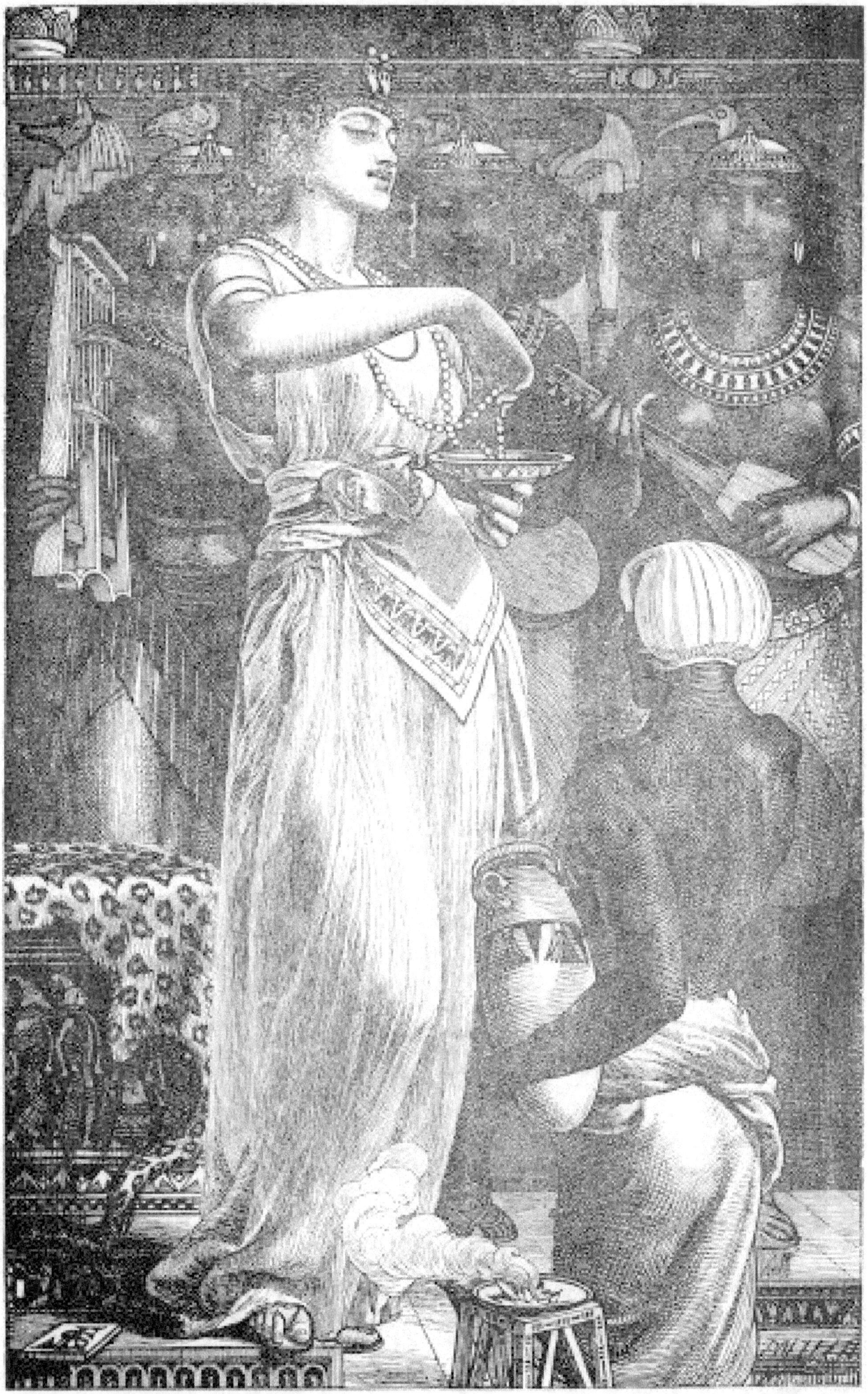

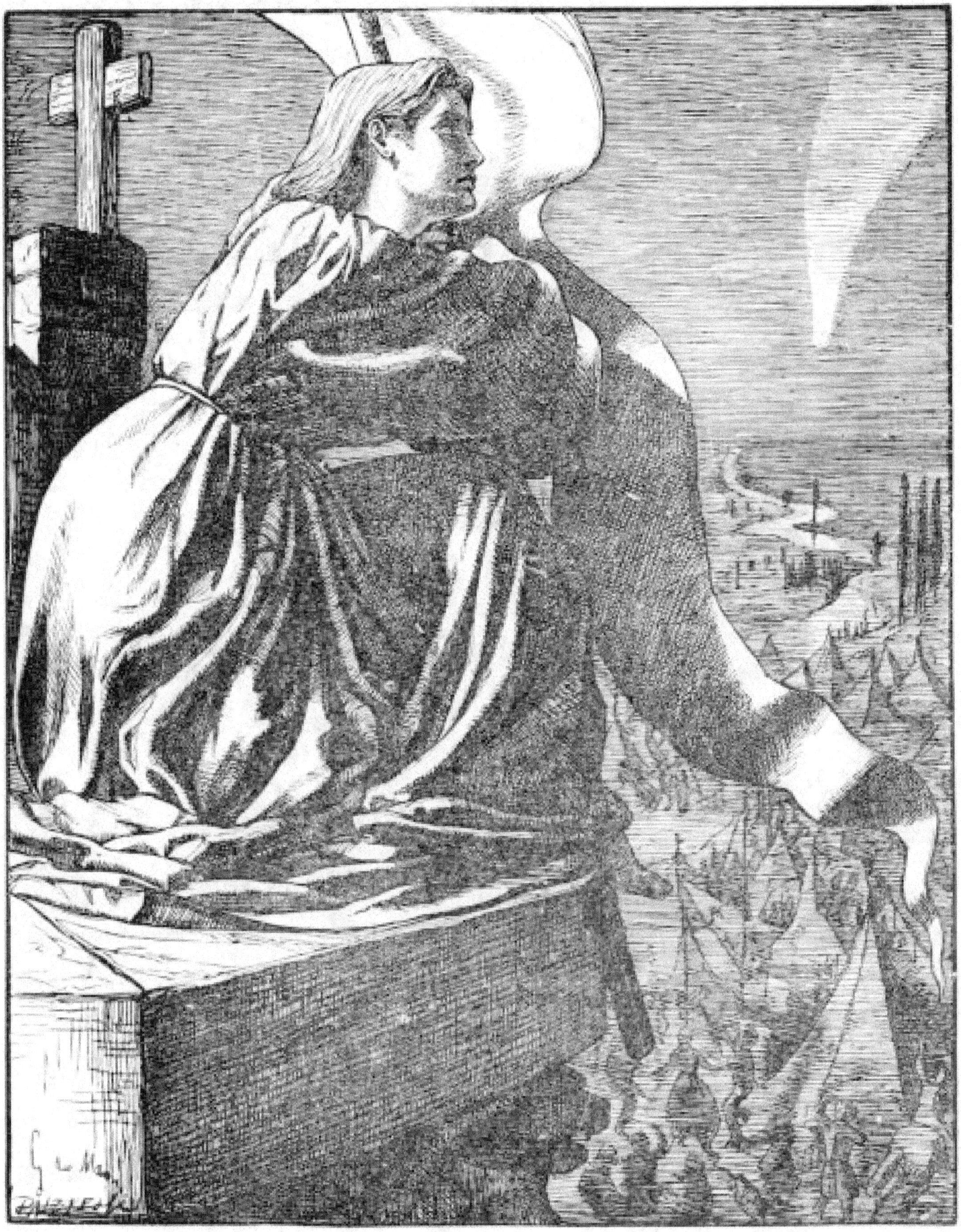

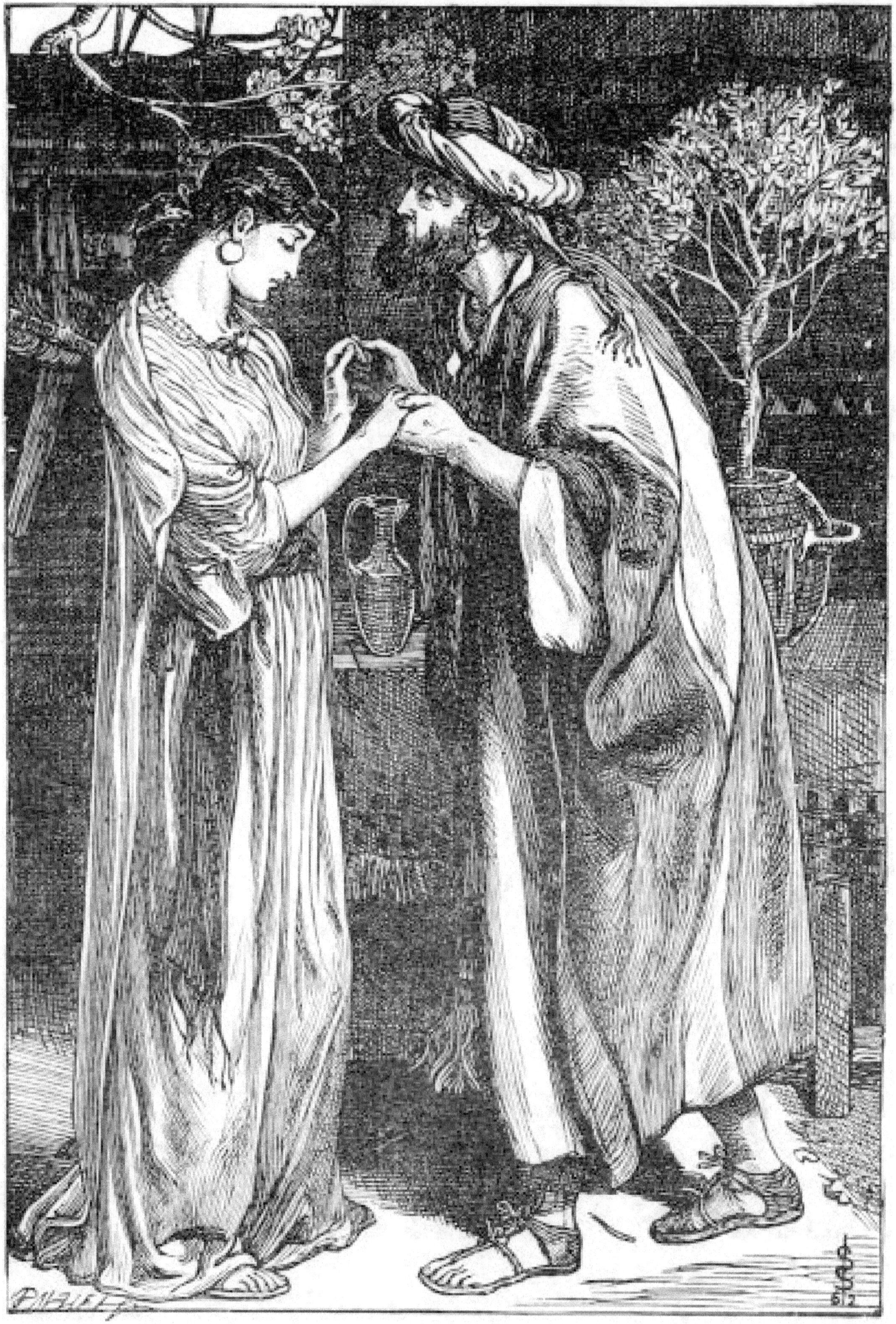

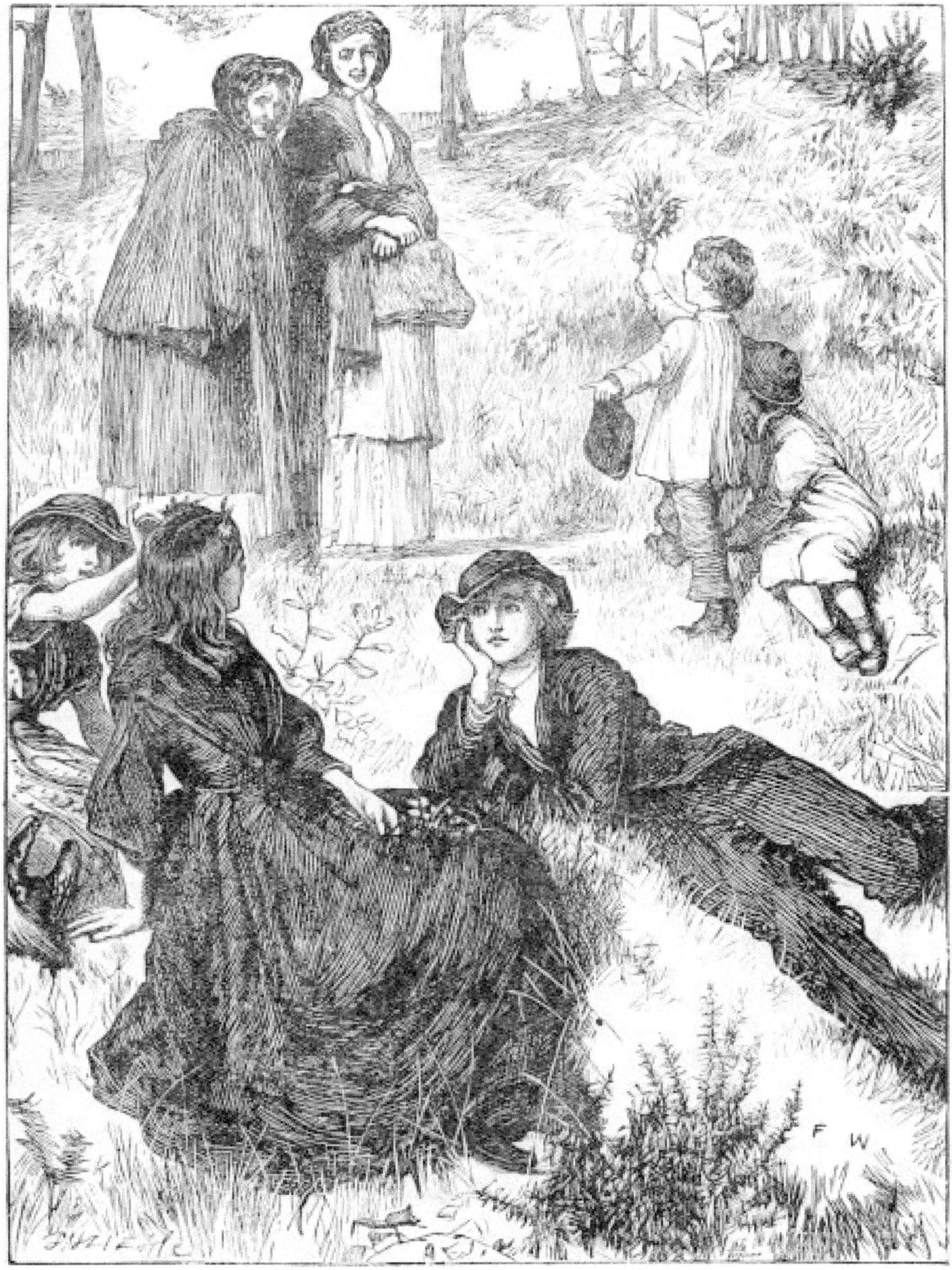
F W

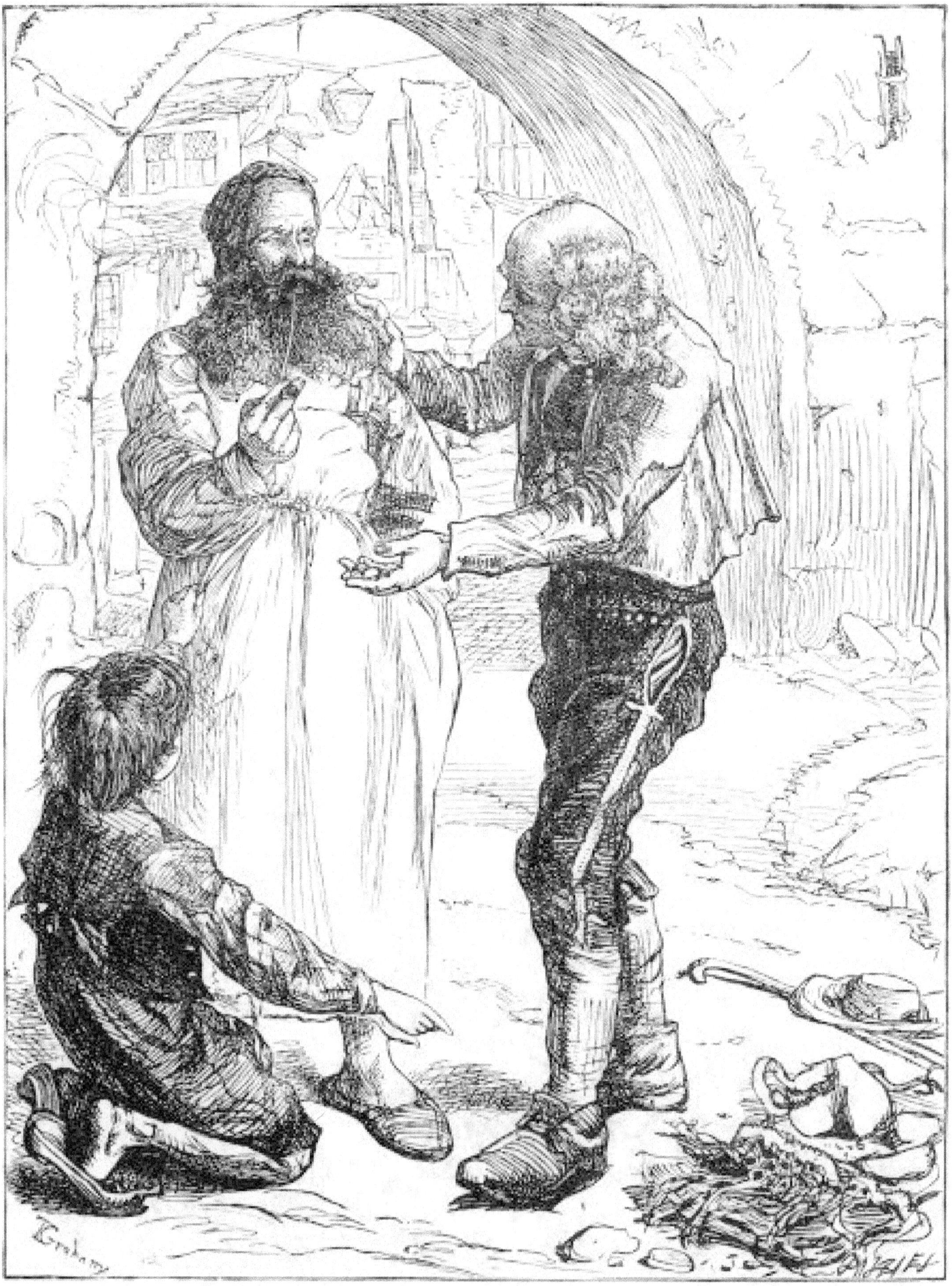

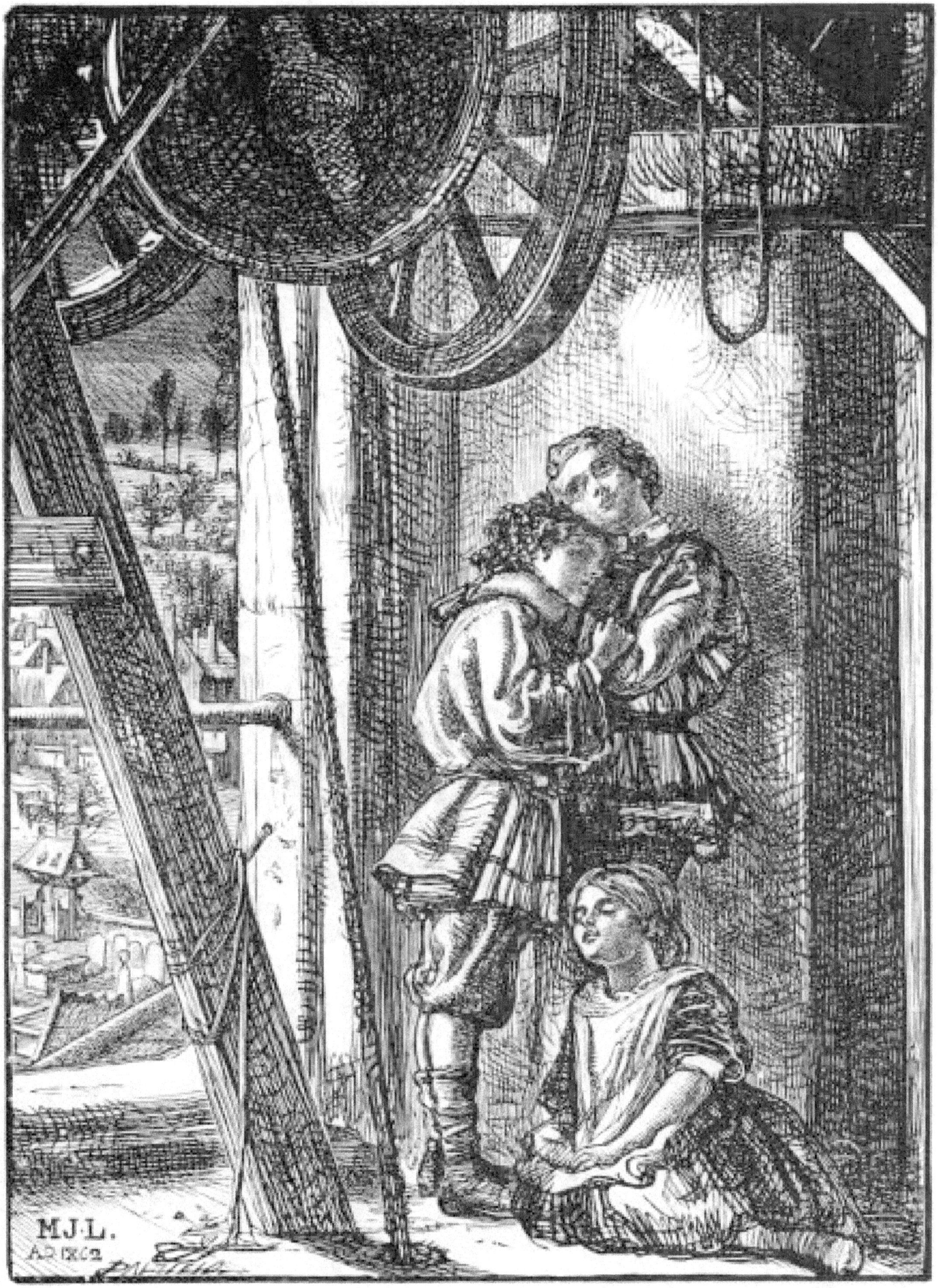
M.J.L.

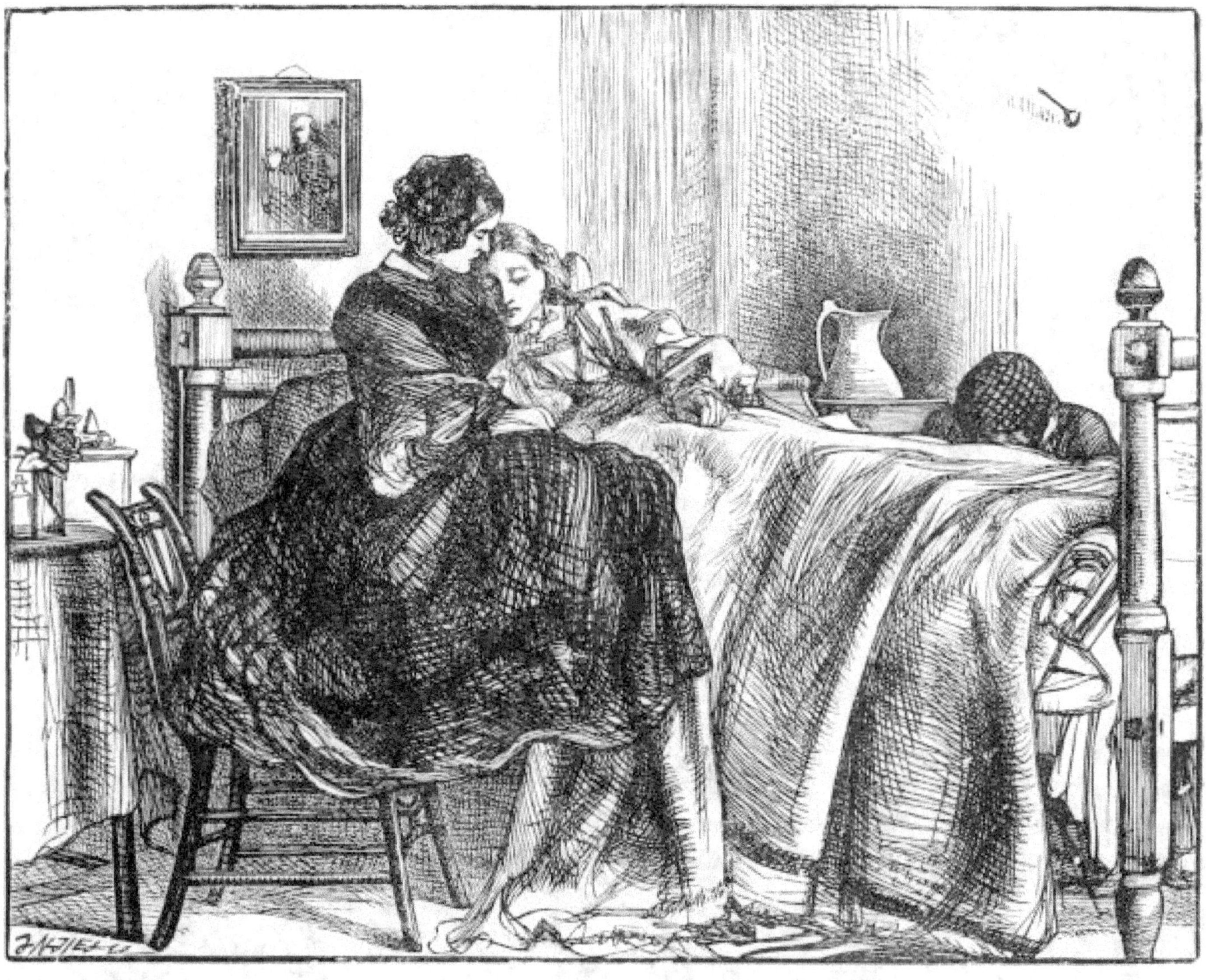

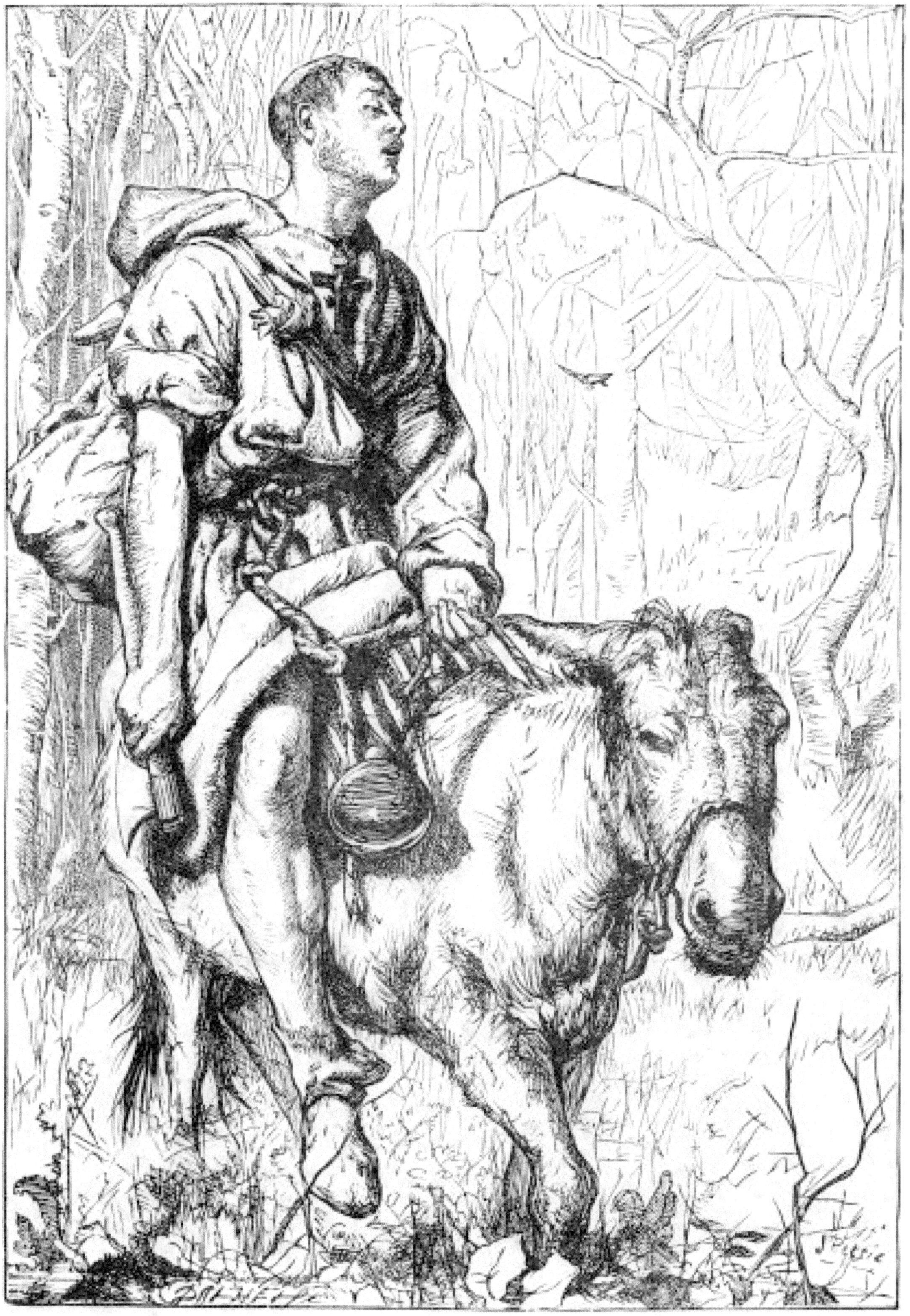

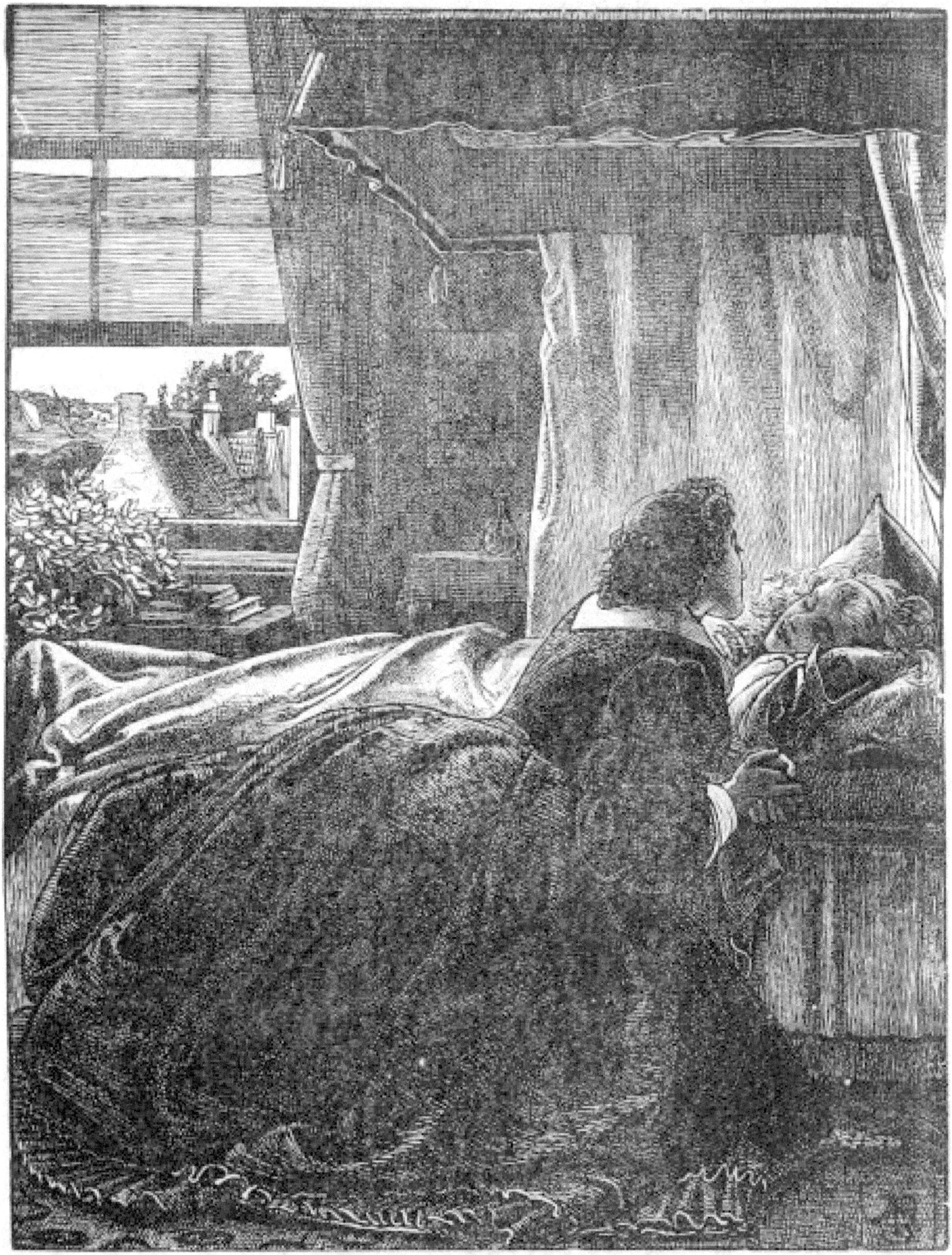

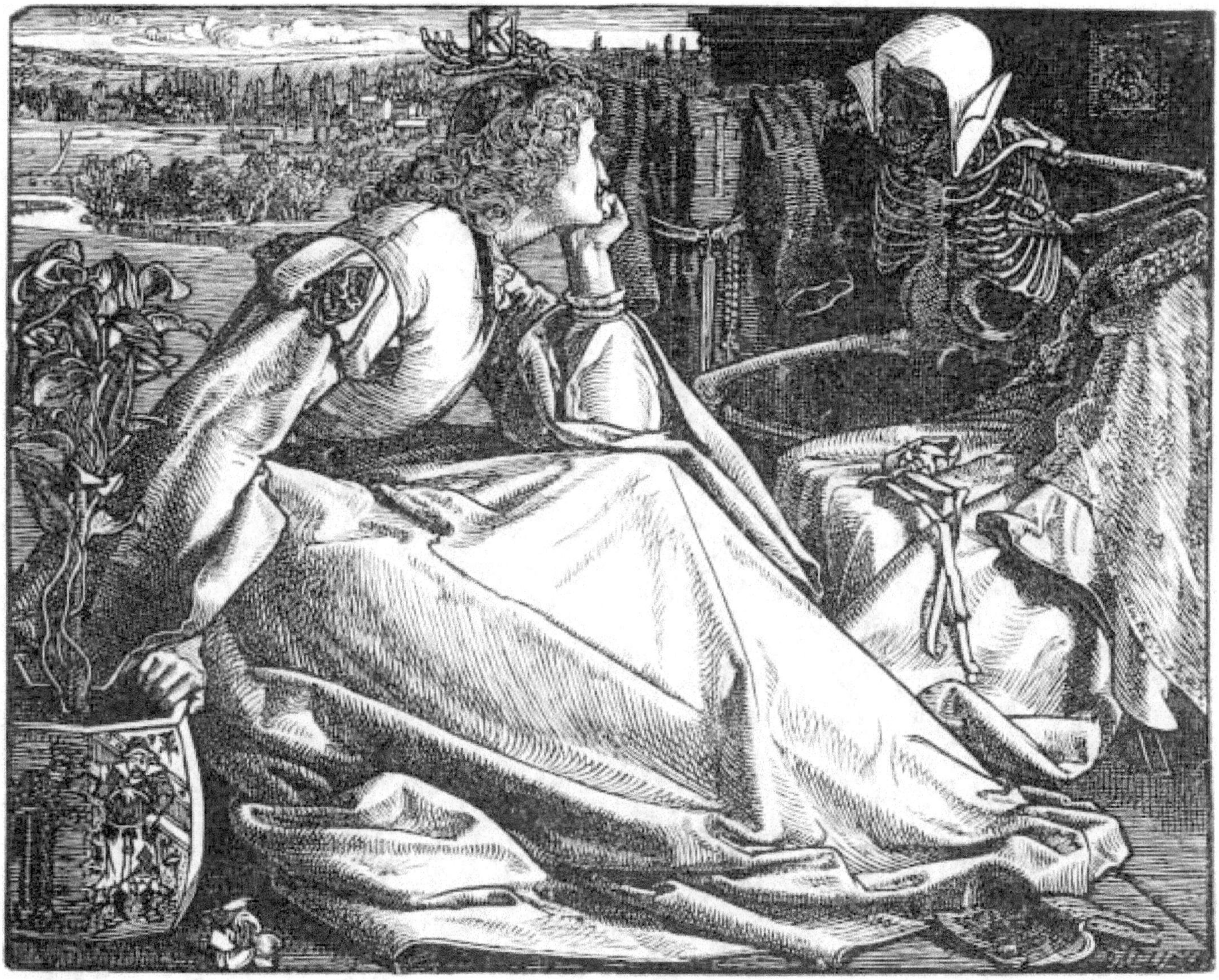

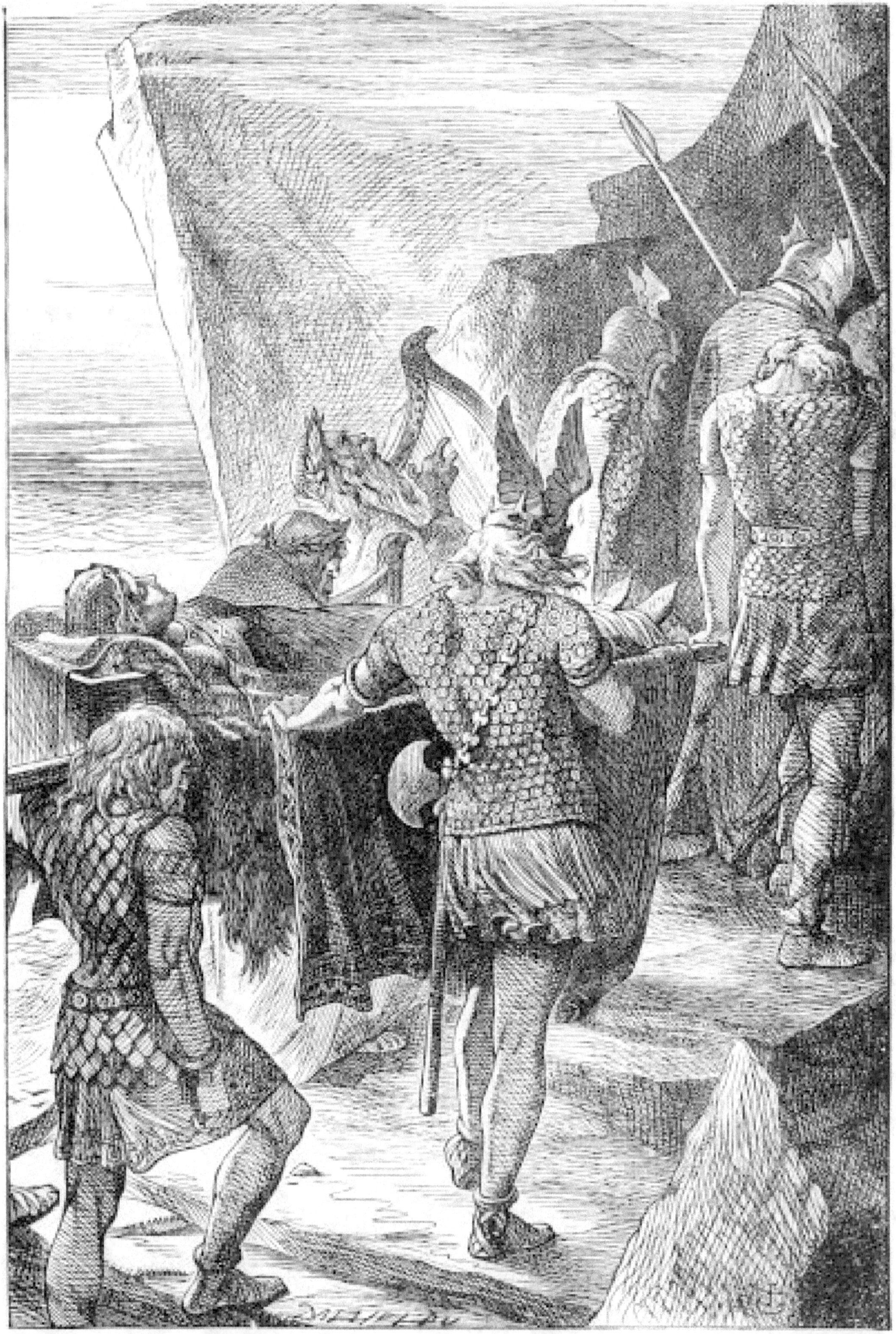

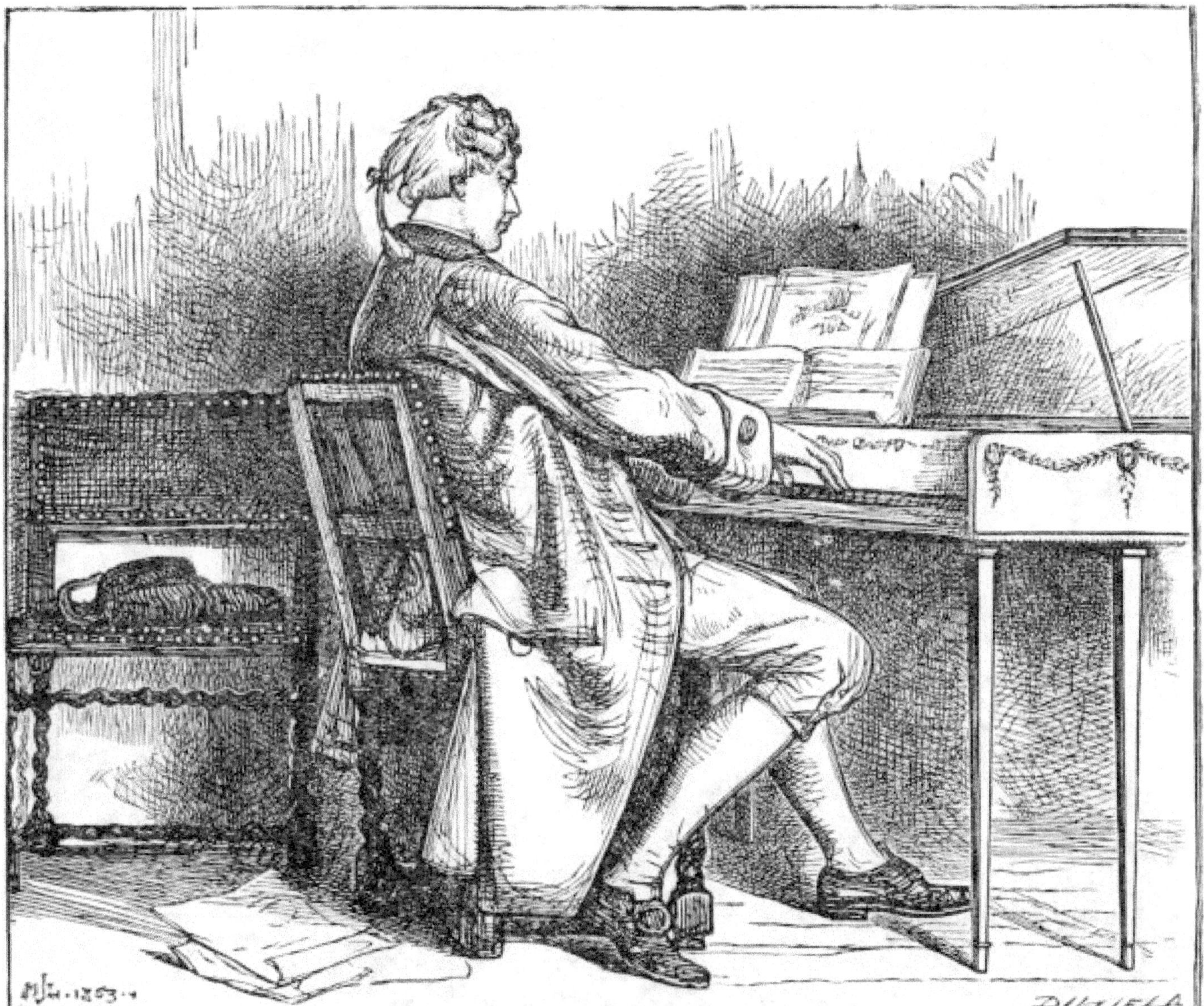
DALZIEL

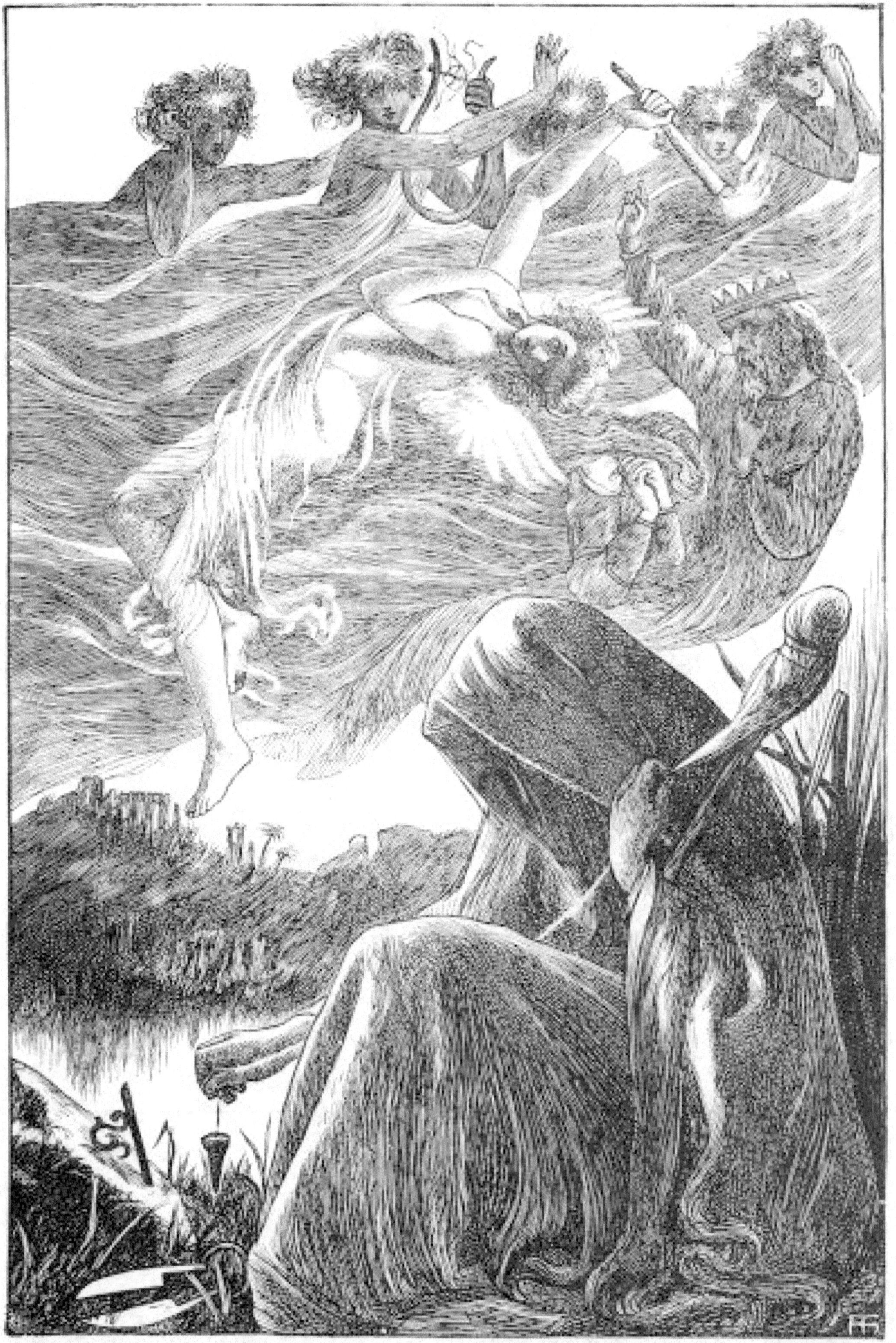

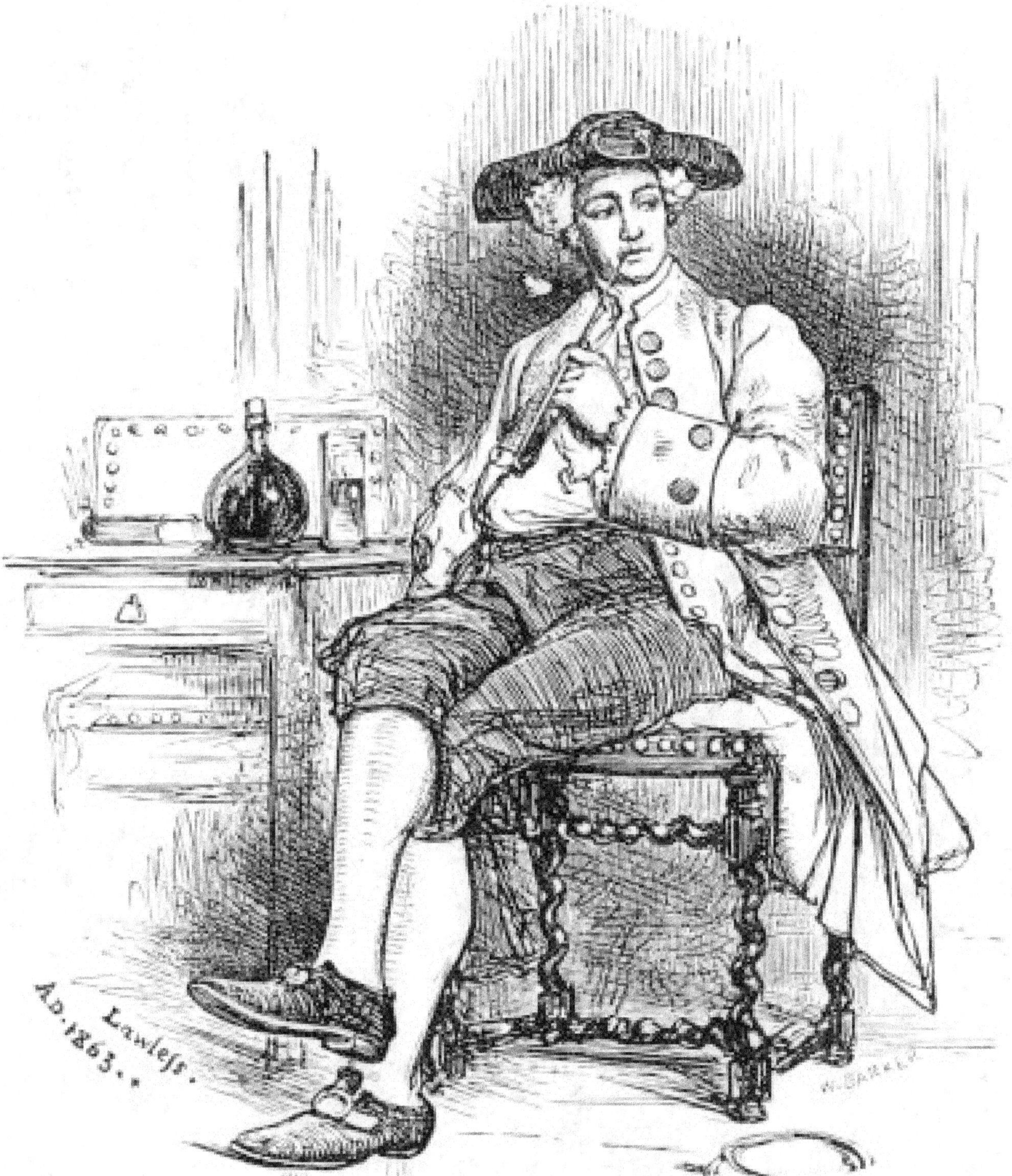
Lawless.
AD. 1863.

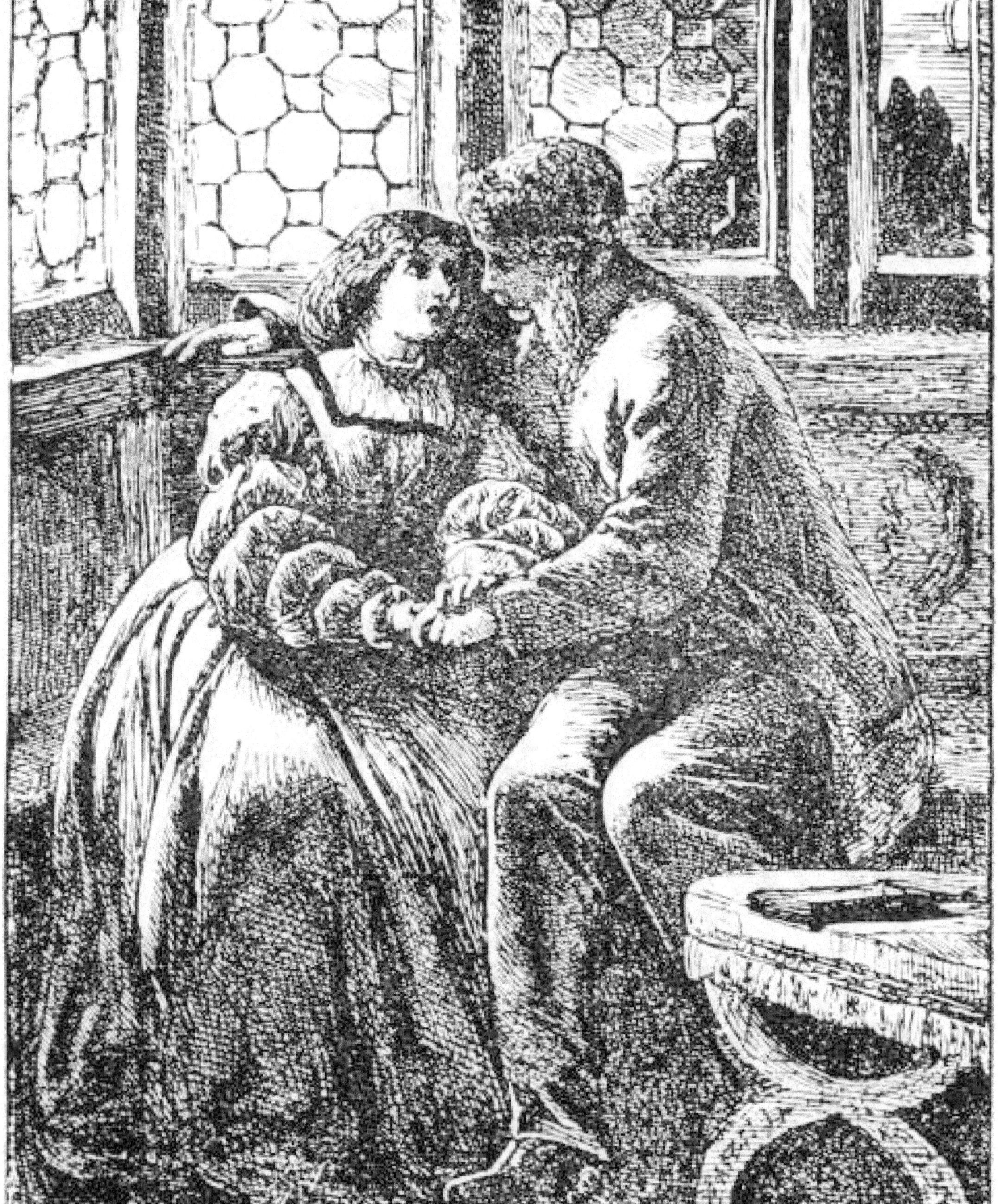

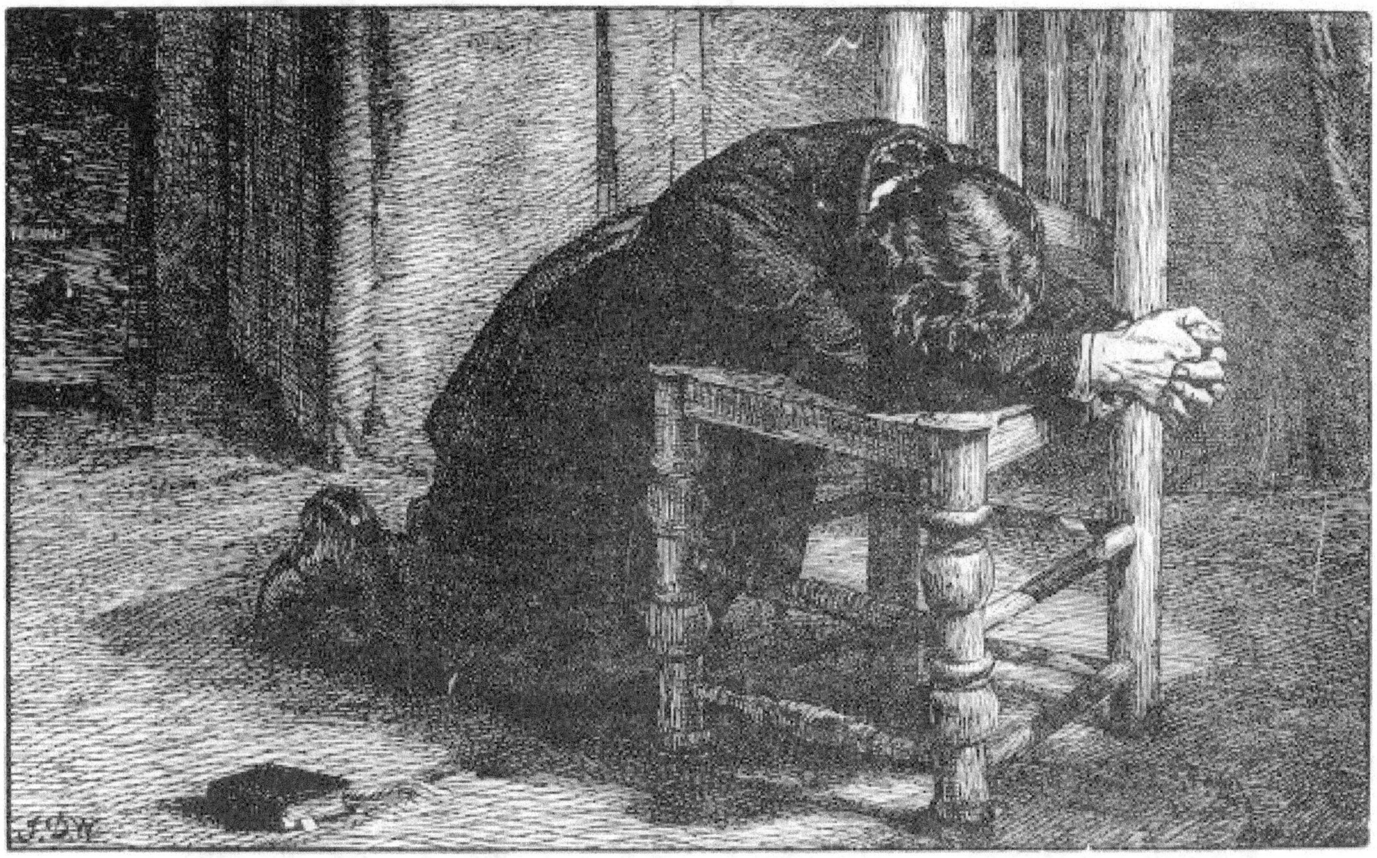

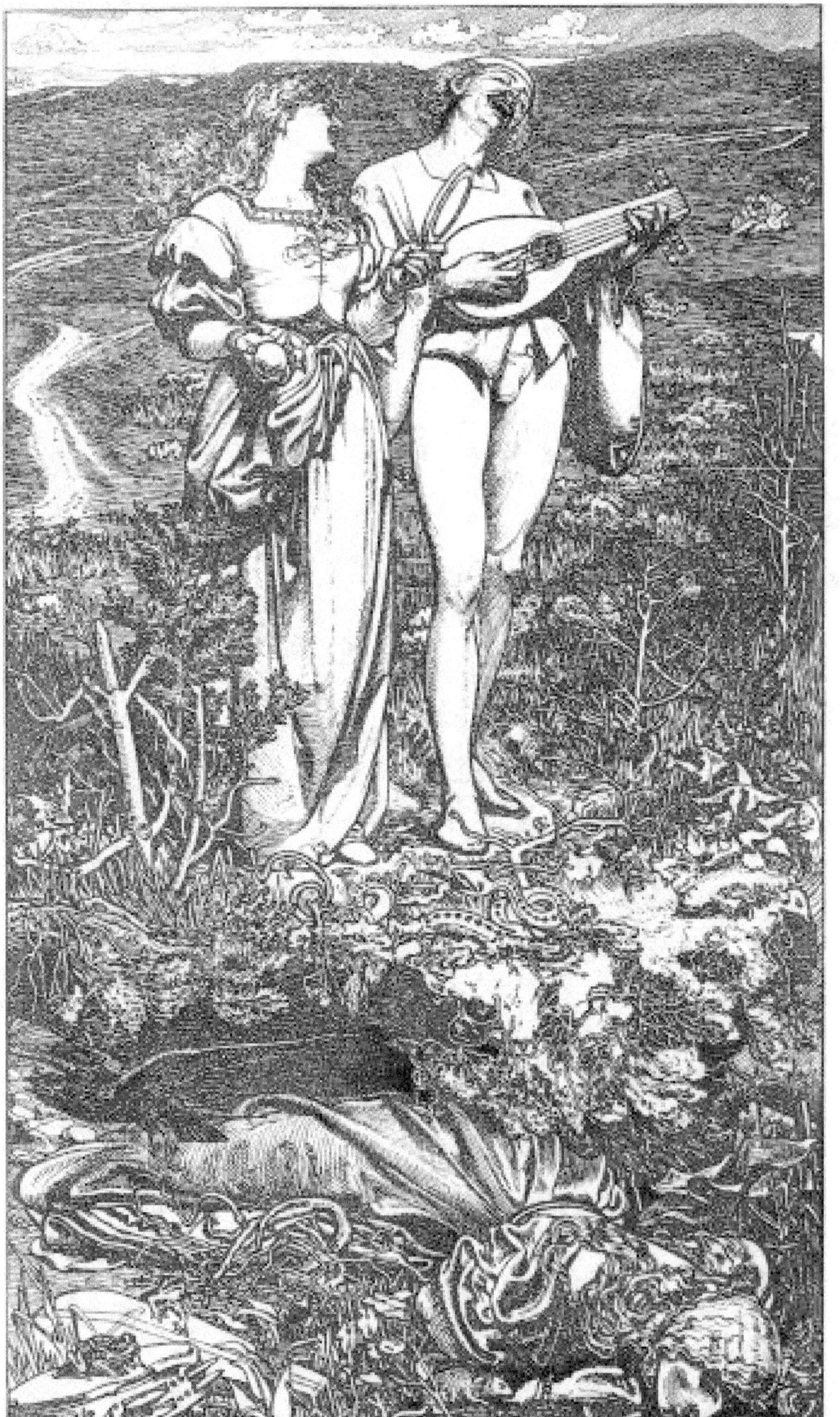

Frederick Sandys del.

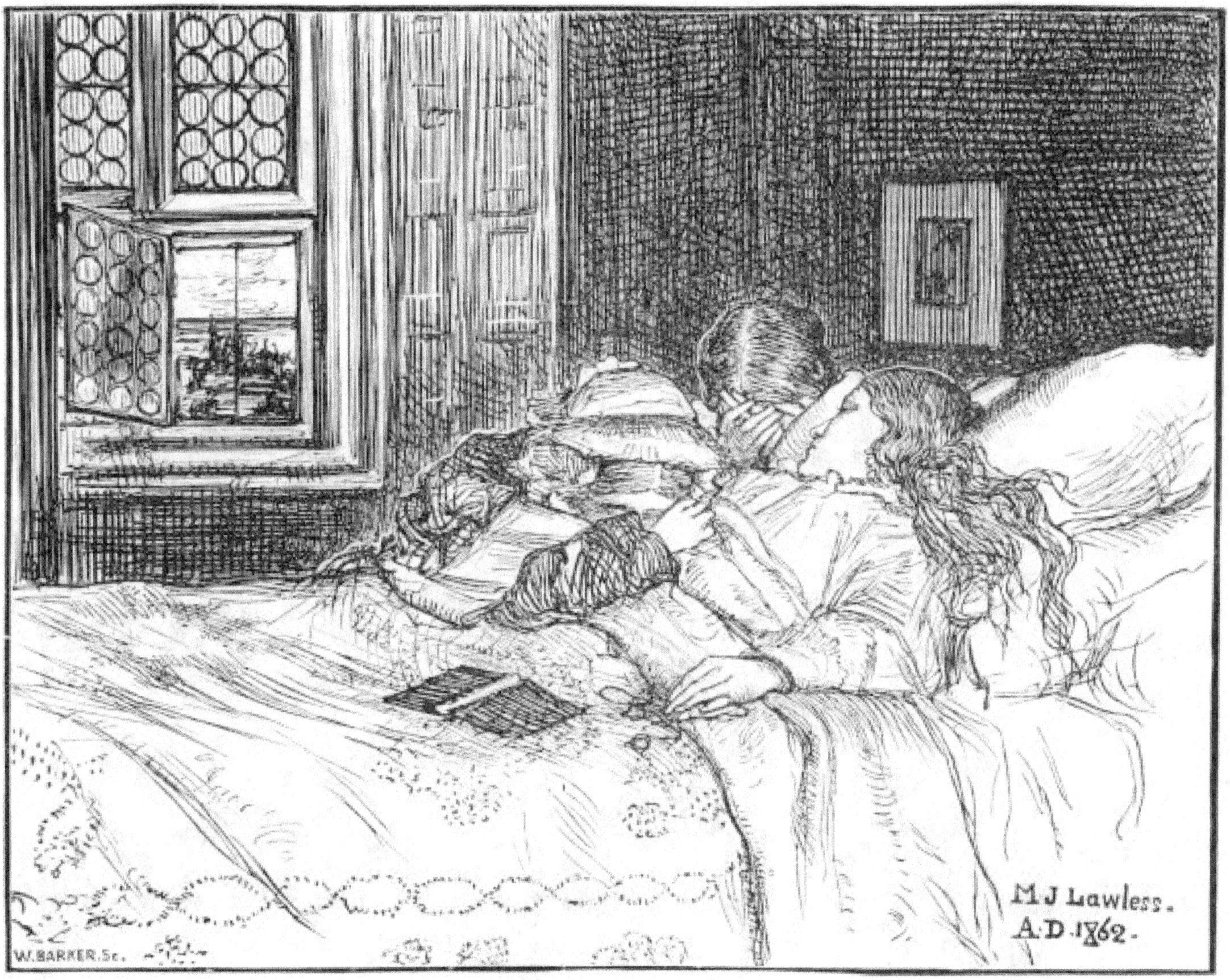
M J Lawless.
A.D. 1862.
W. BARKER. Sc.

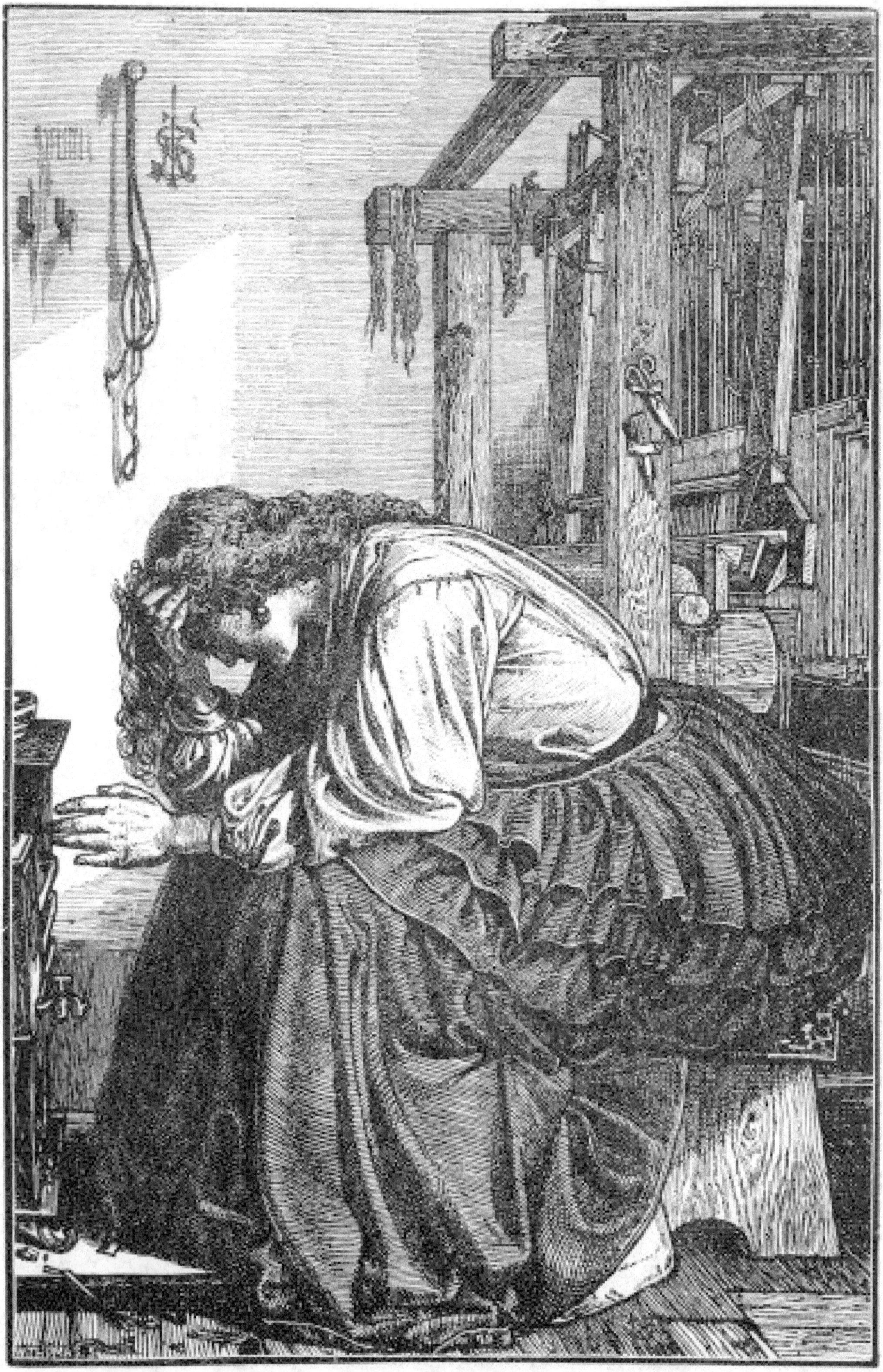

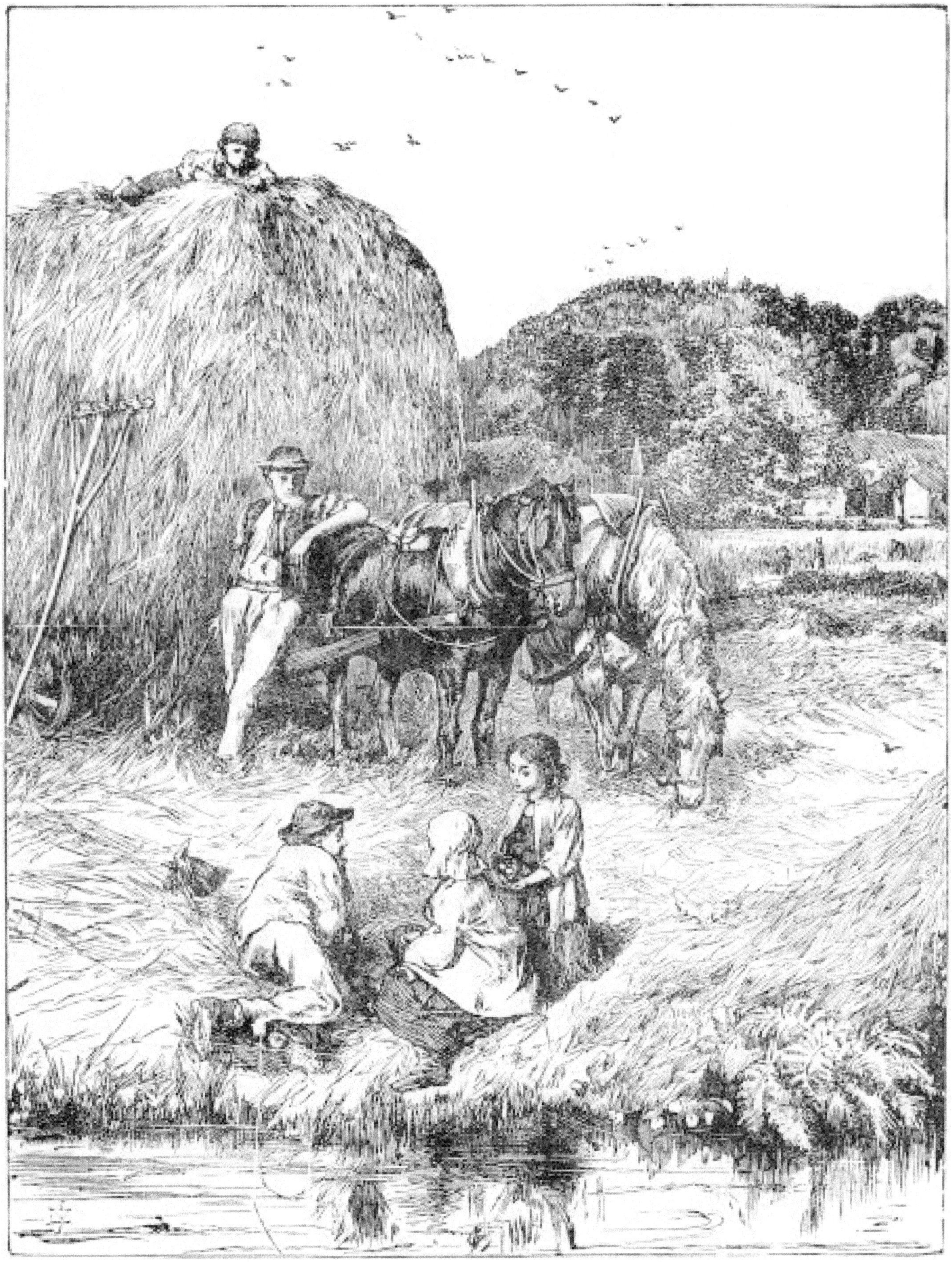

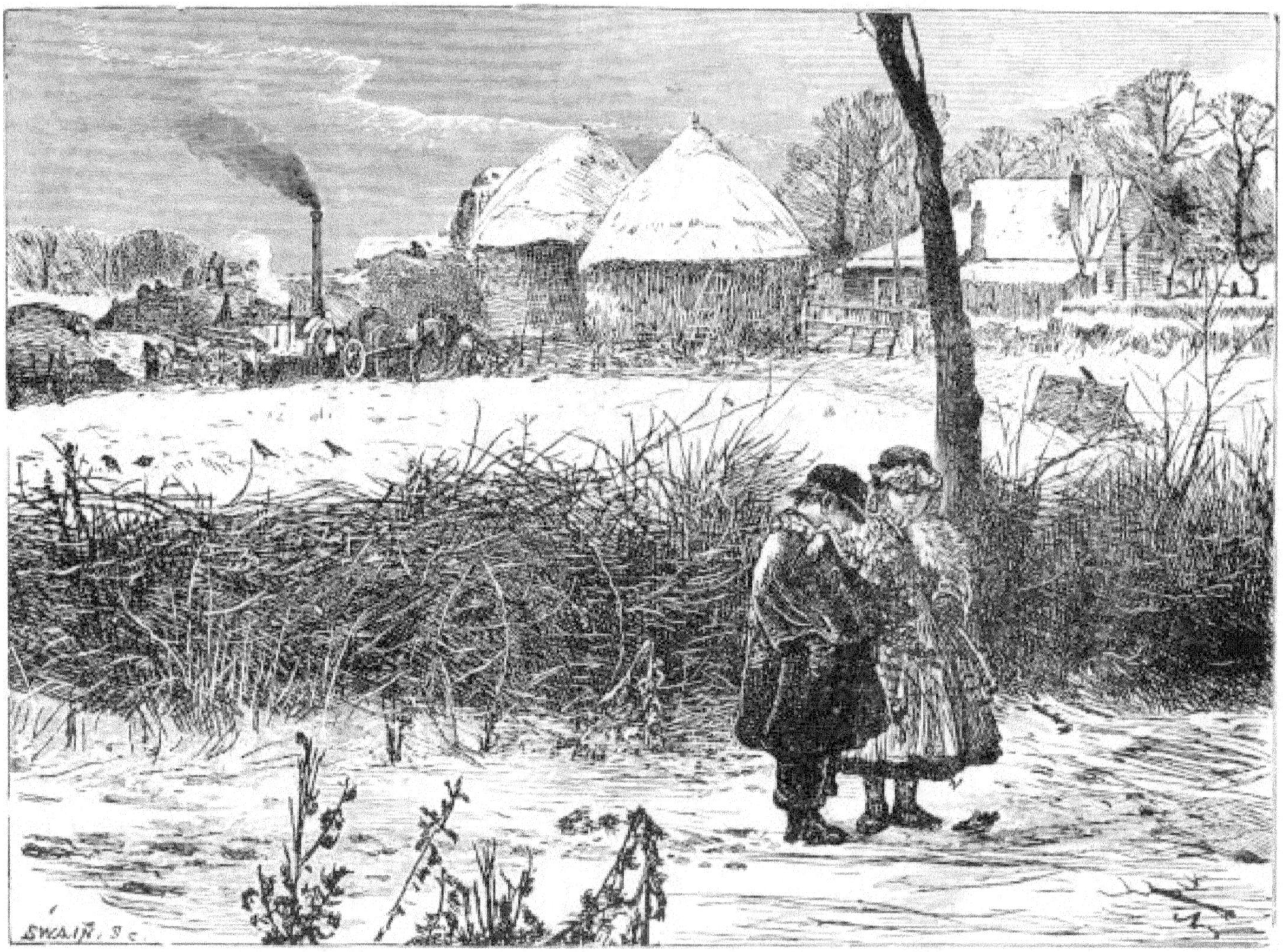
SWAIN, Sc

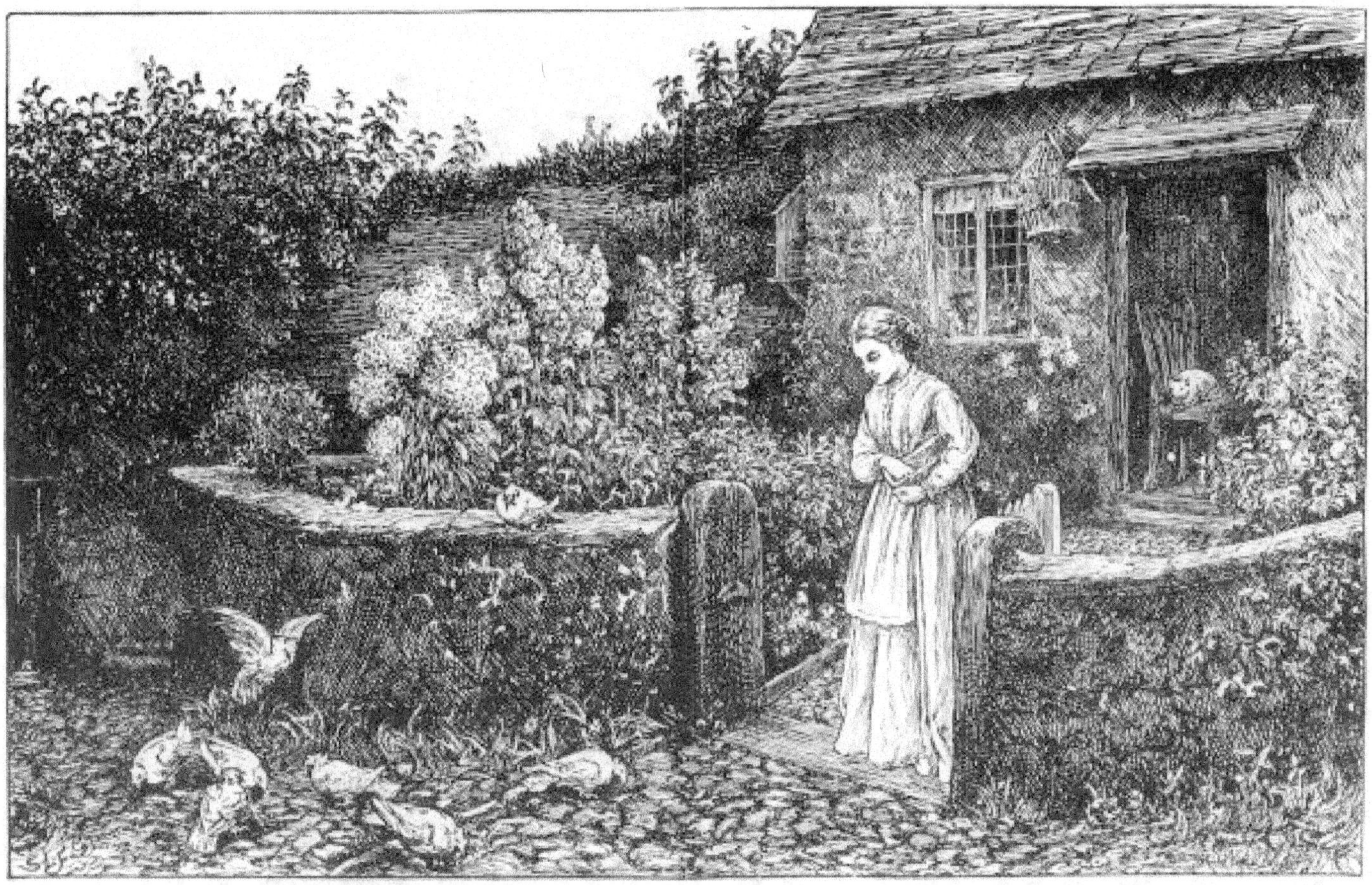

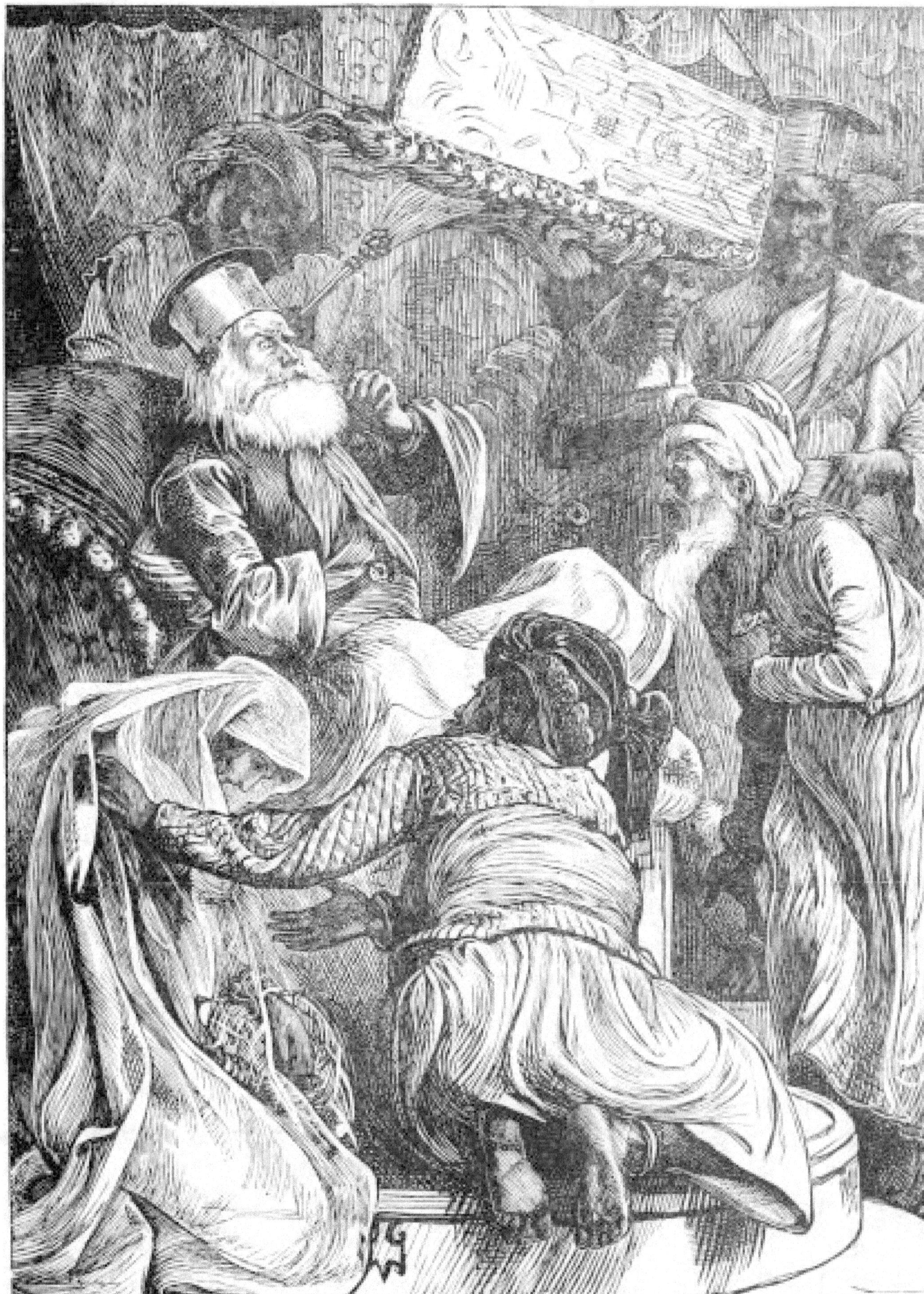

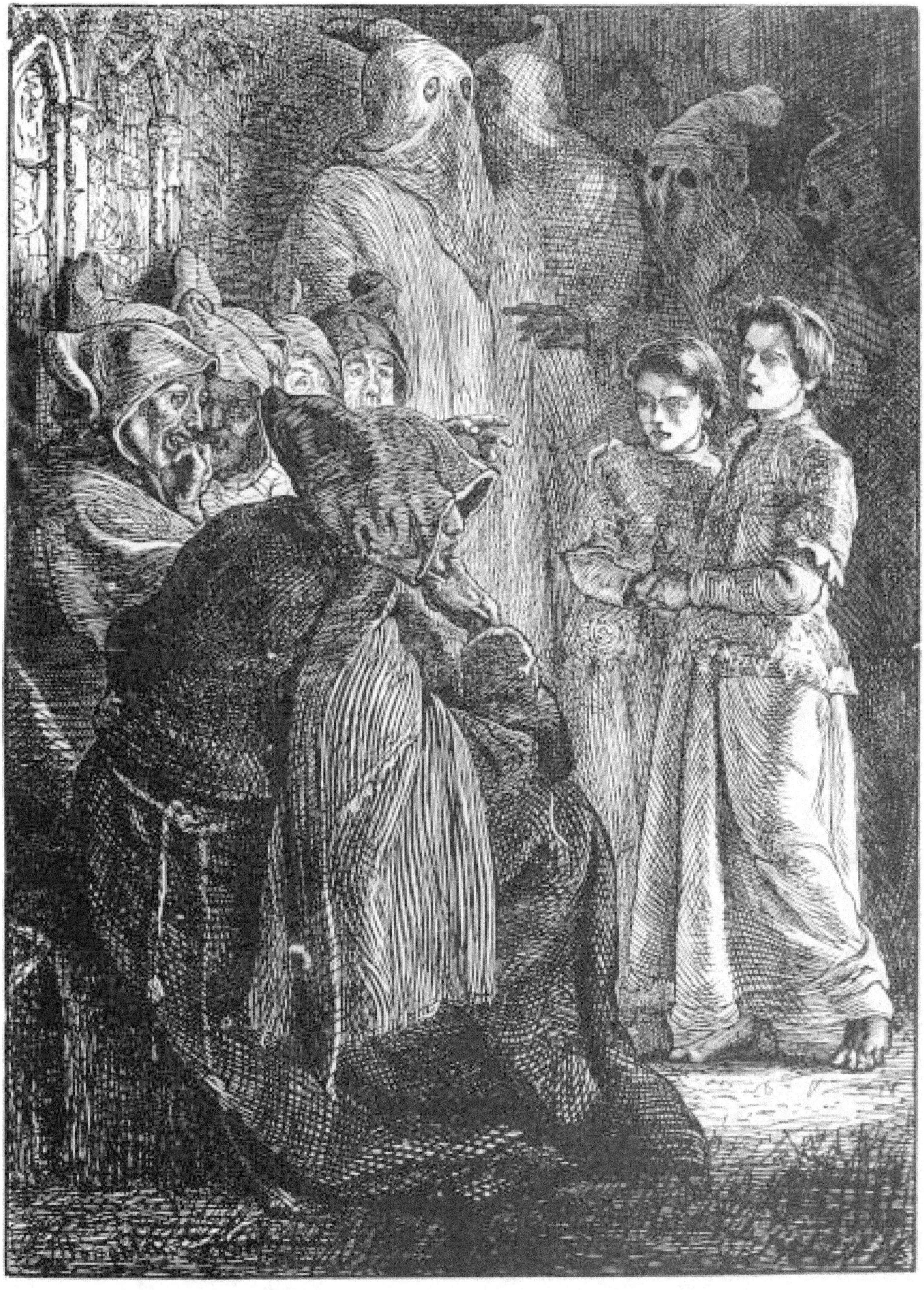

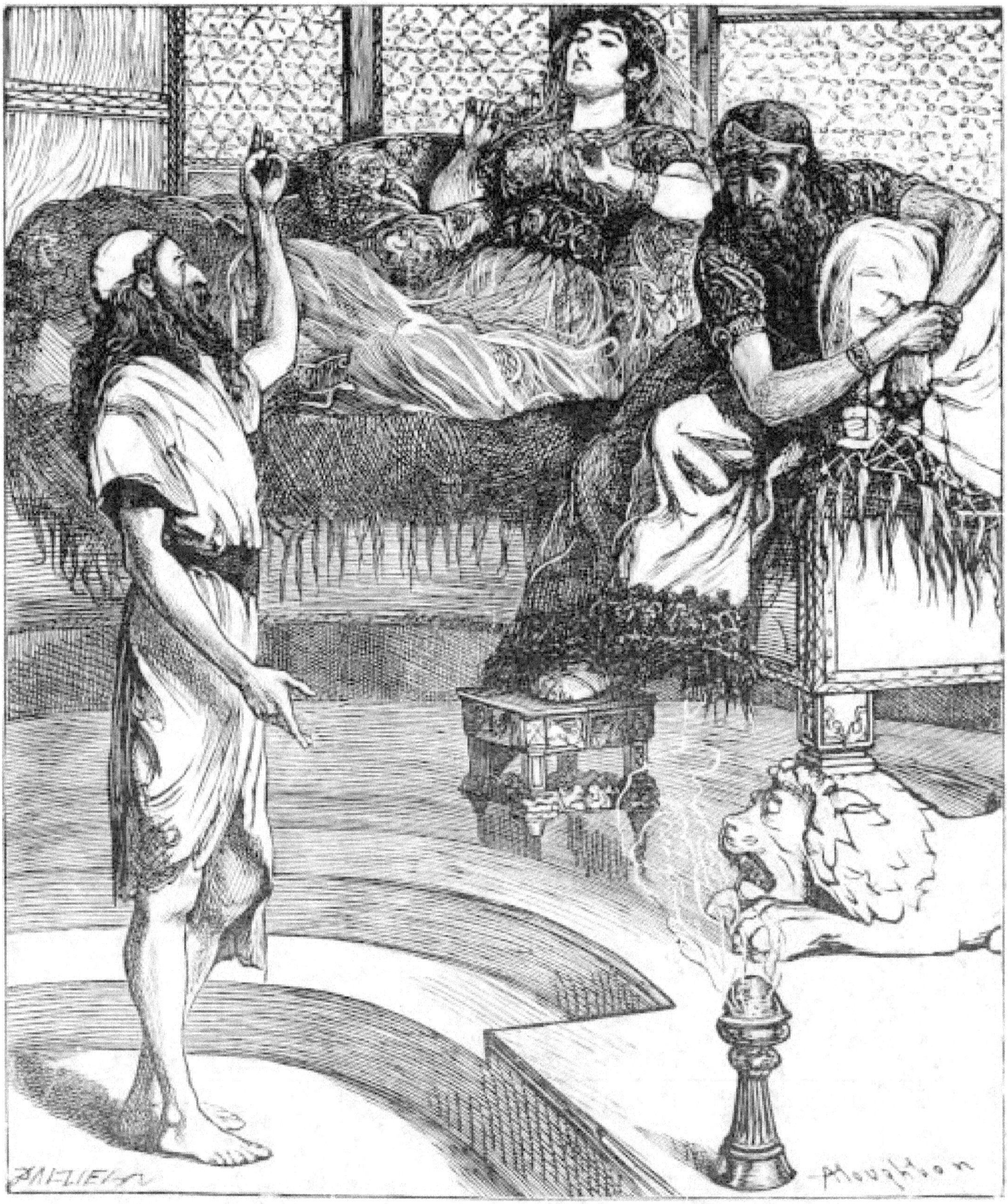
DALZIEL
Houghton

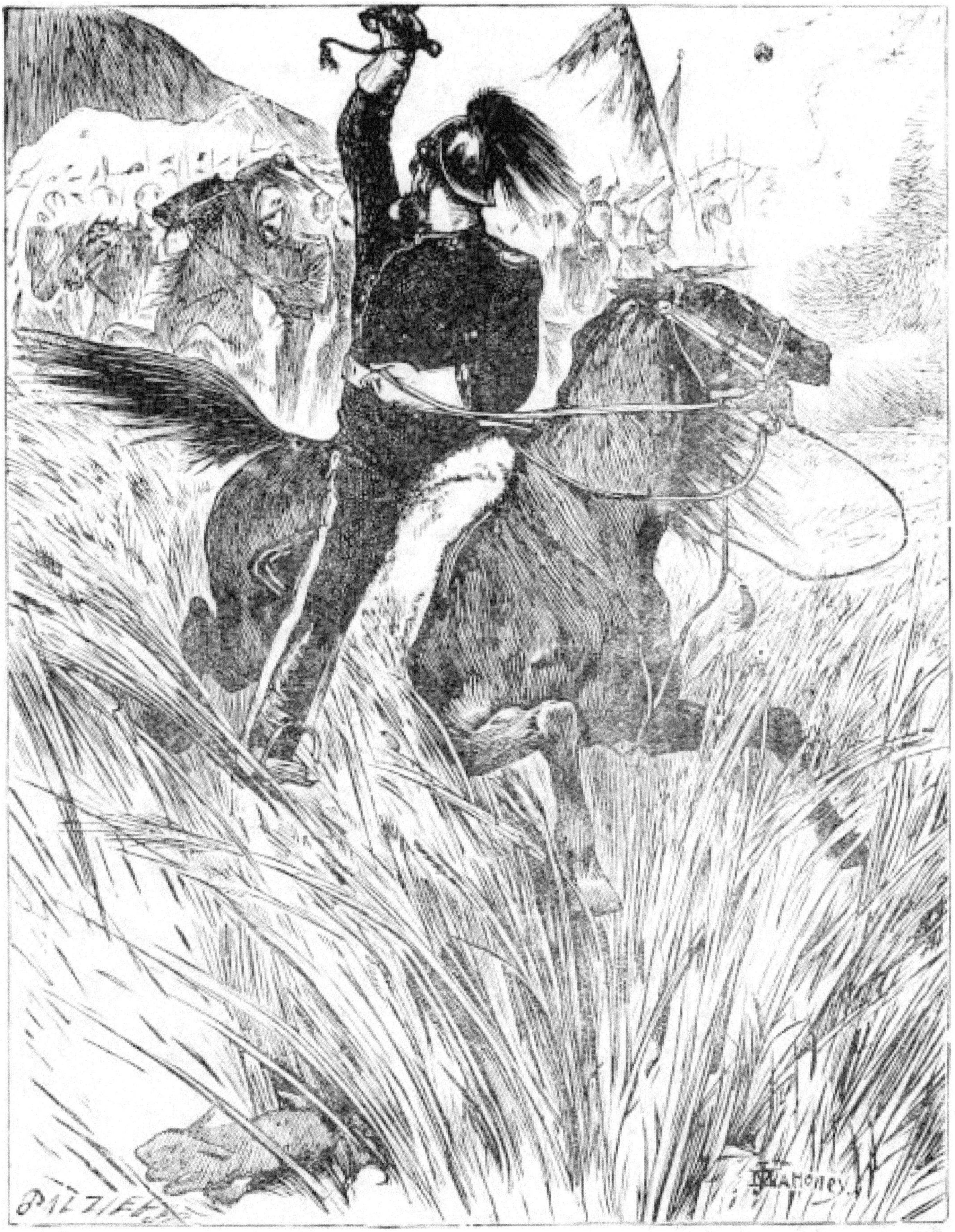

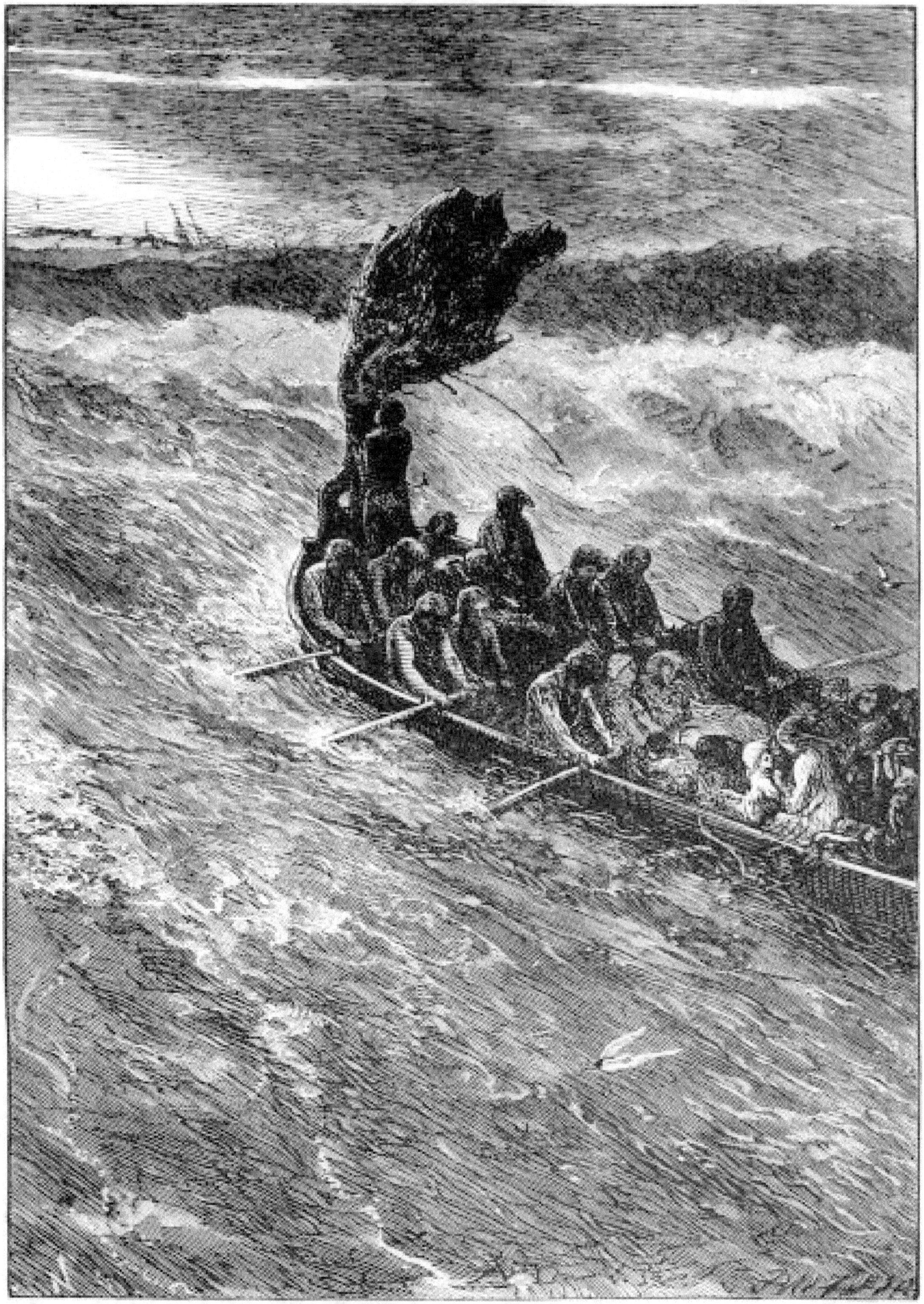

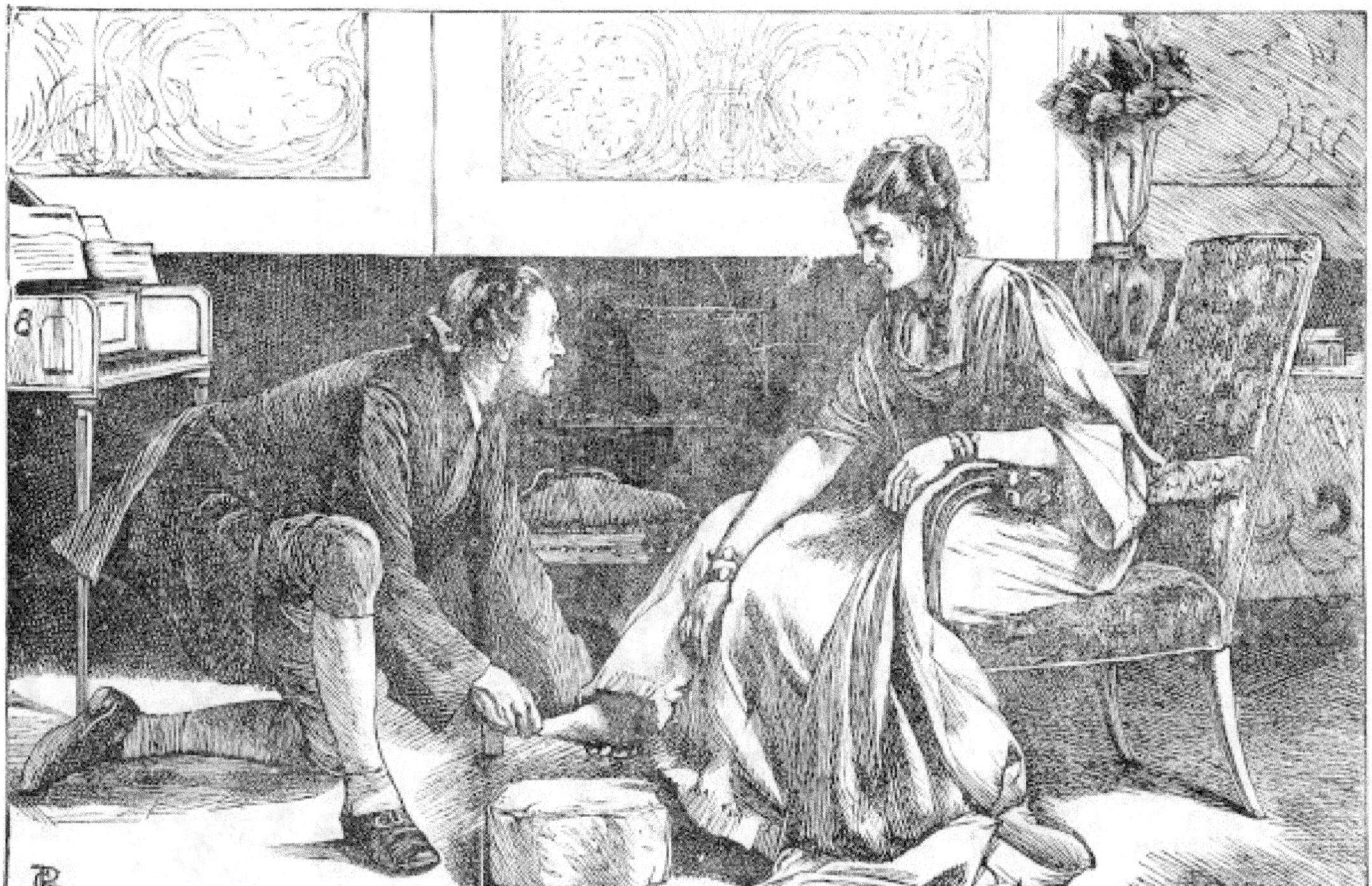

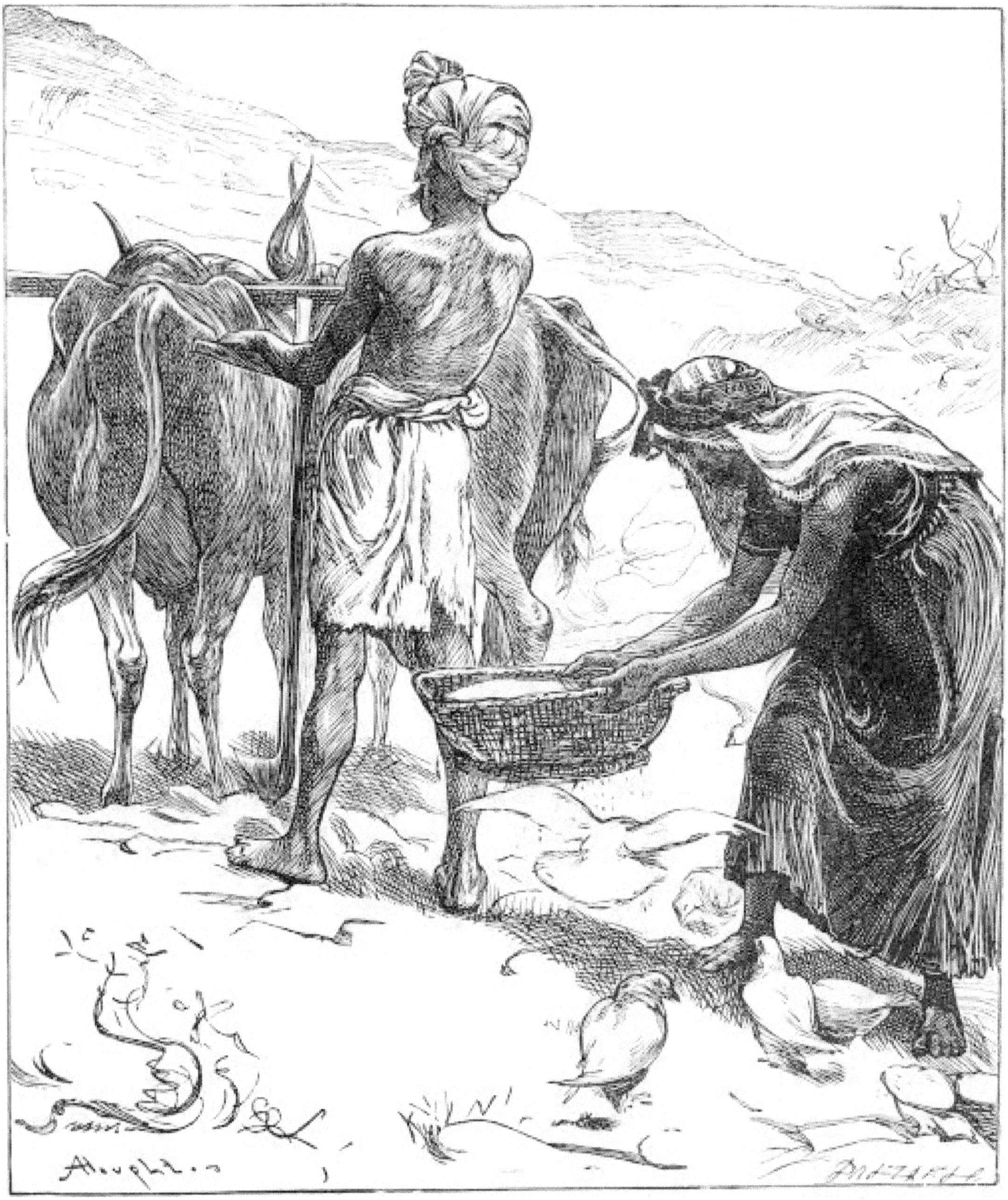

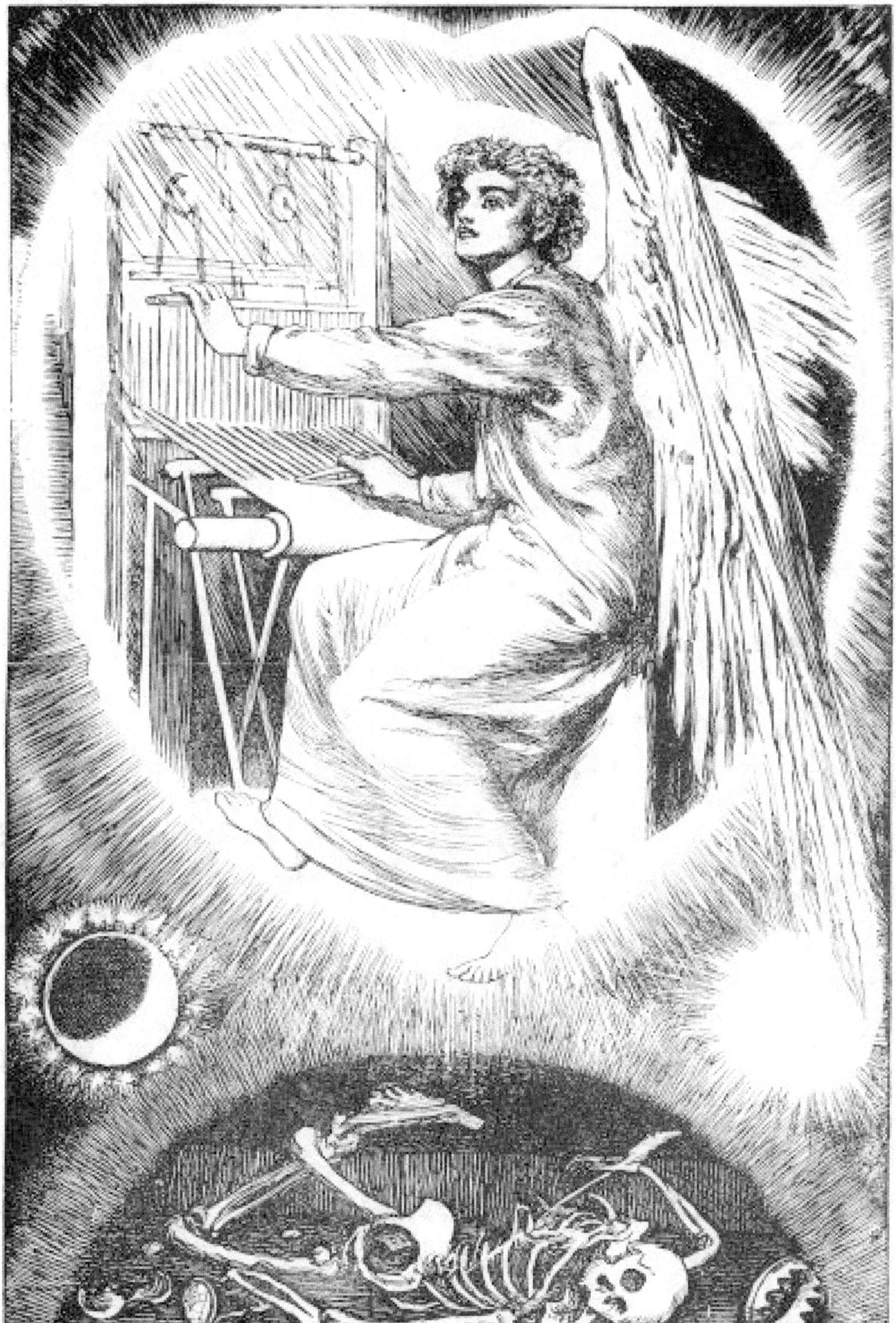

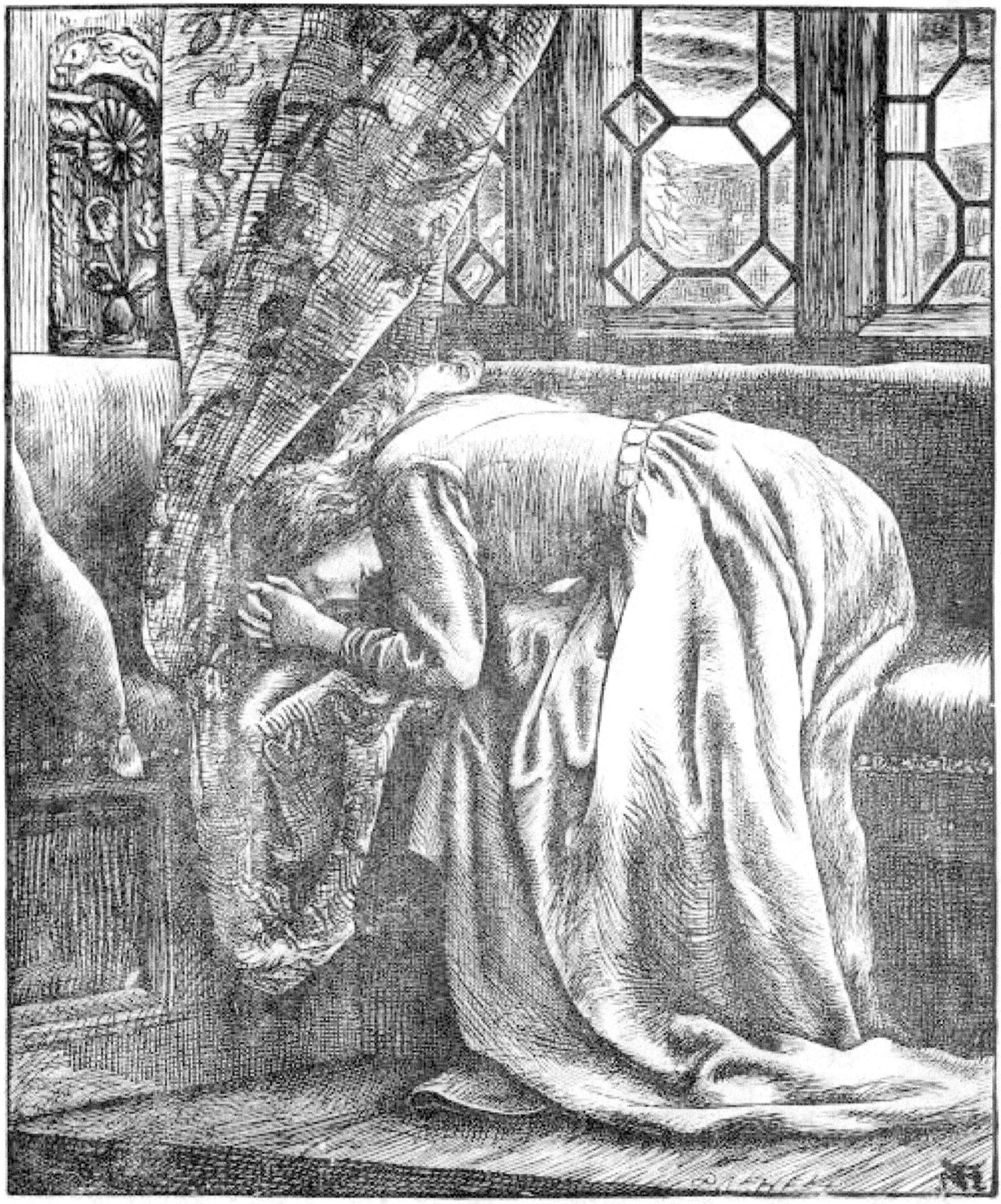

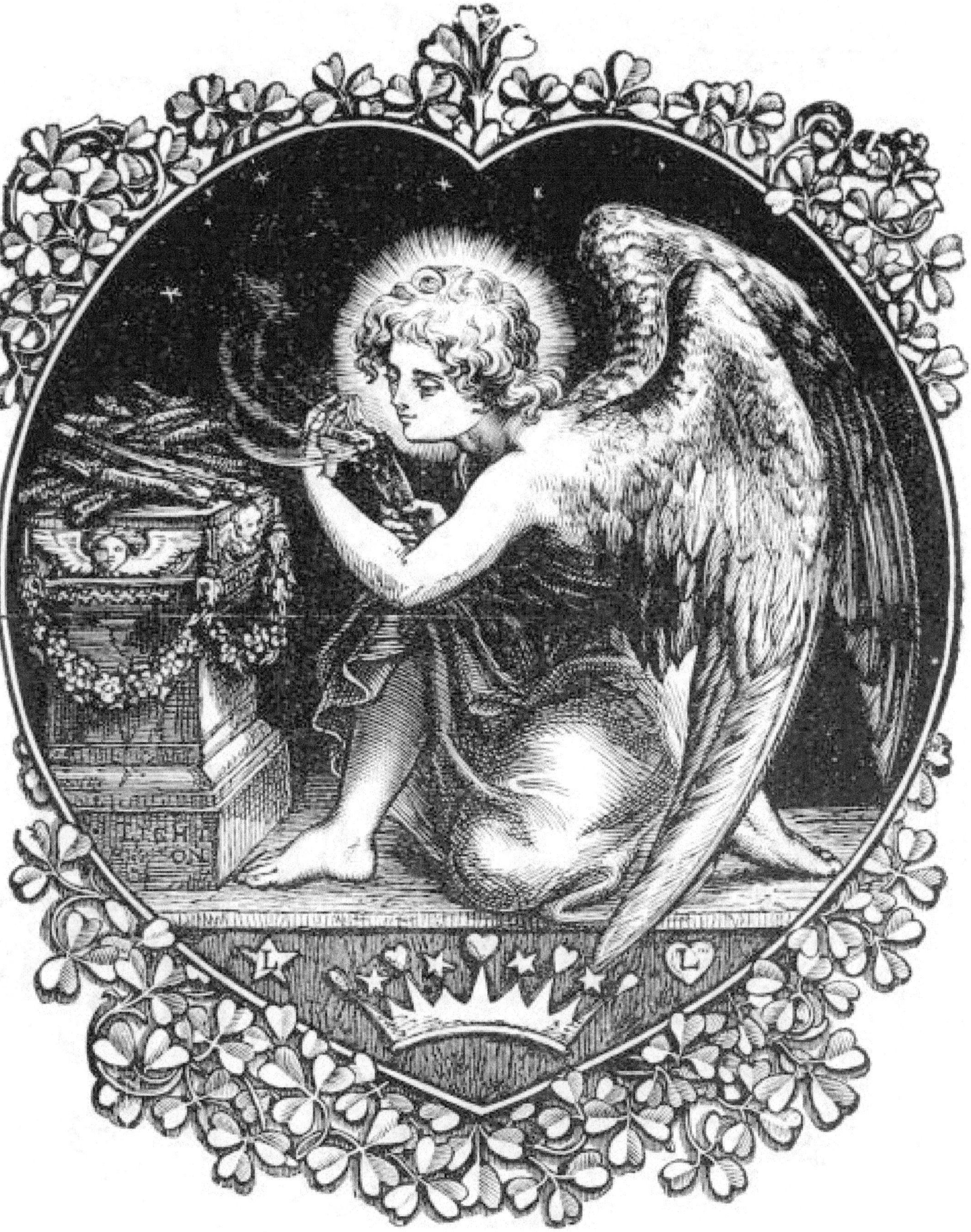

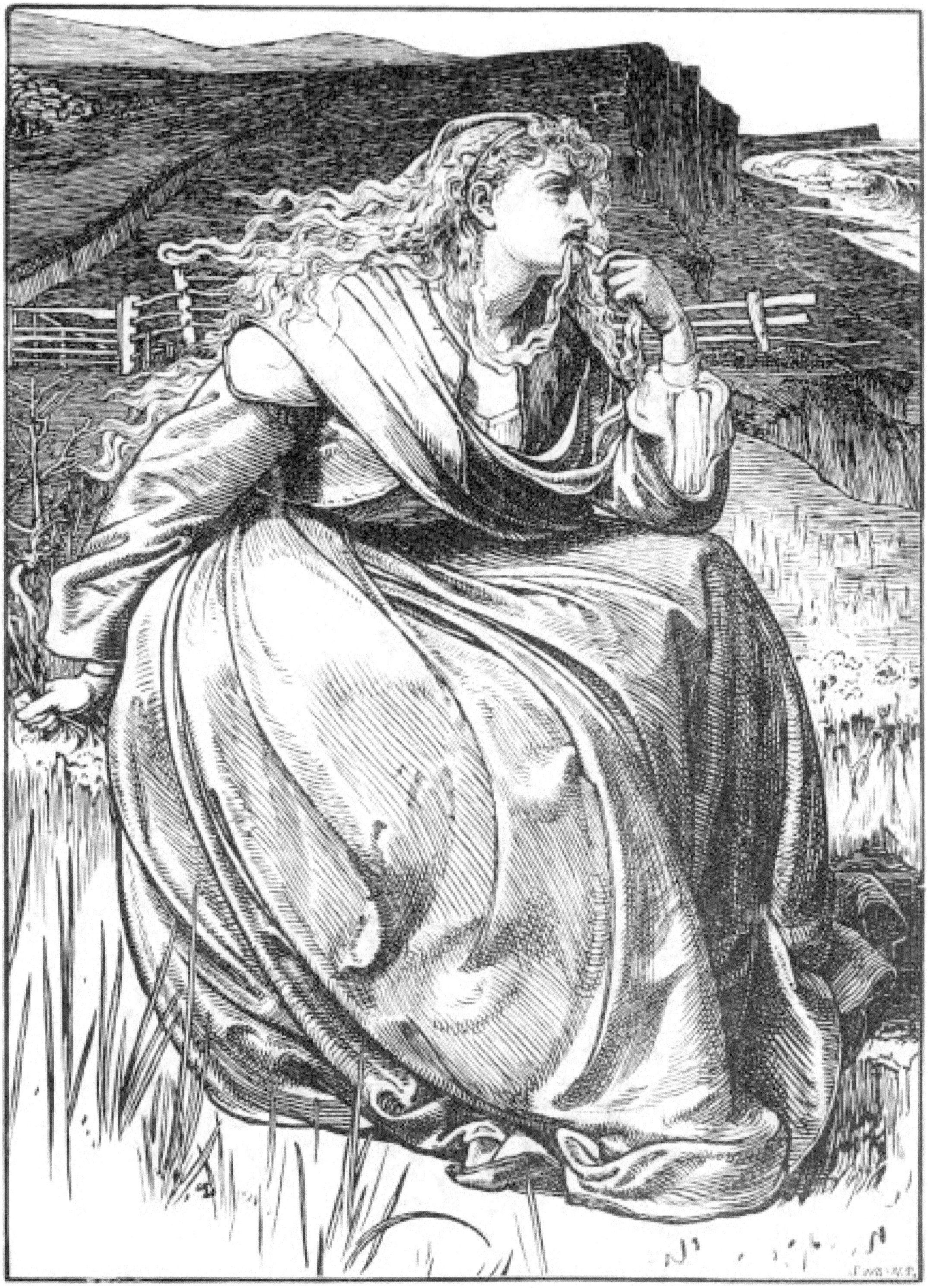

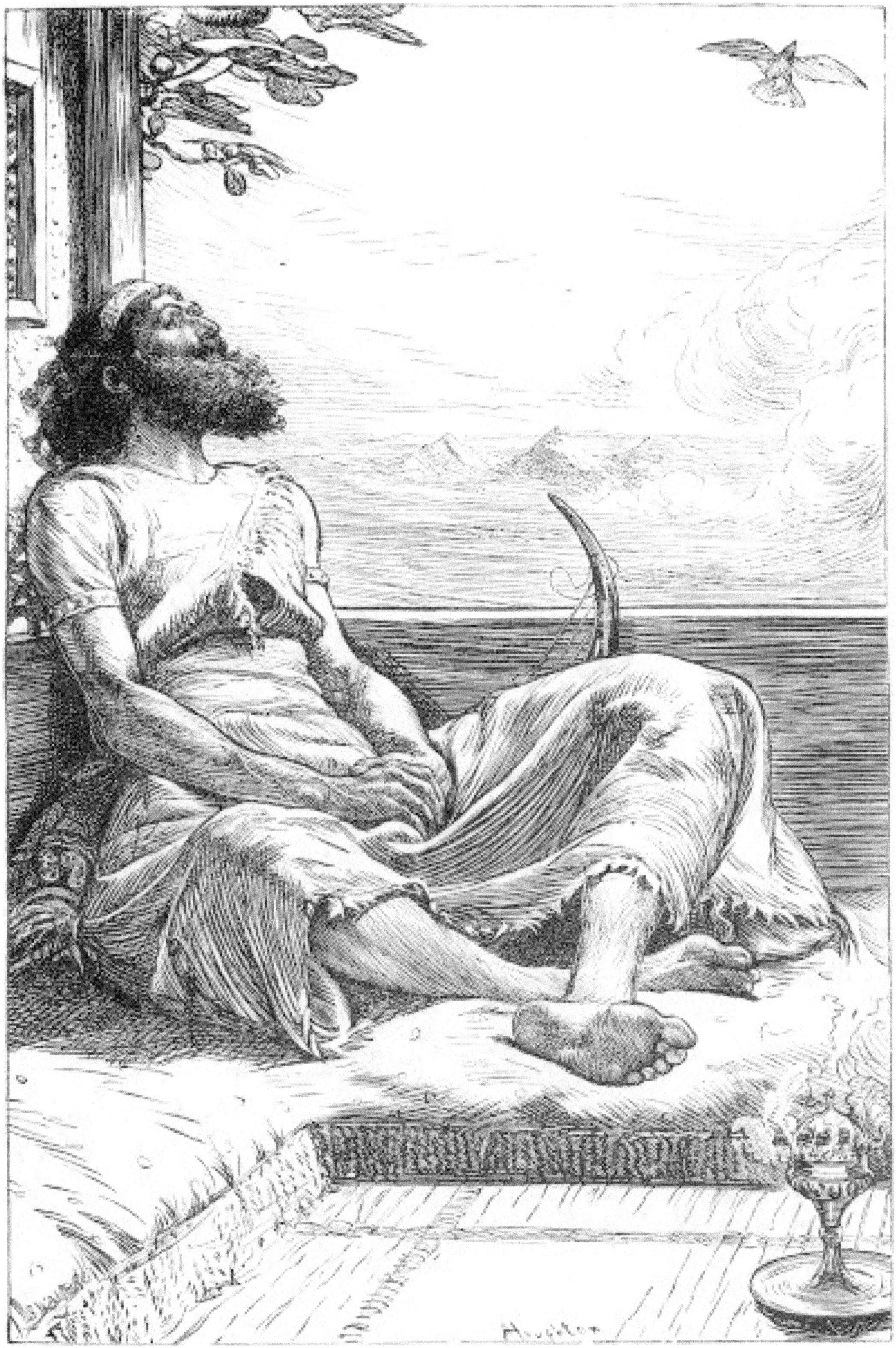

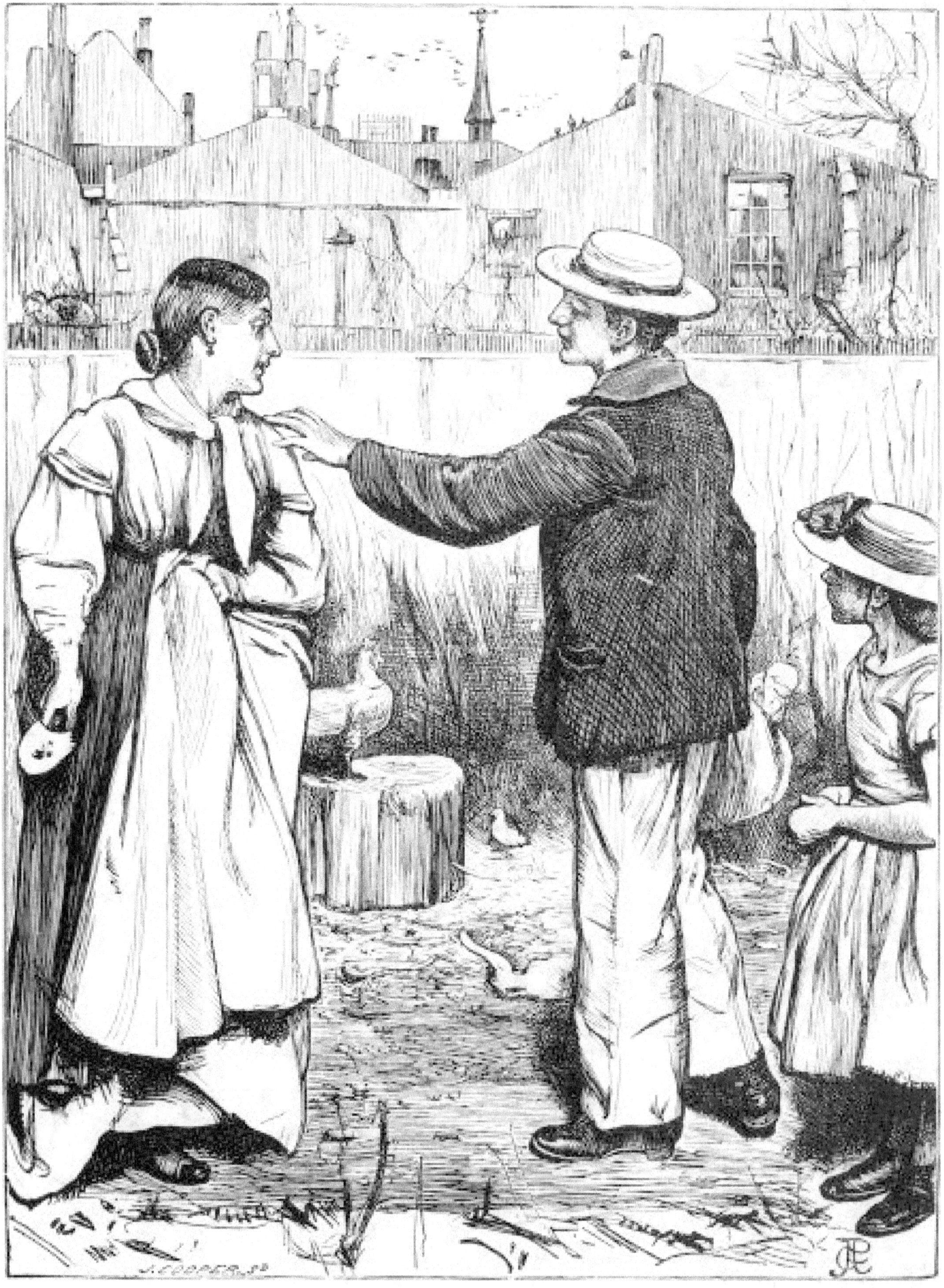

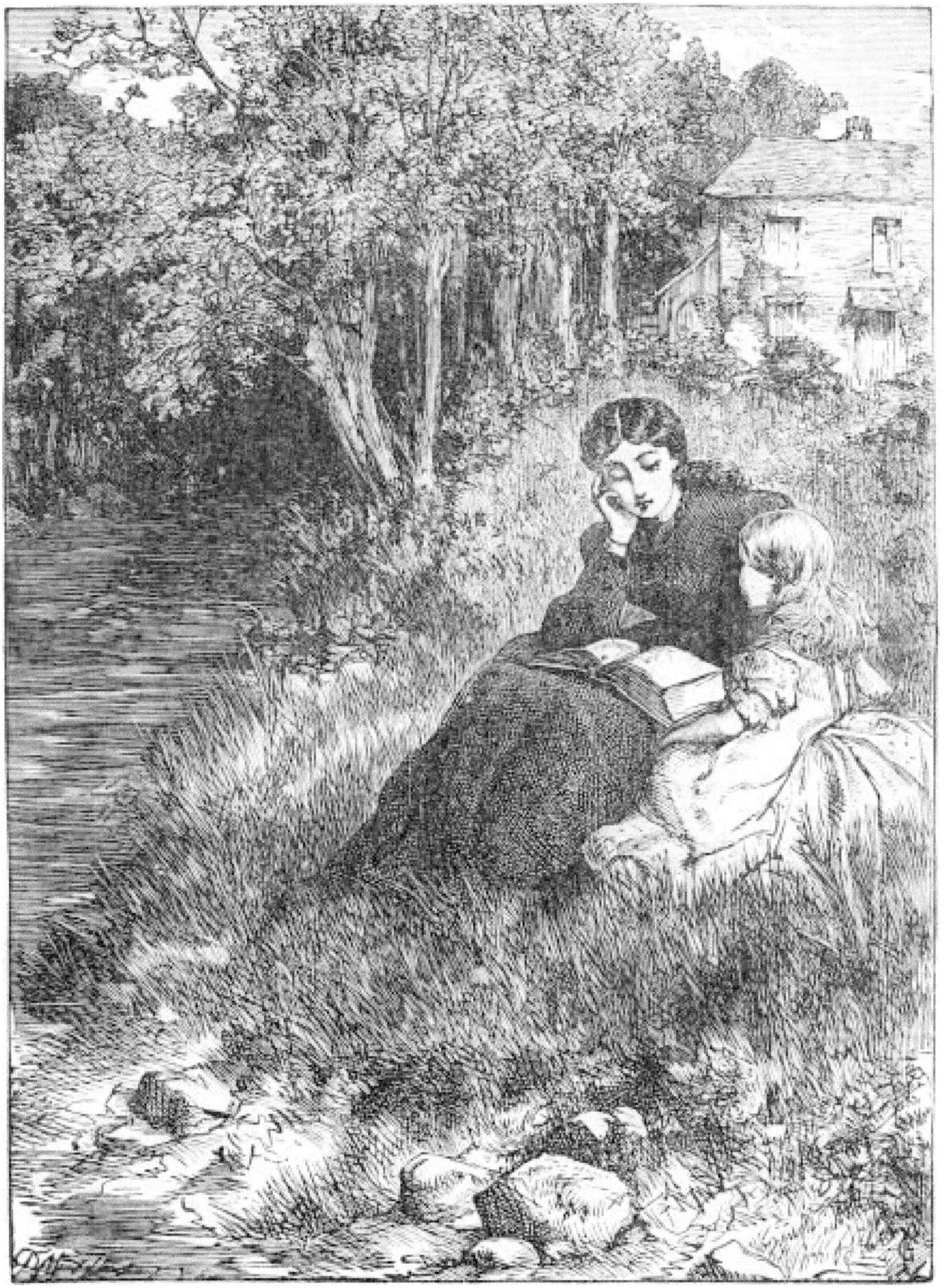

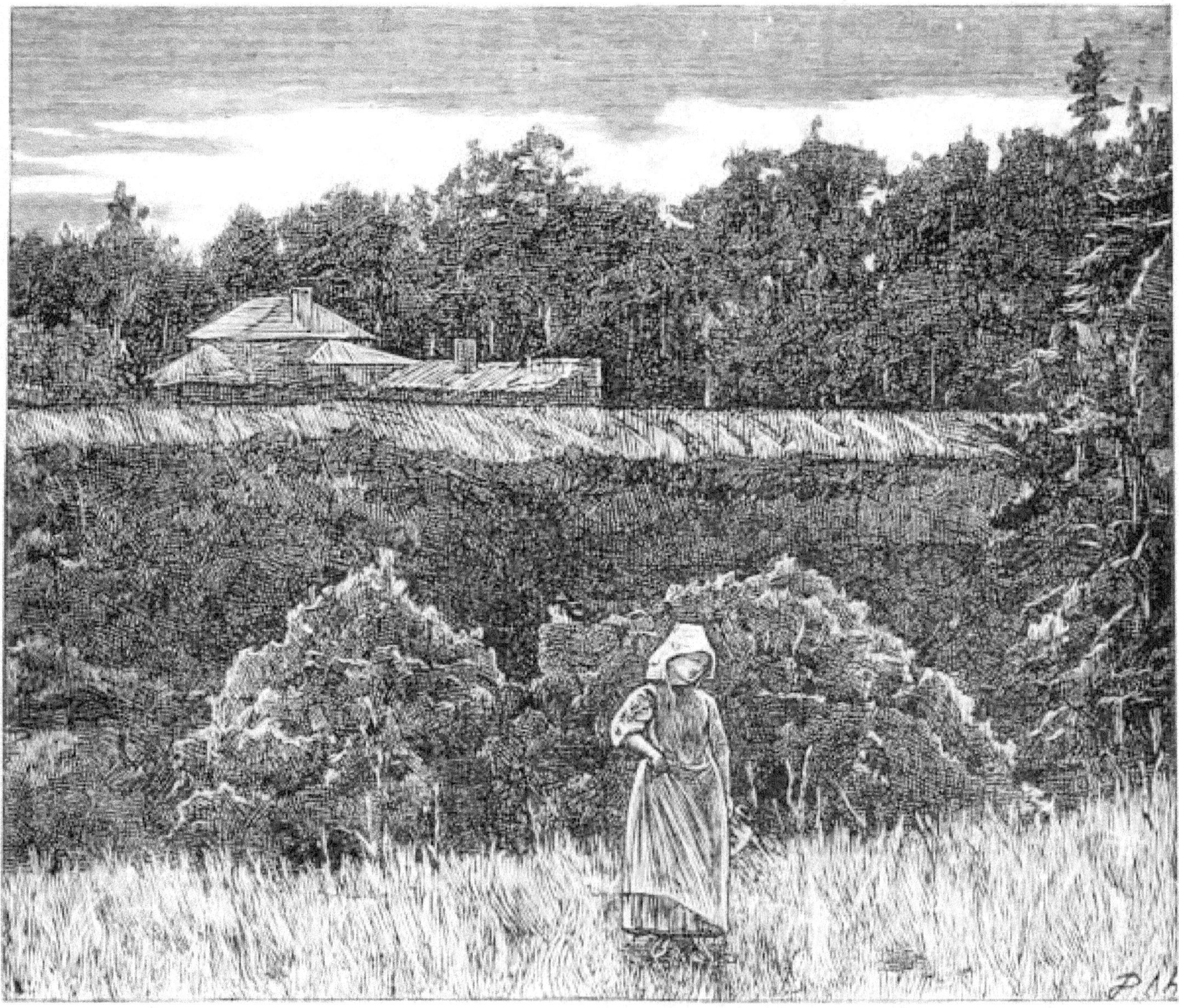

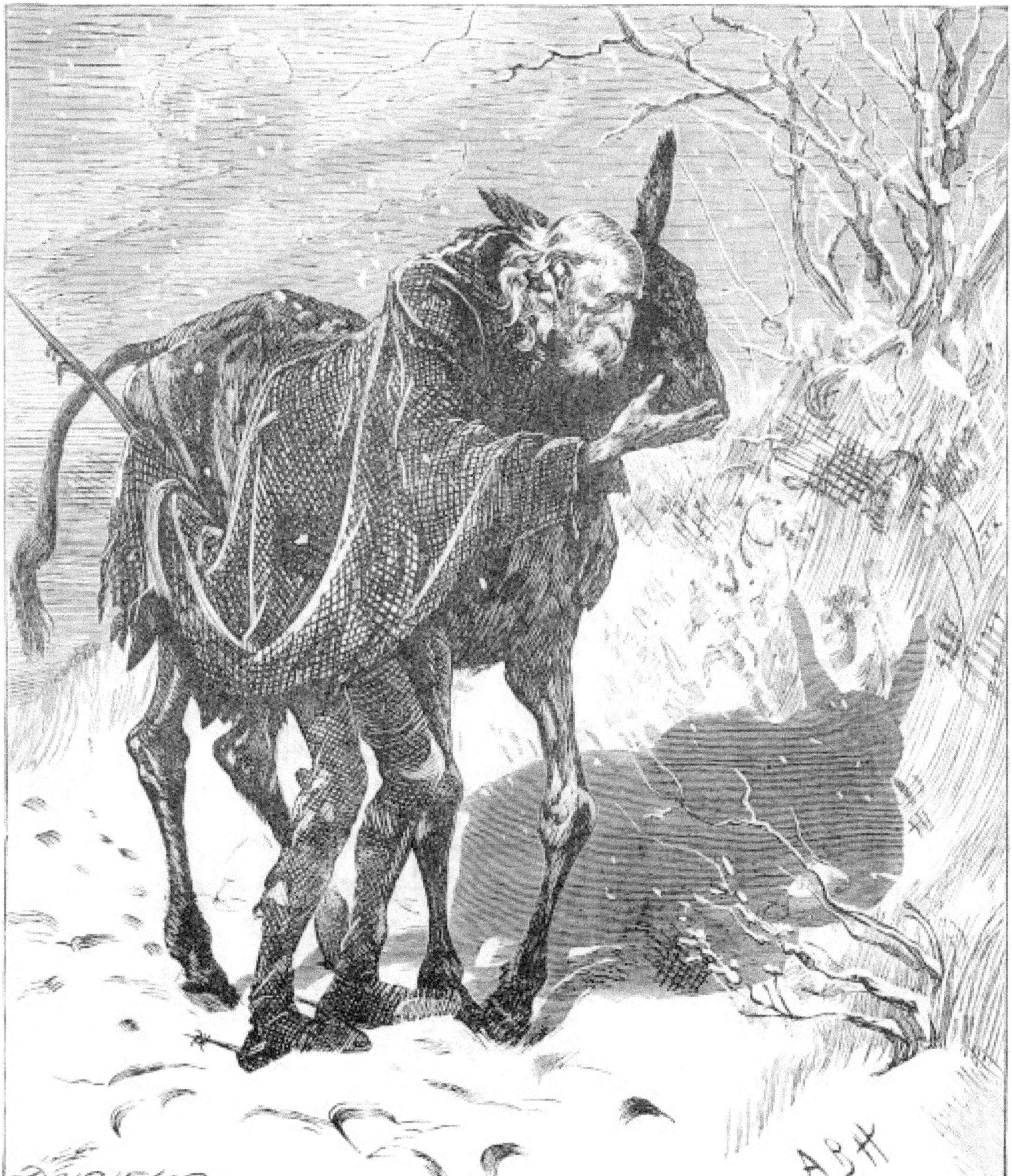
ABH

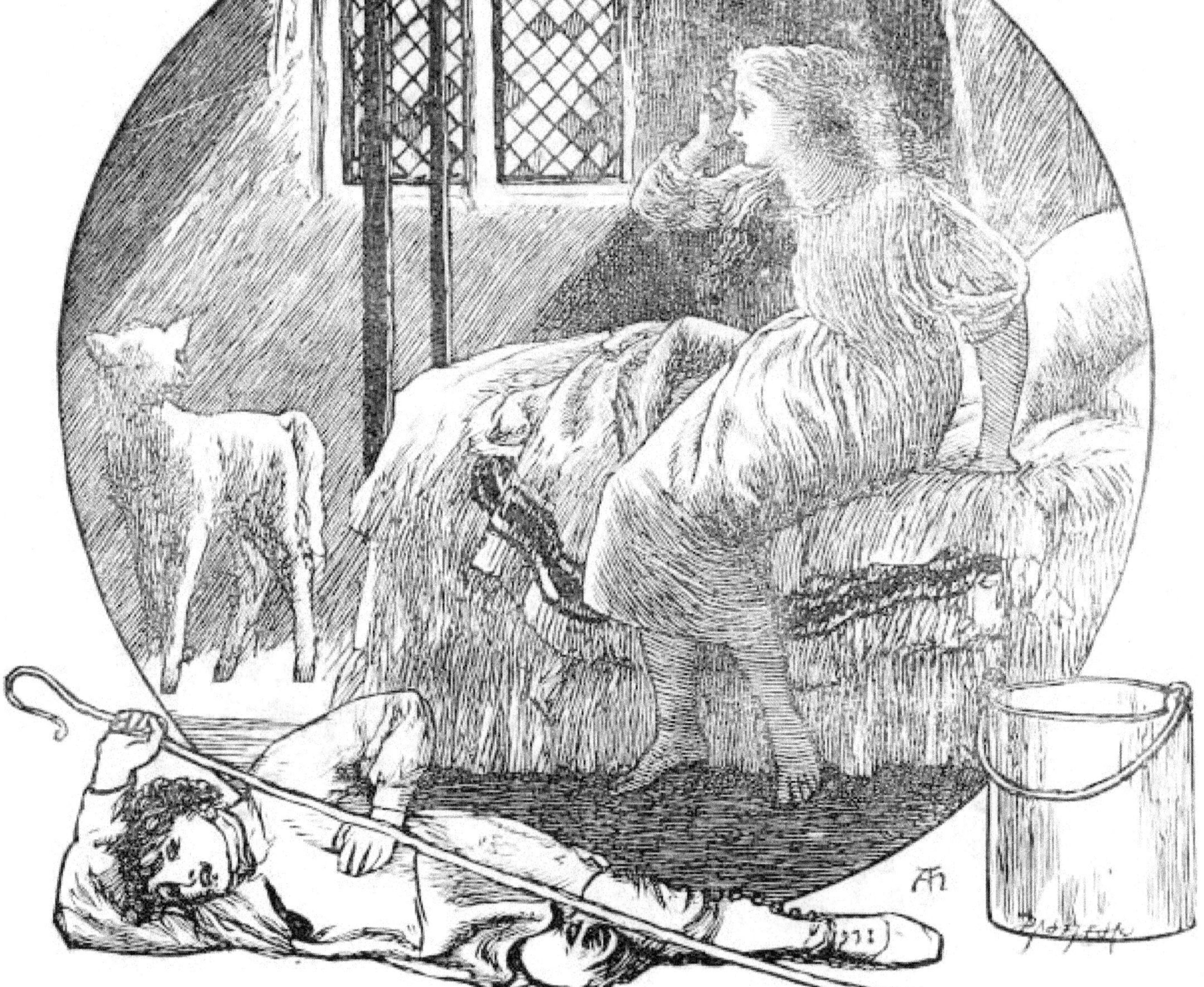

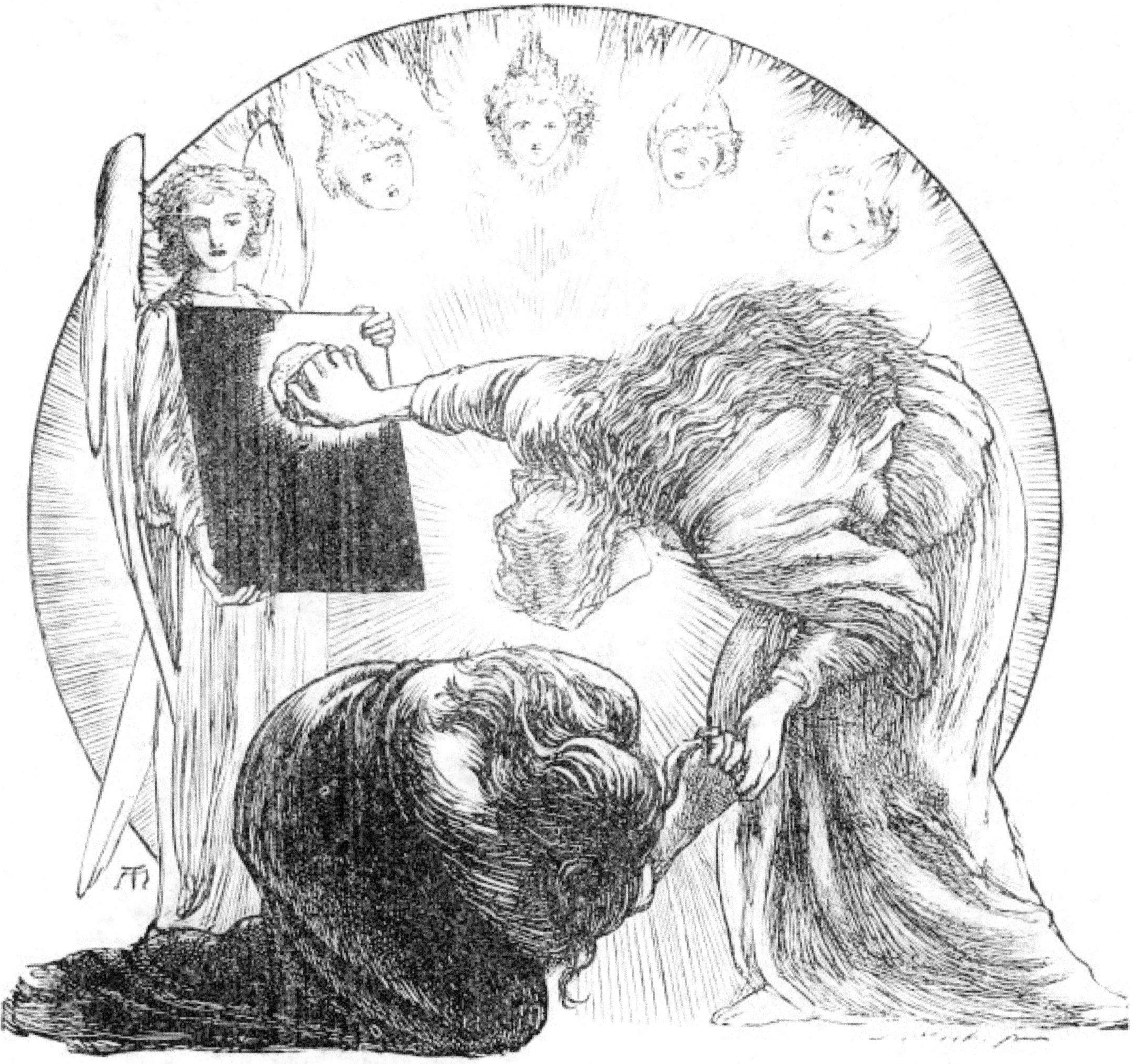

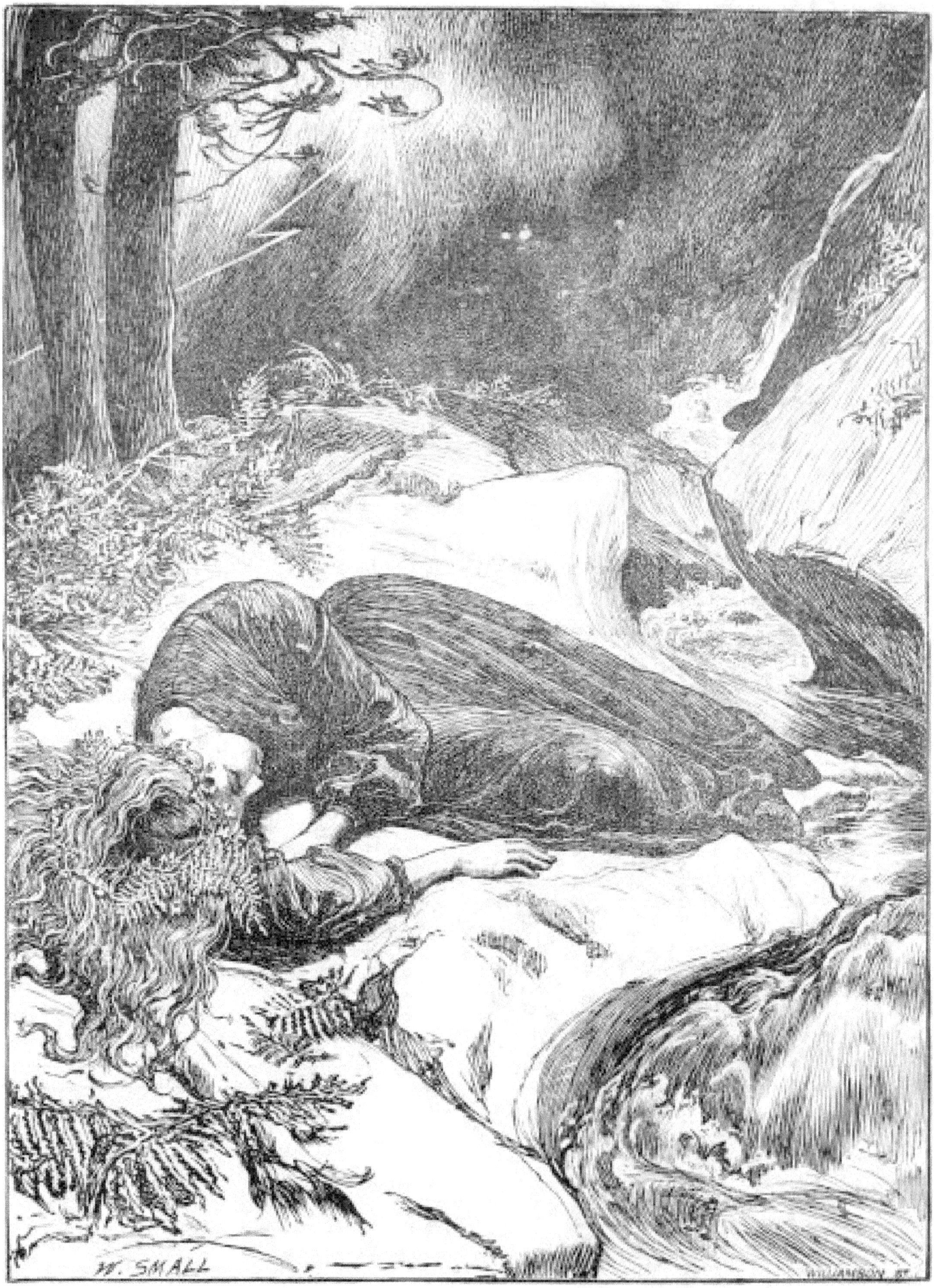
W. SMALL

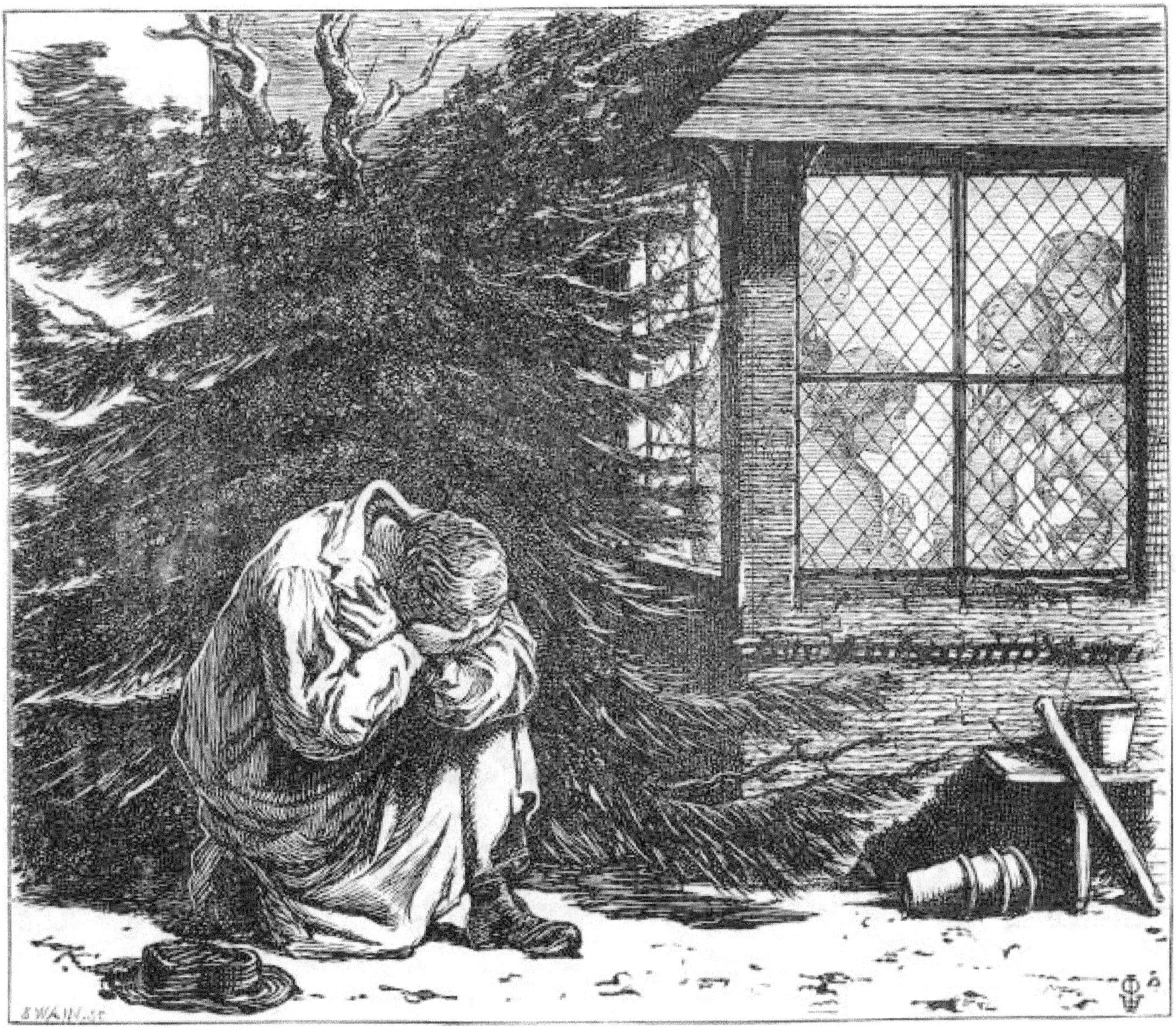
SWAIN sc

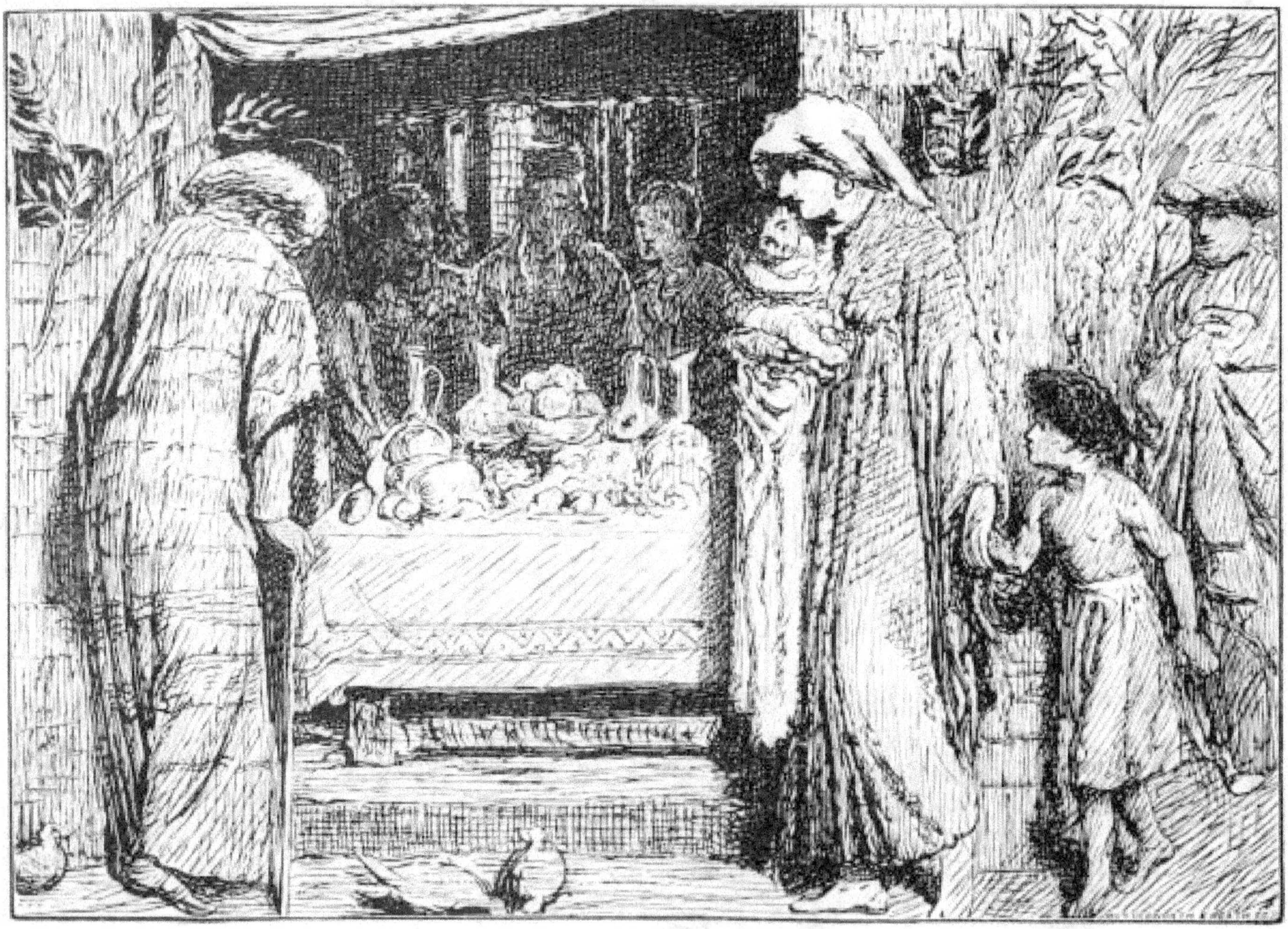

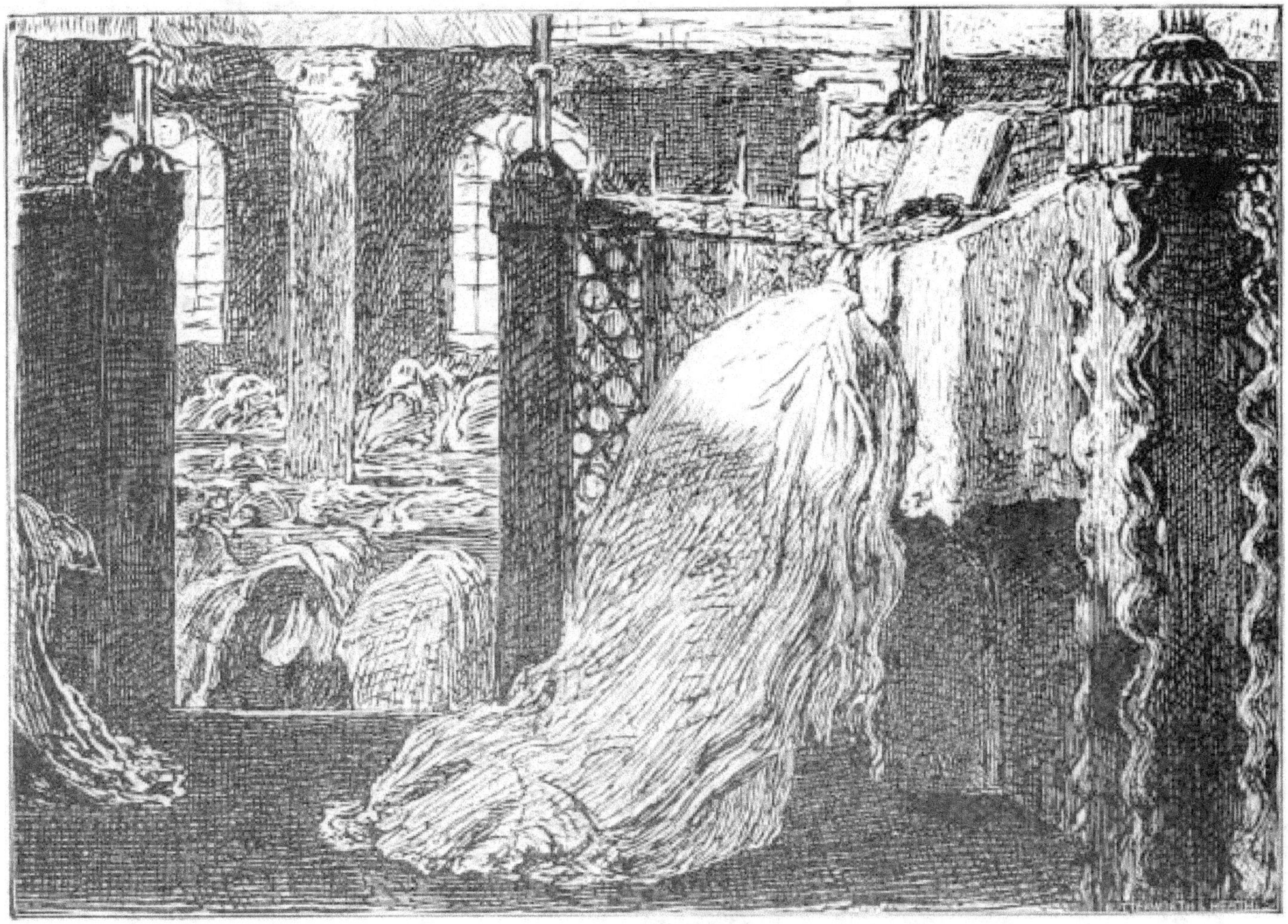

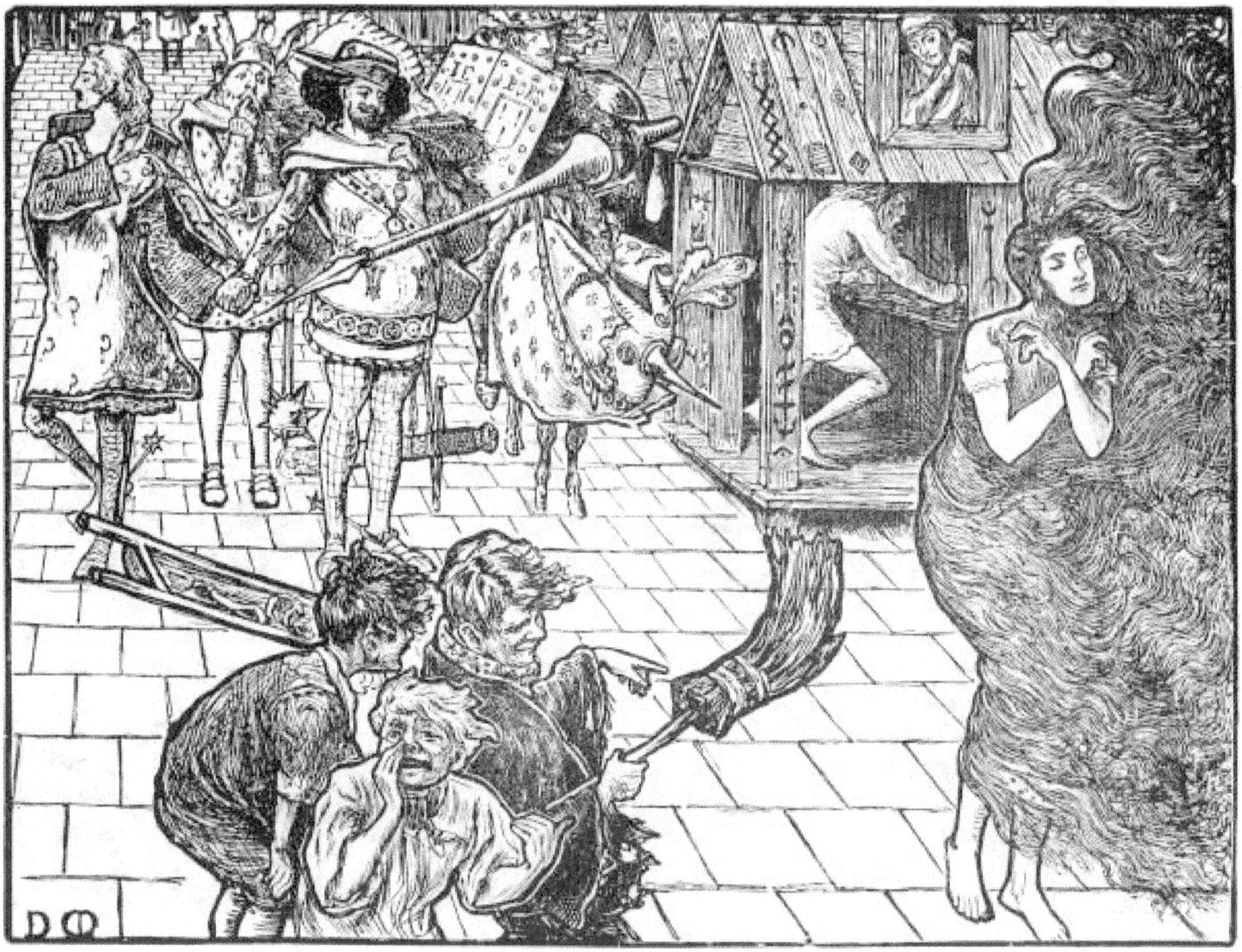

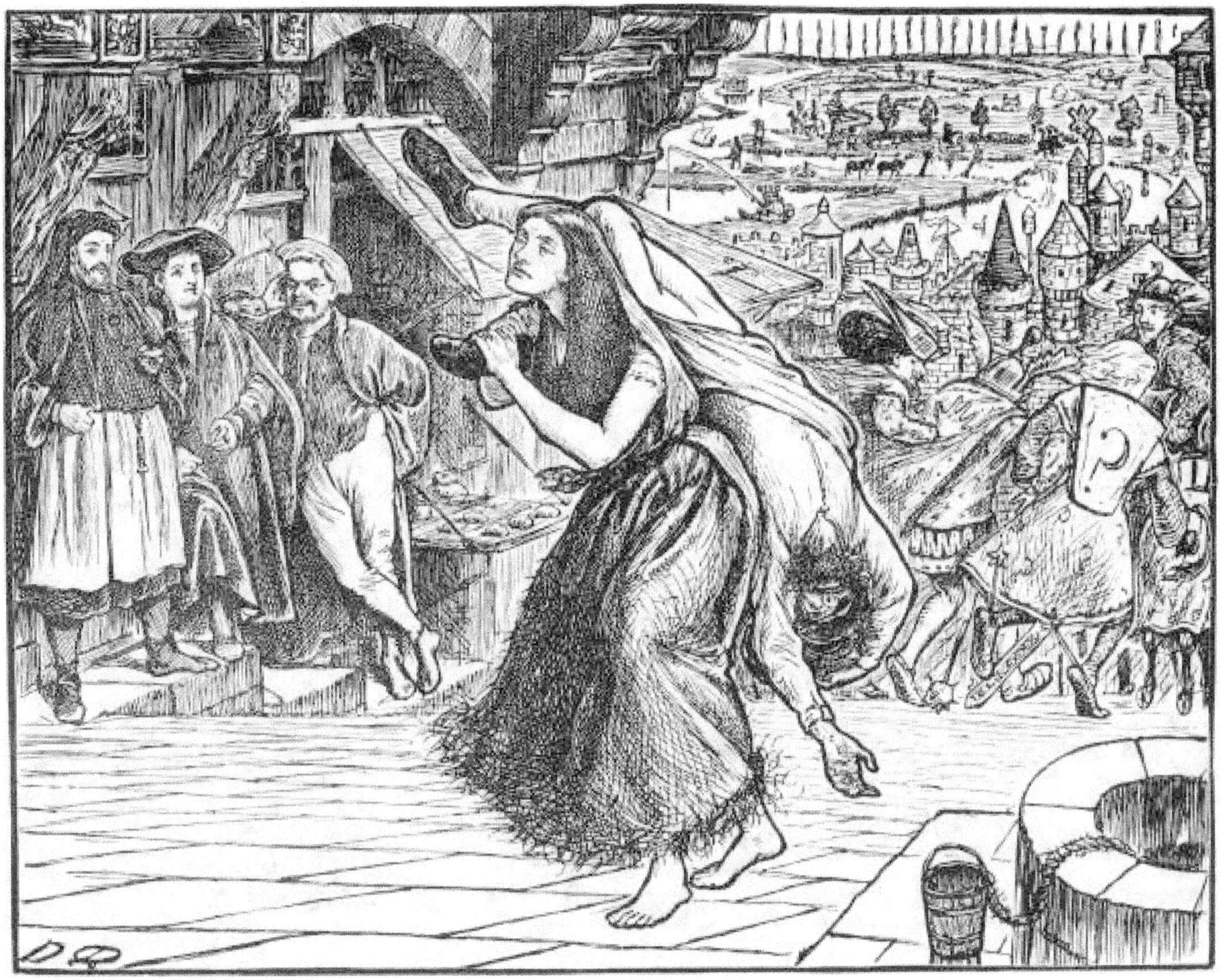

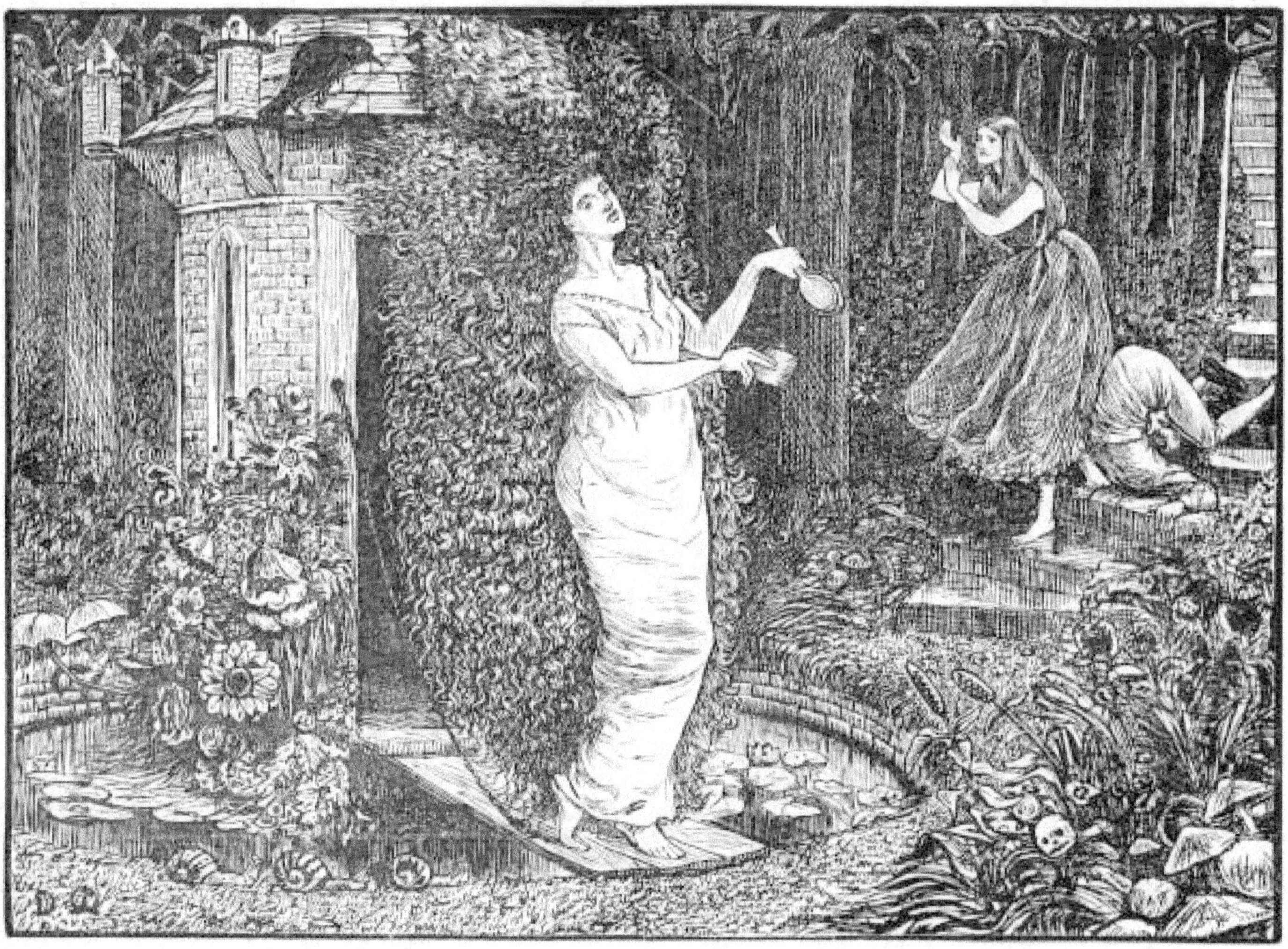

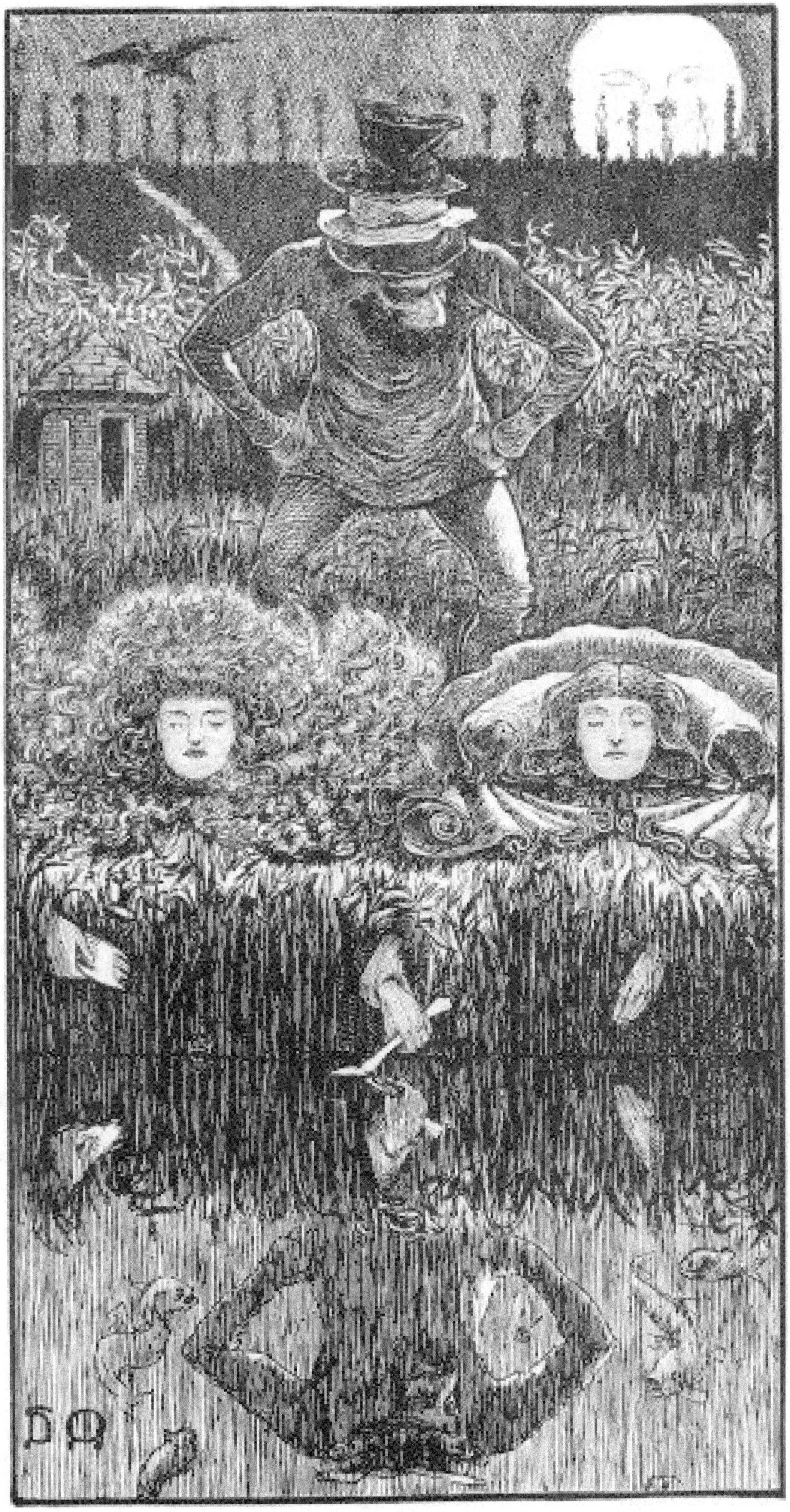

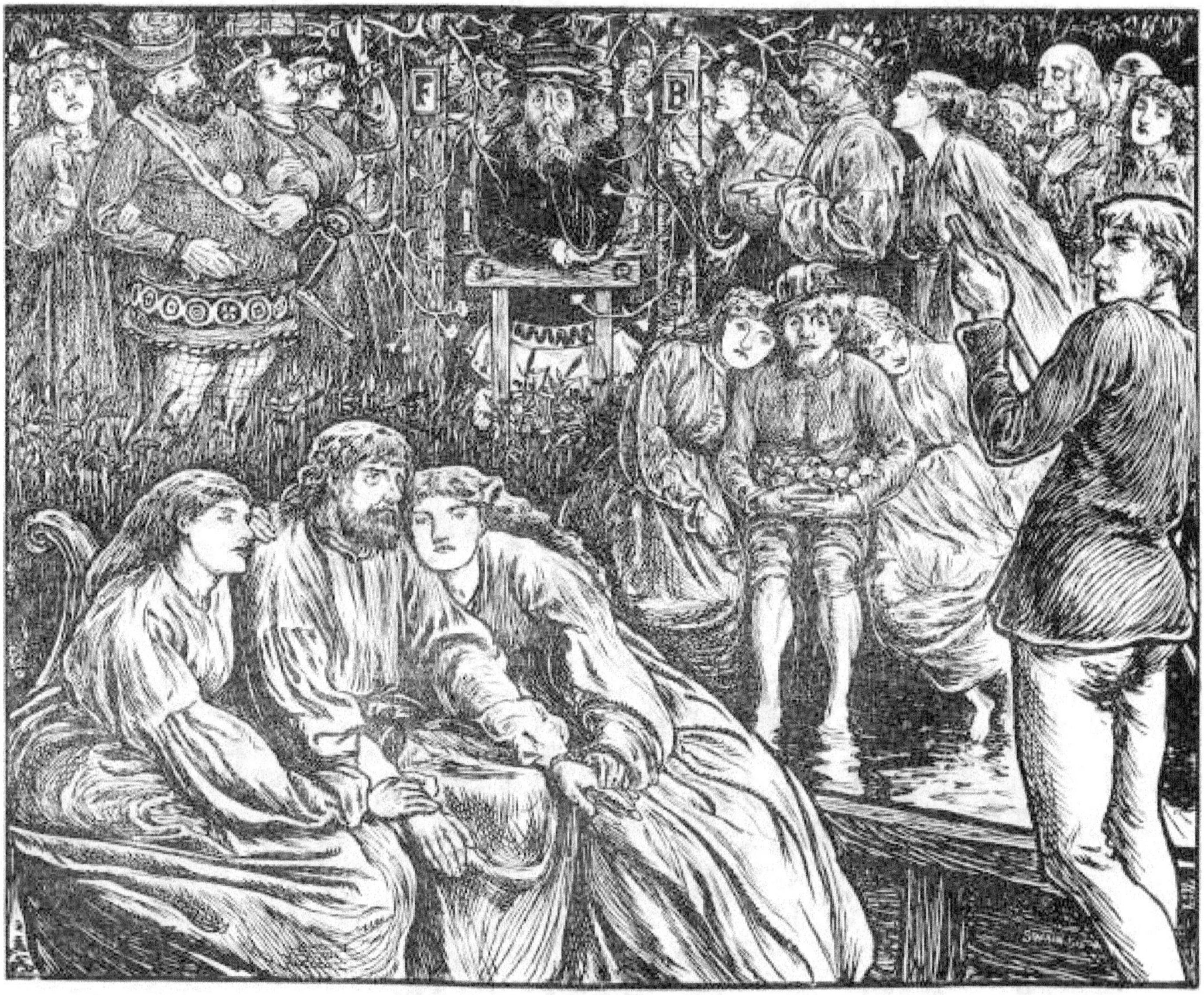
F
B

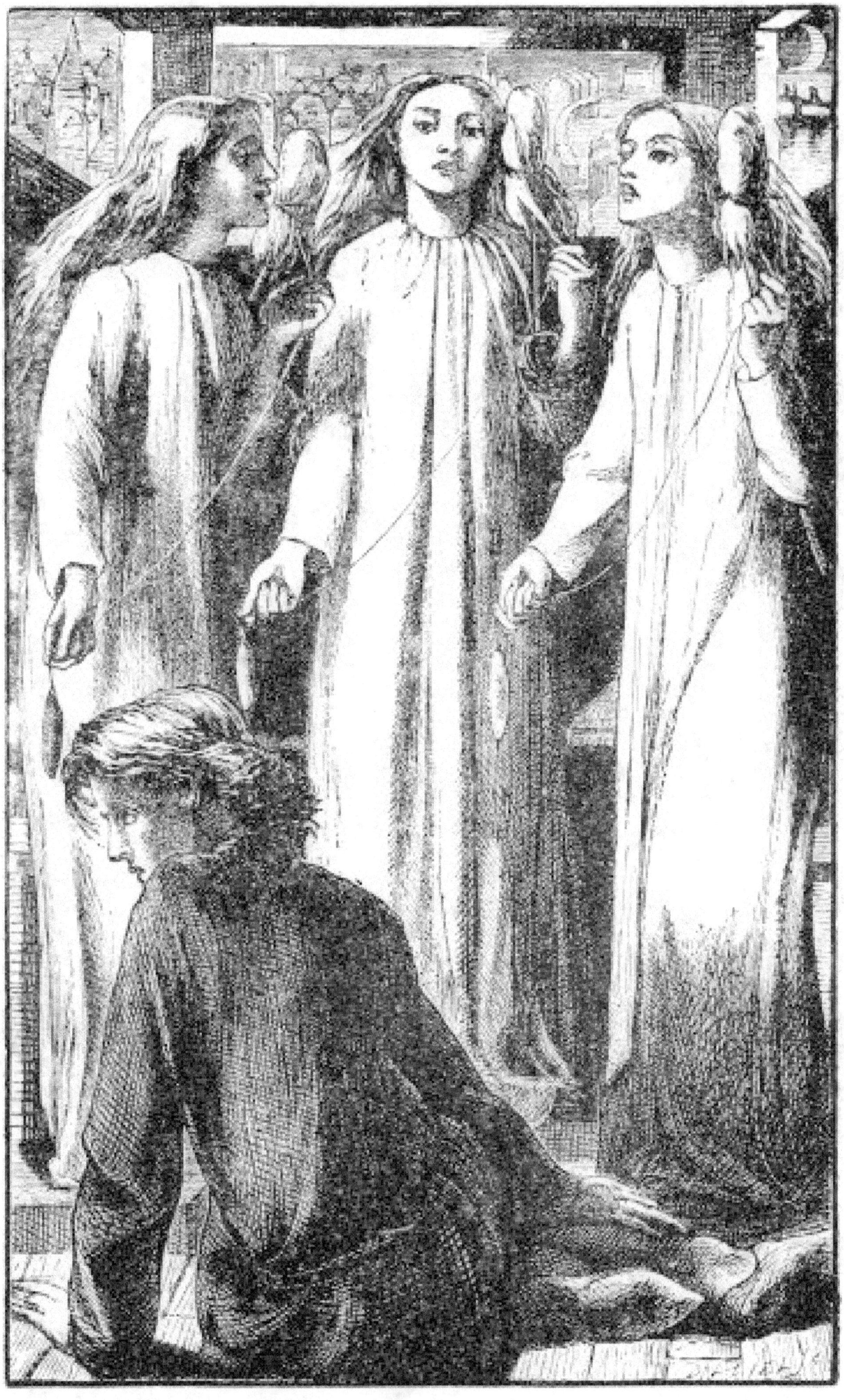

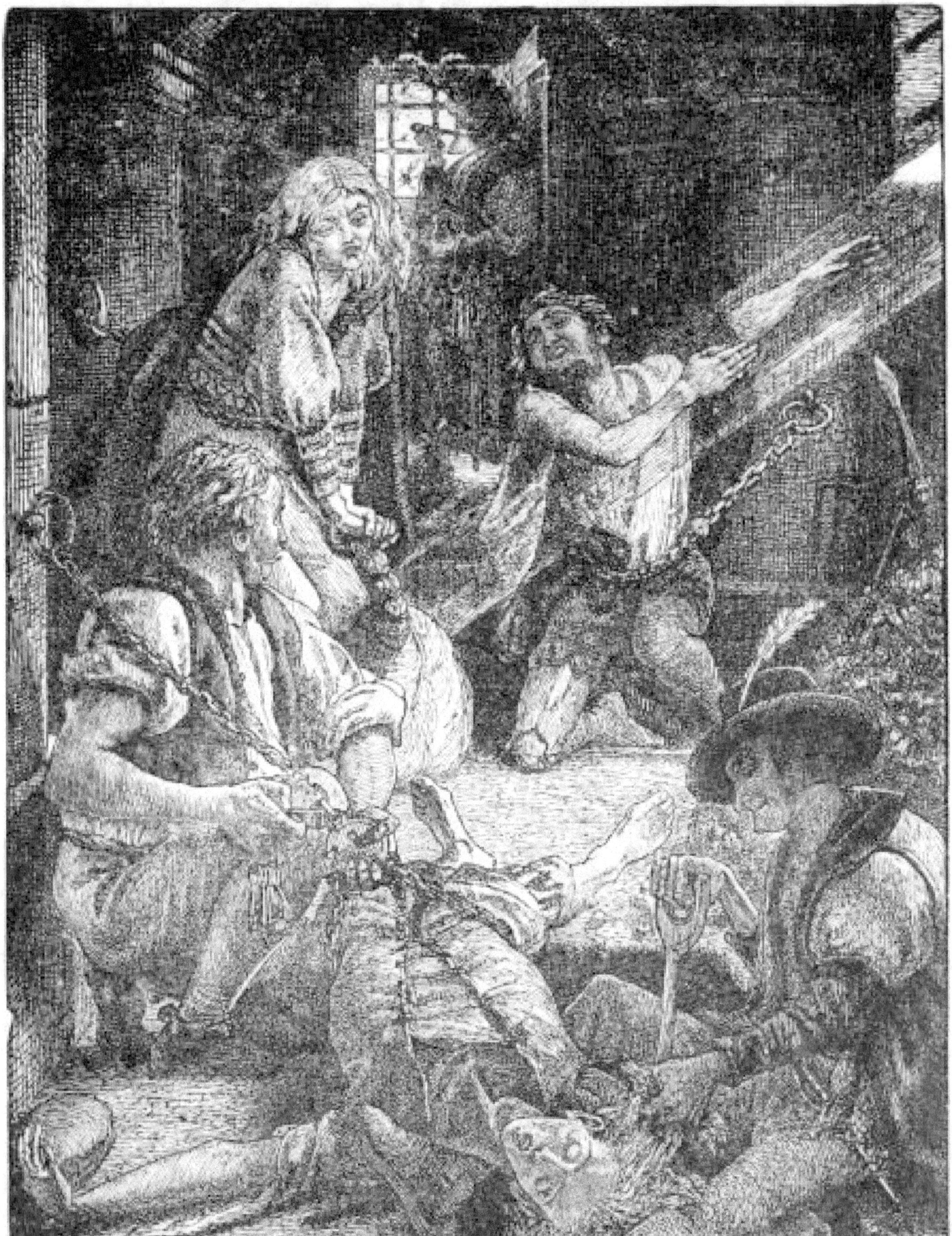

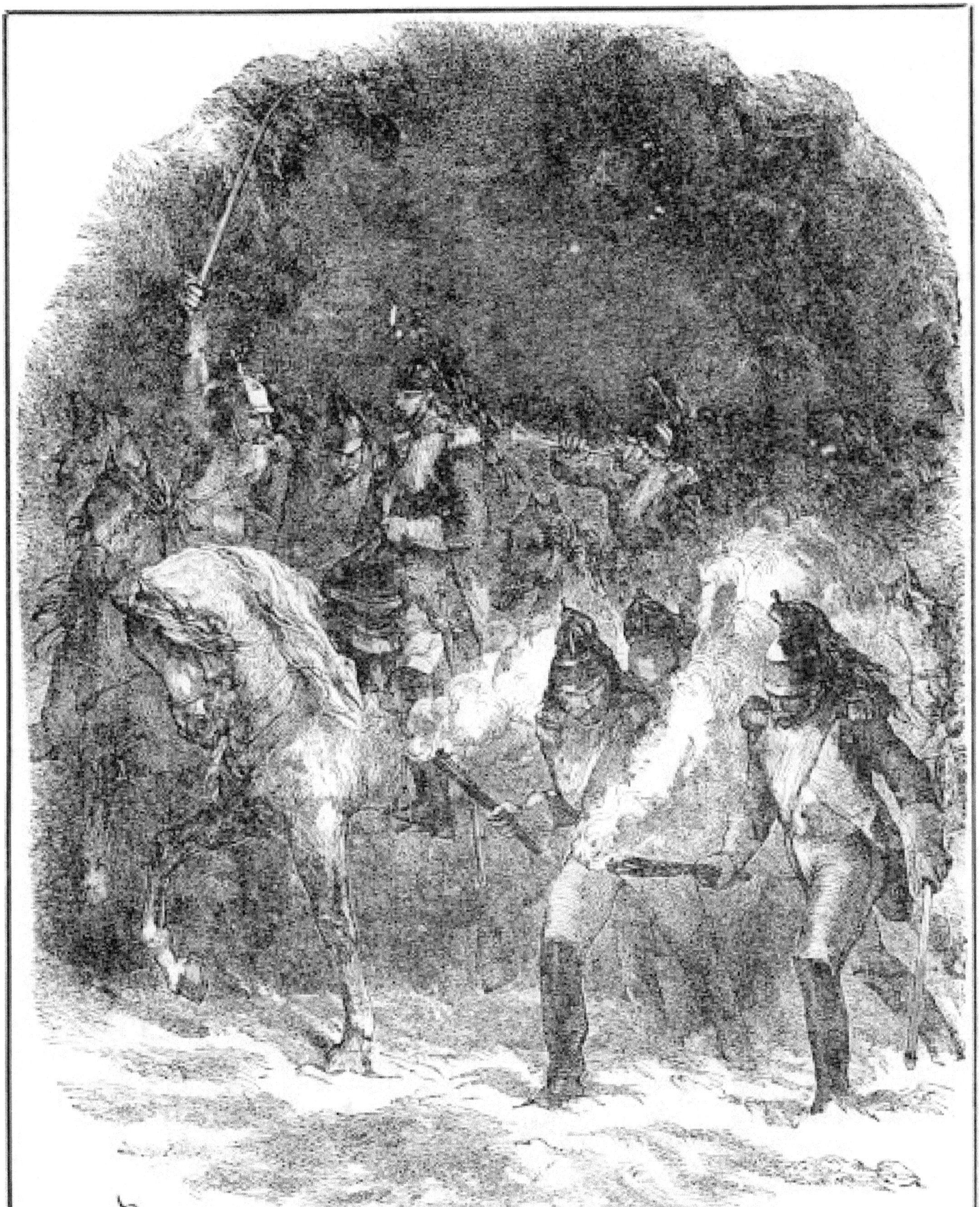

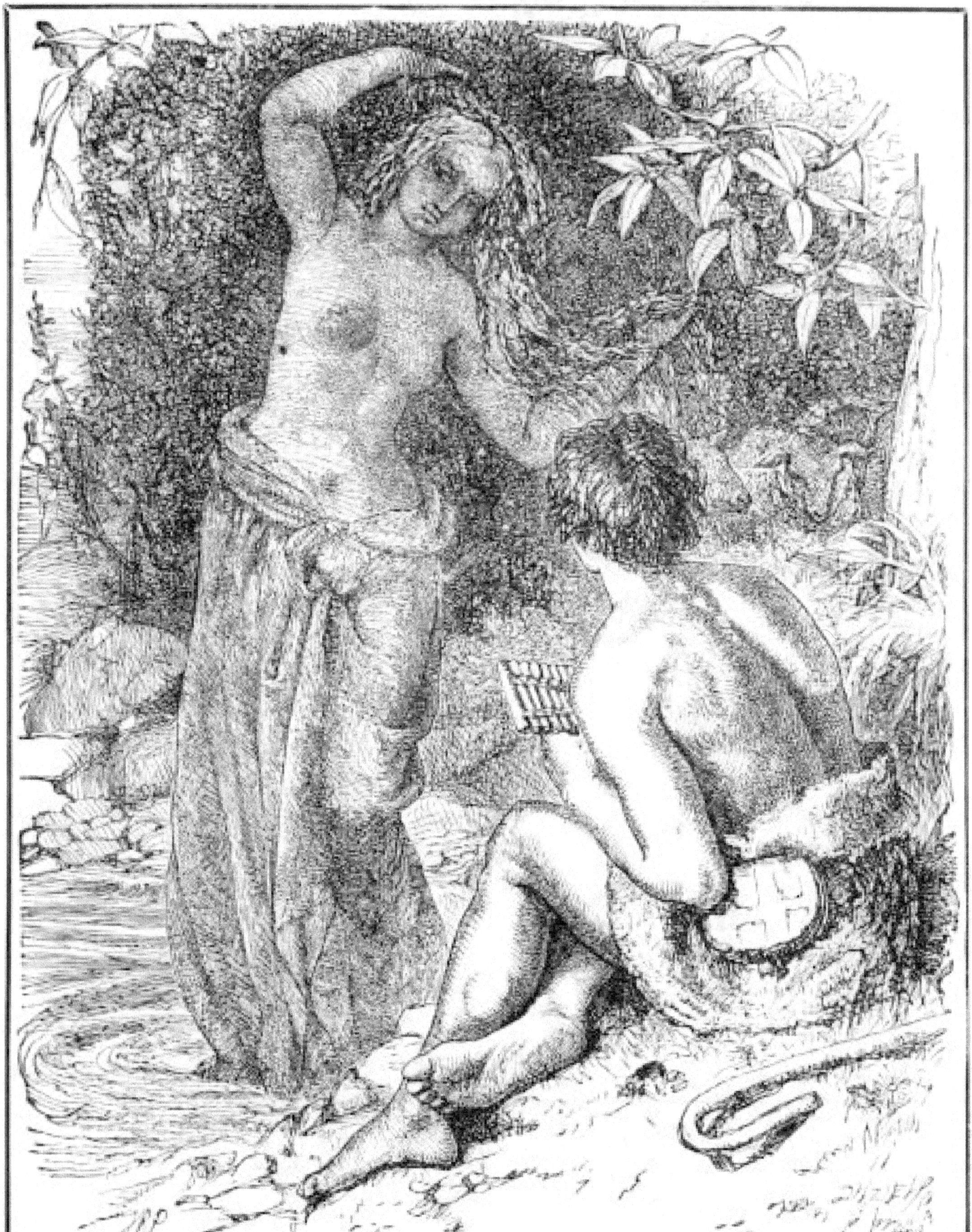

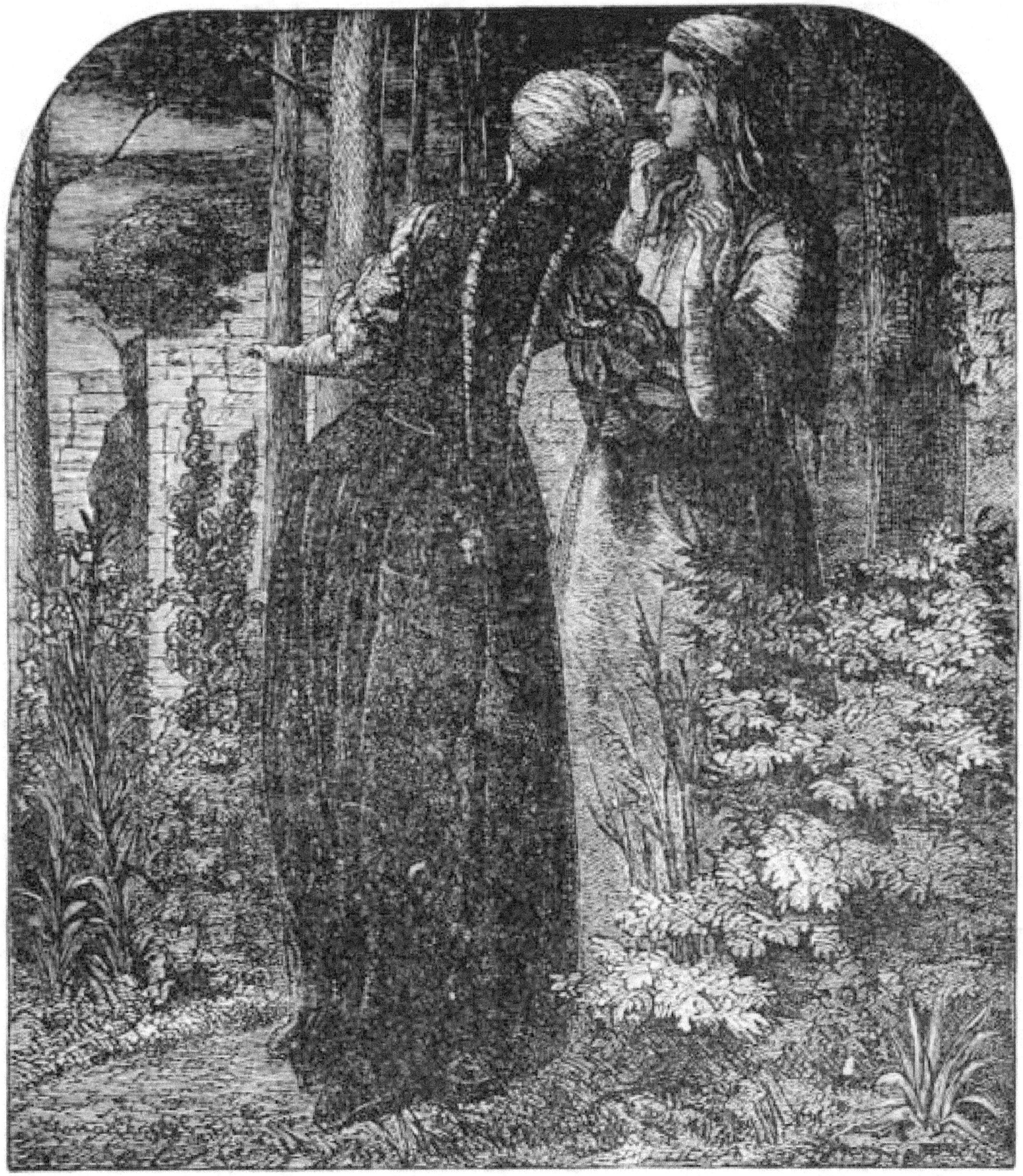

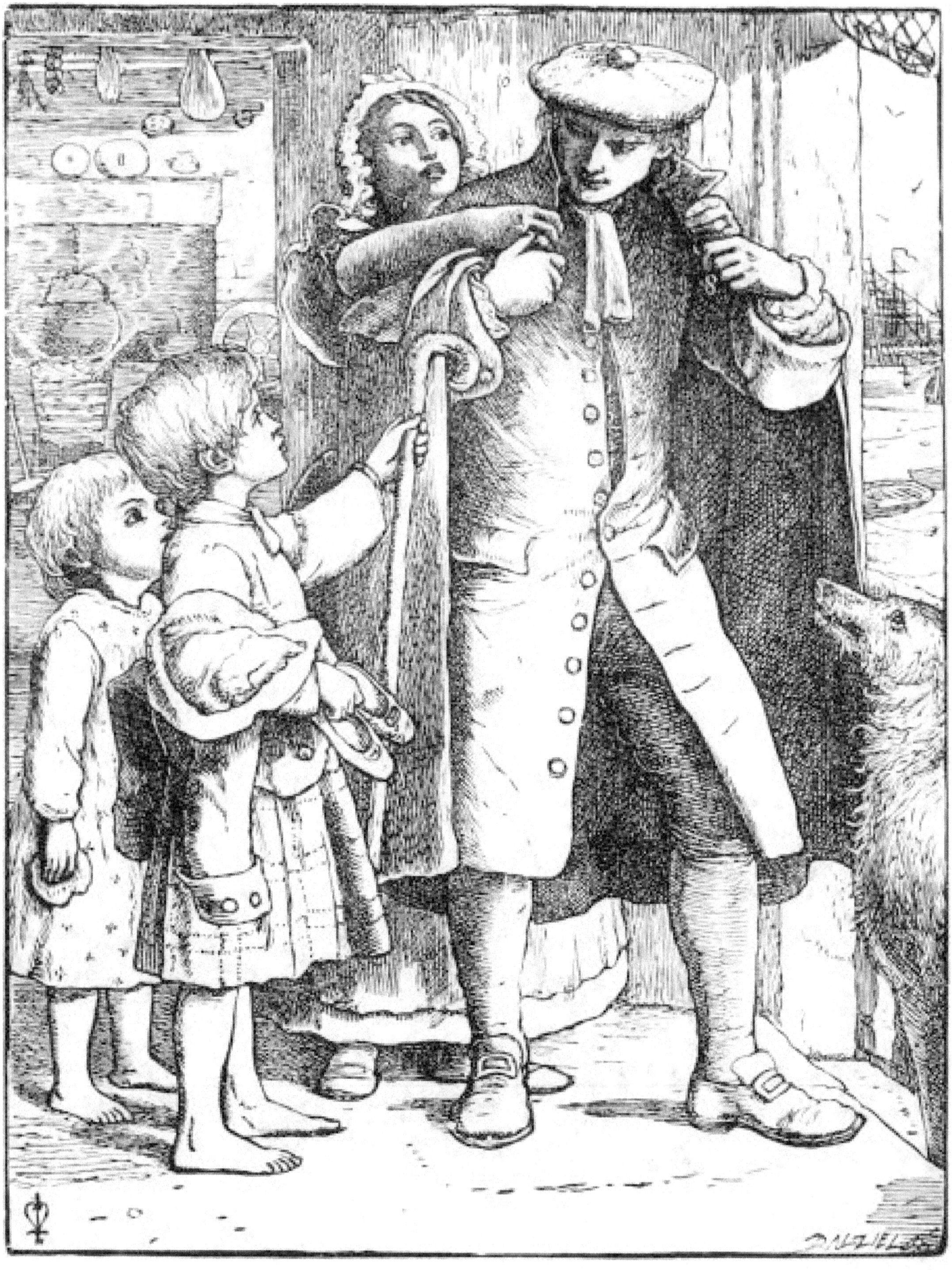

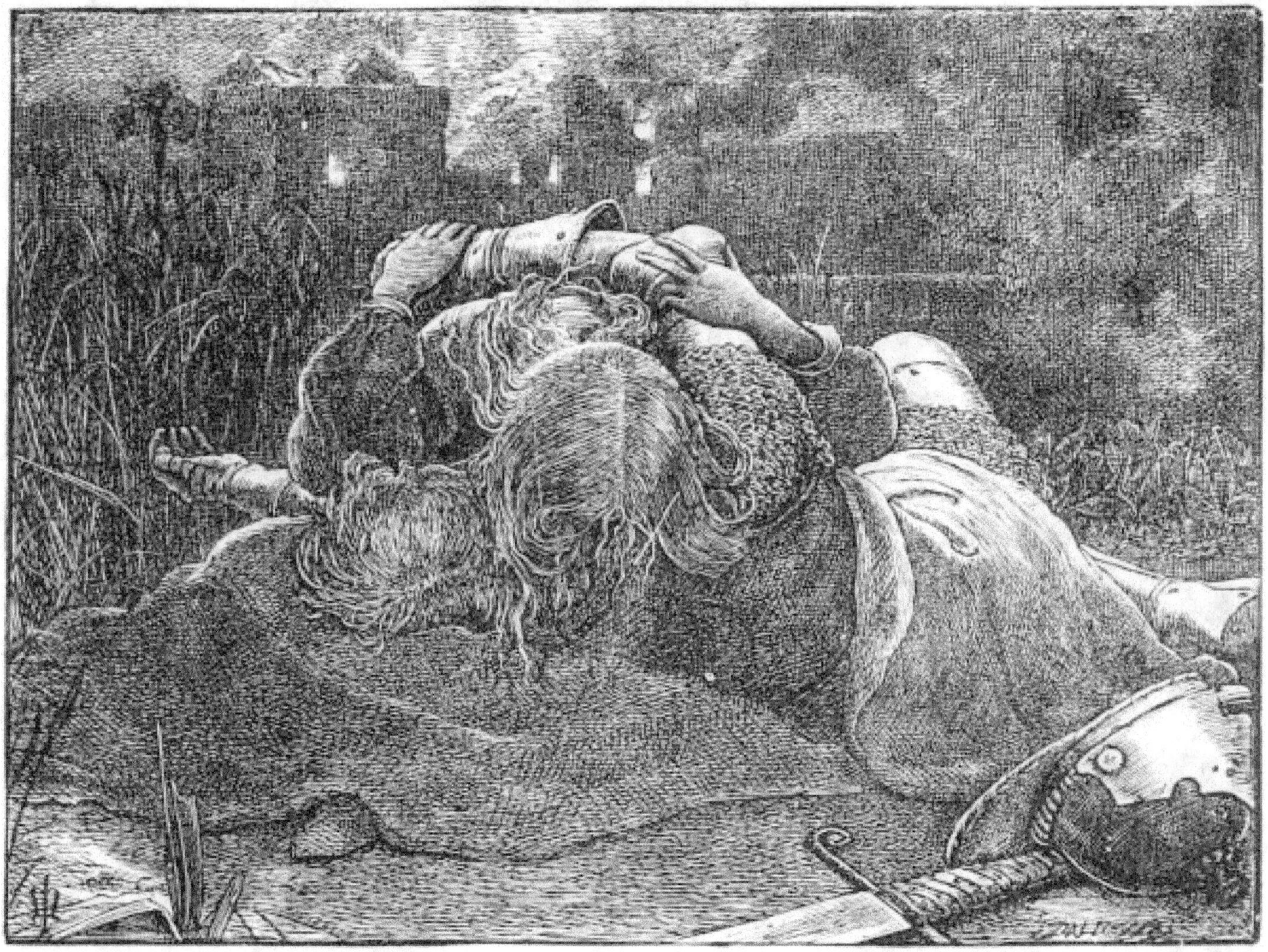

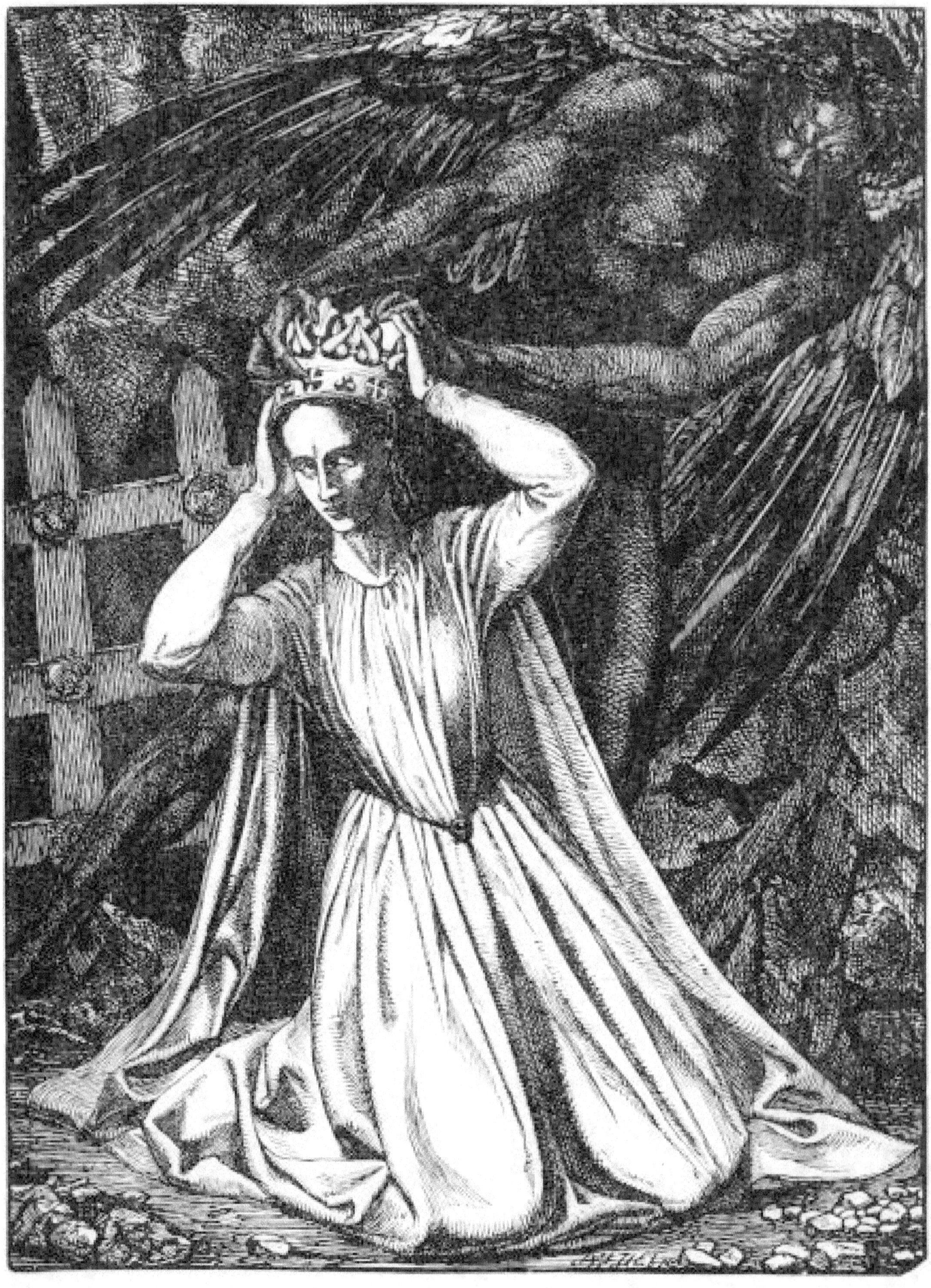

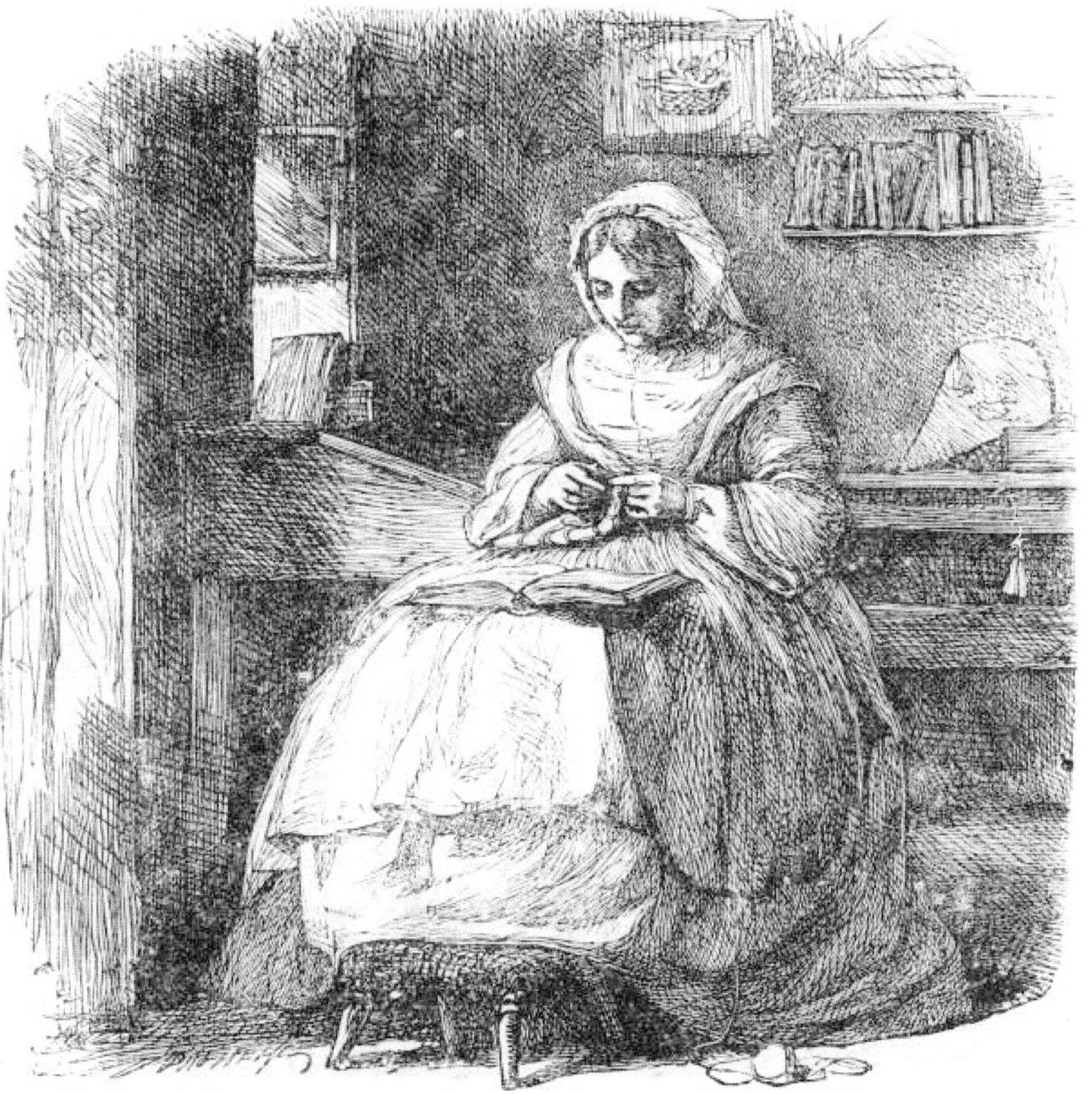

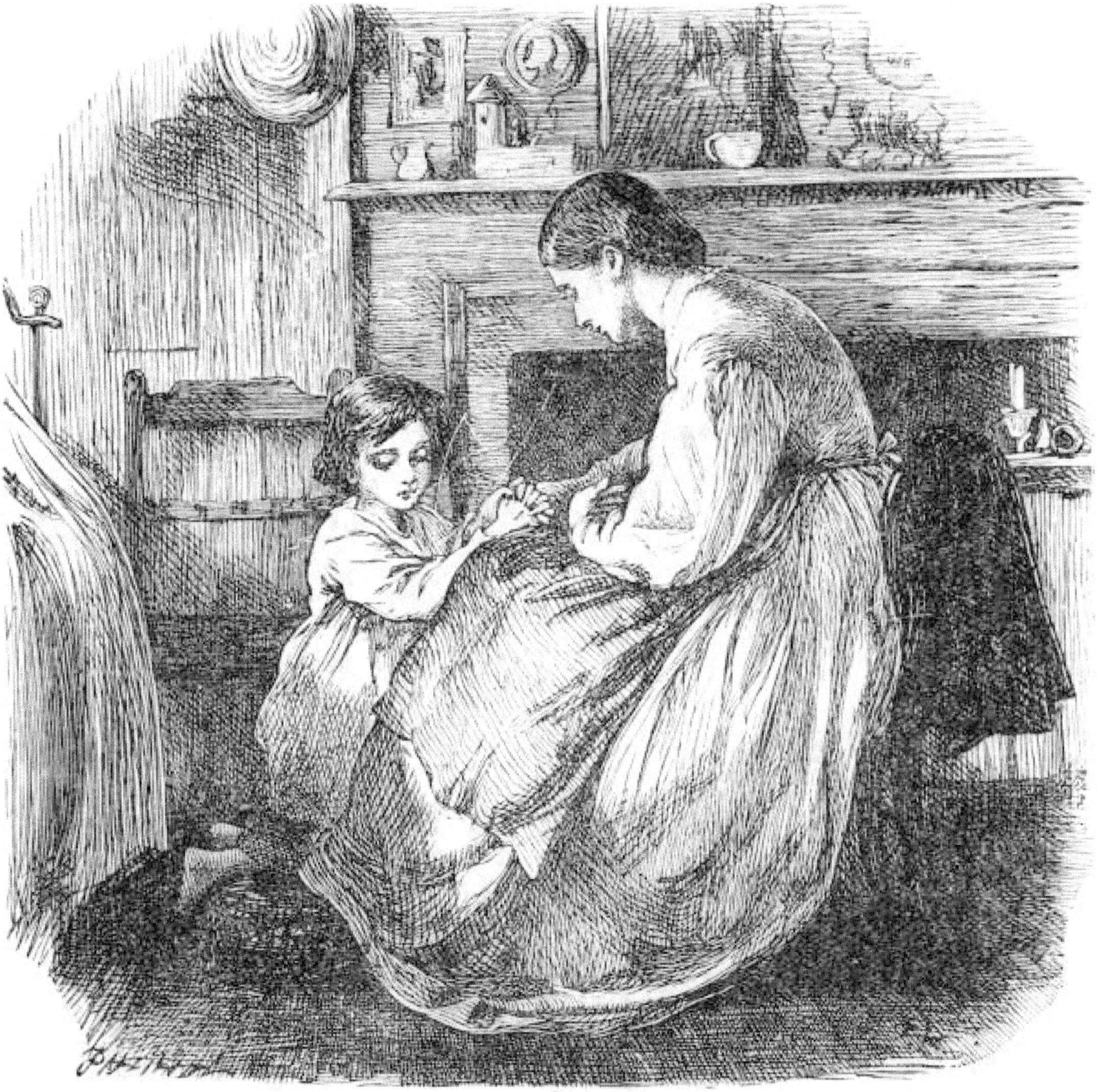

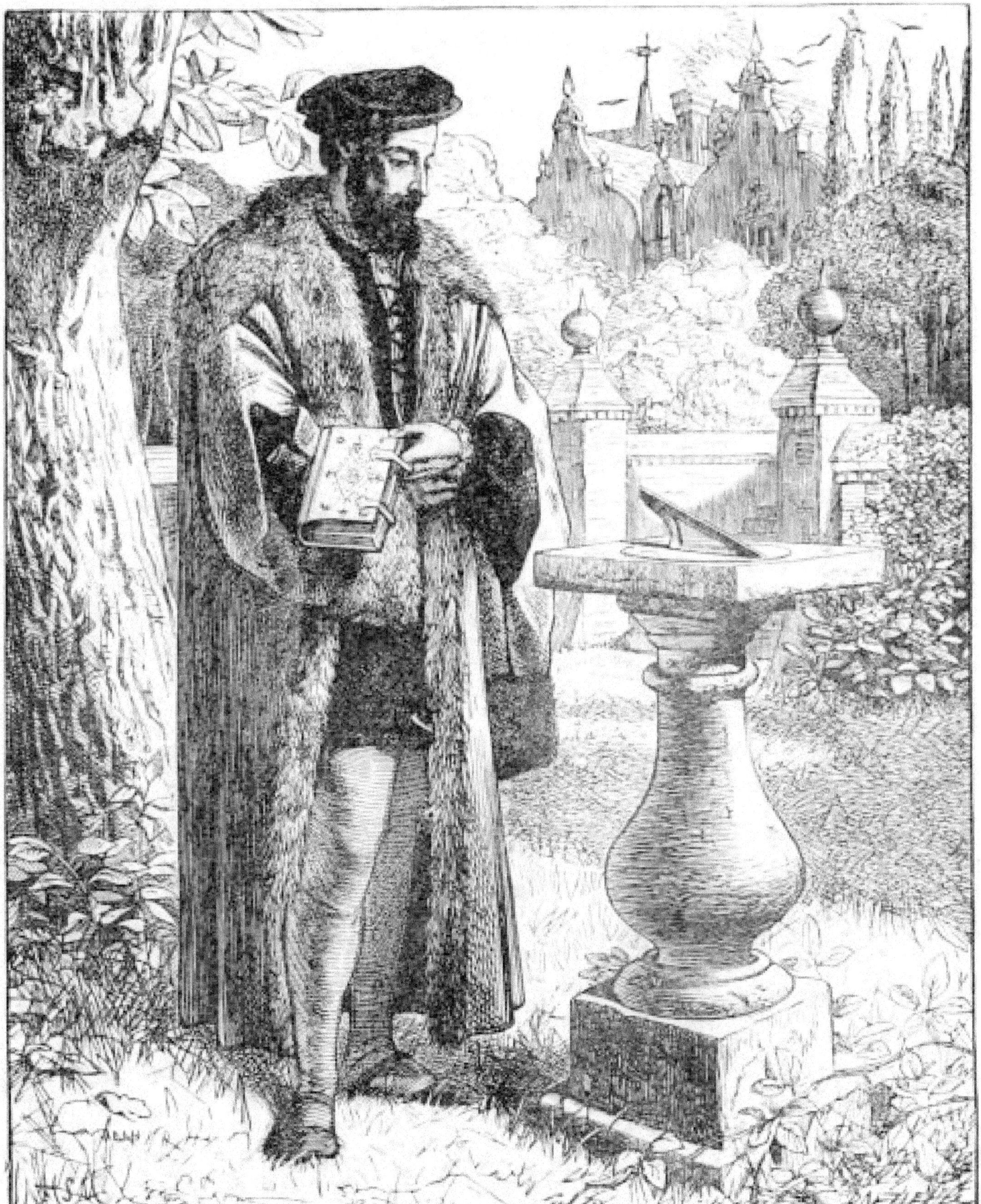

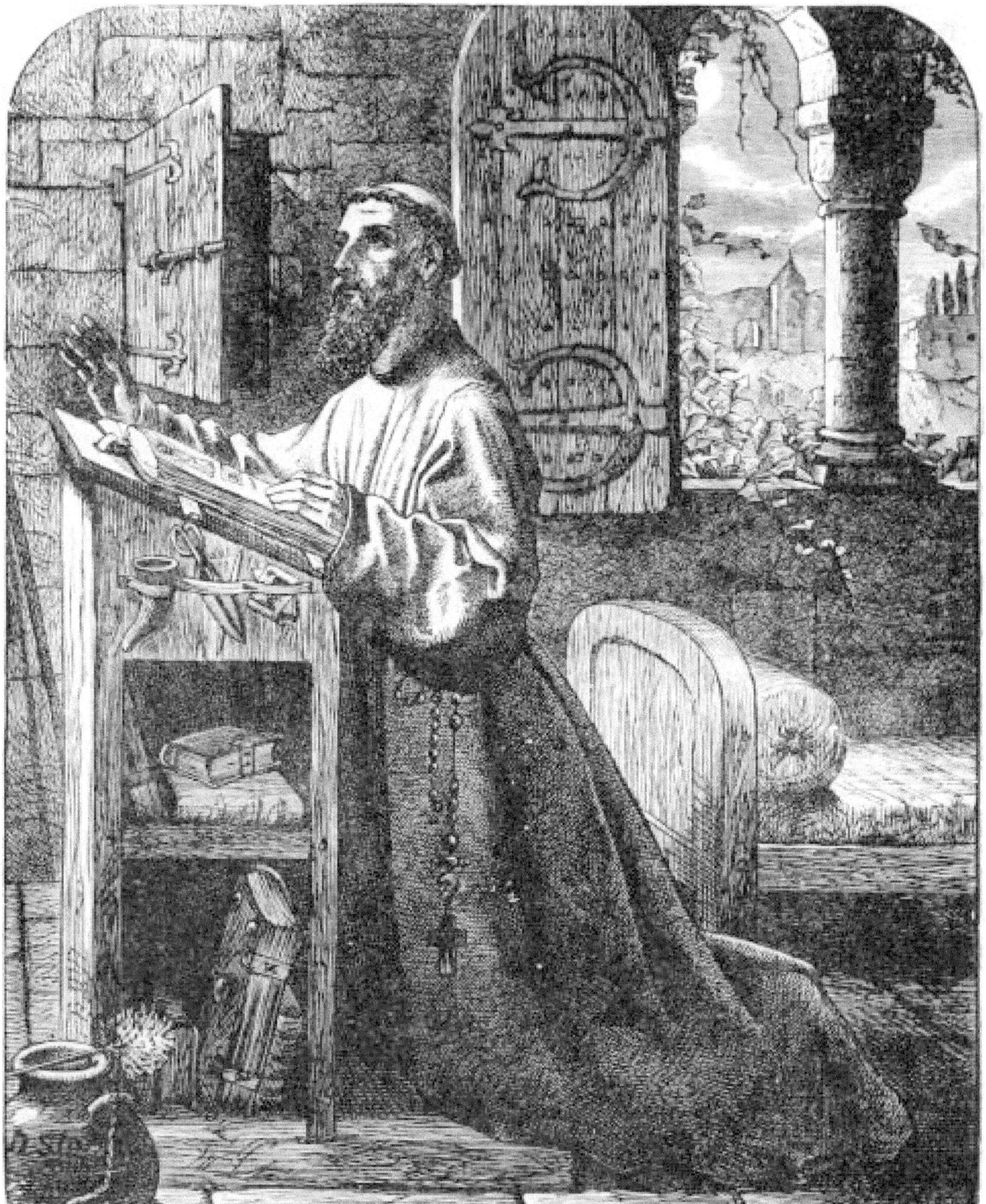

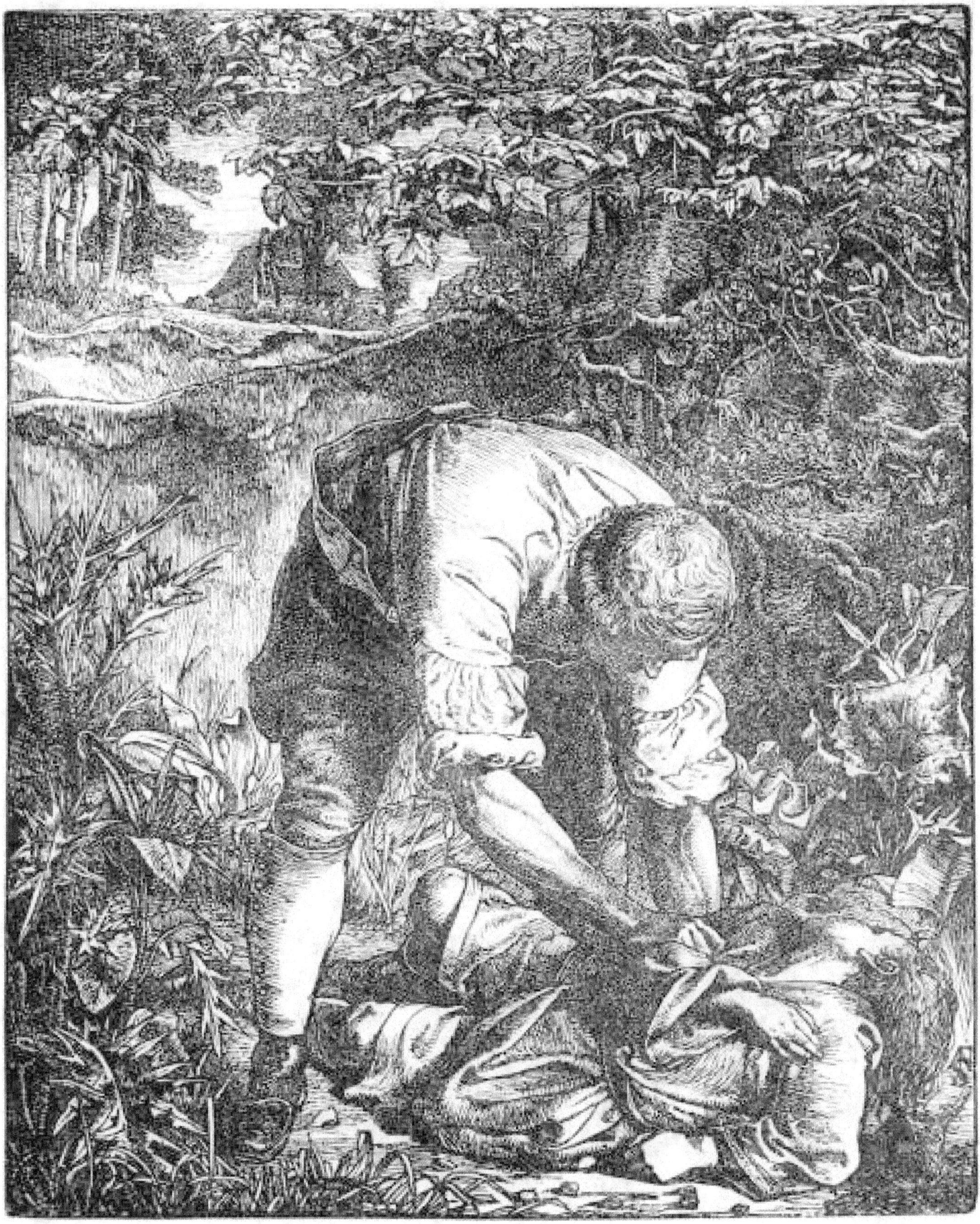

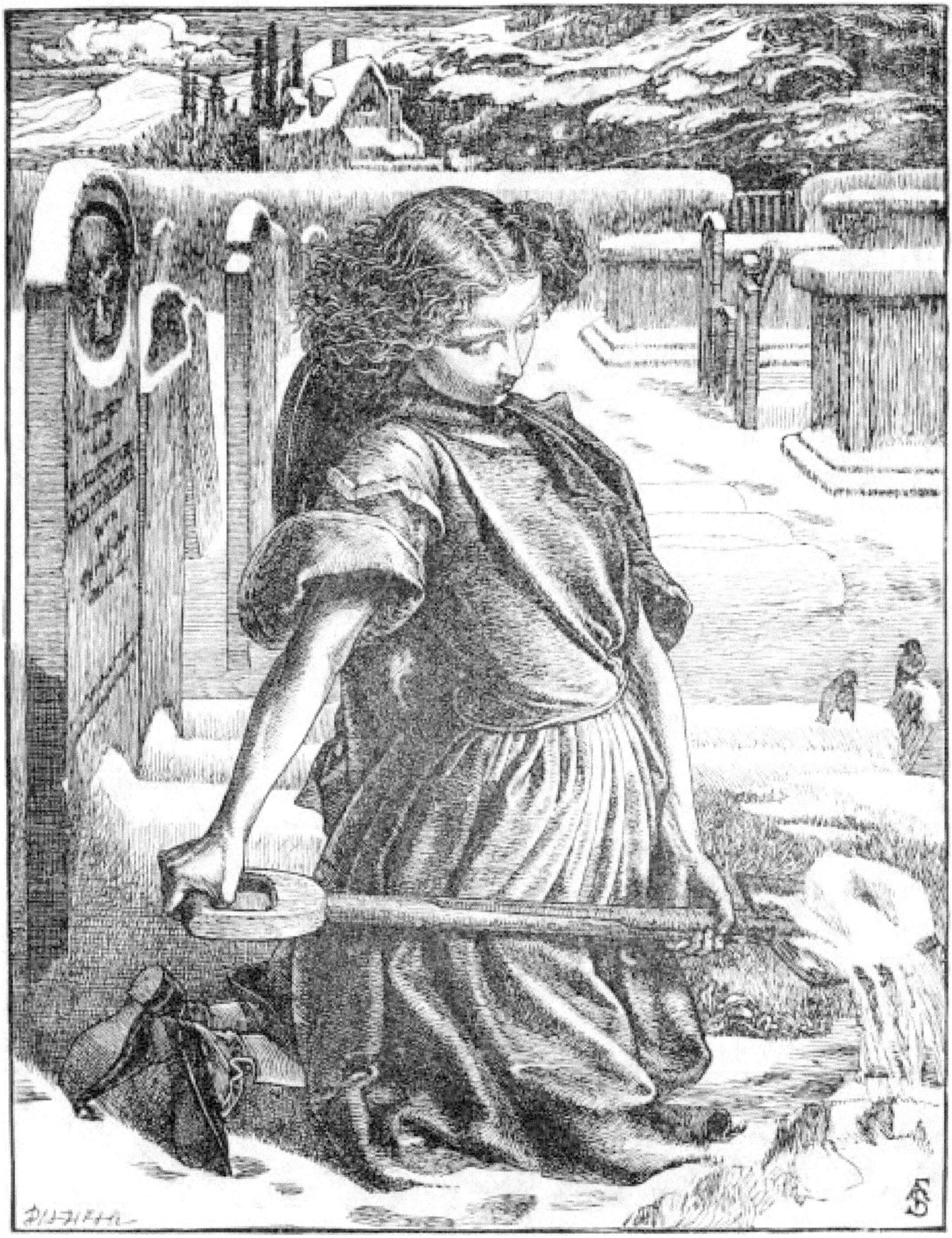

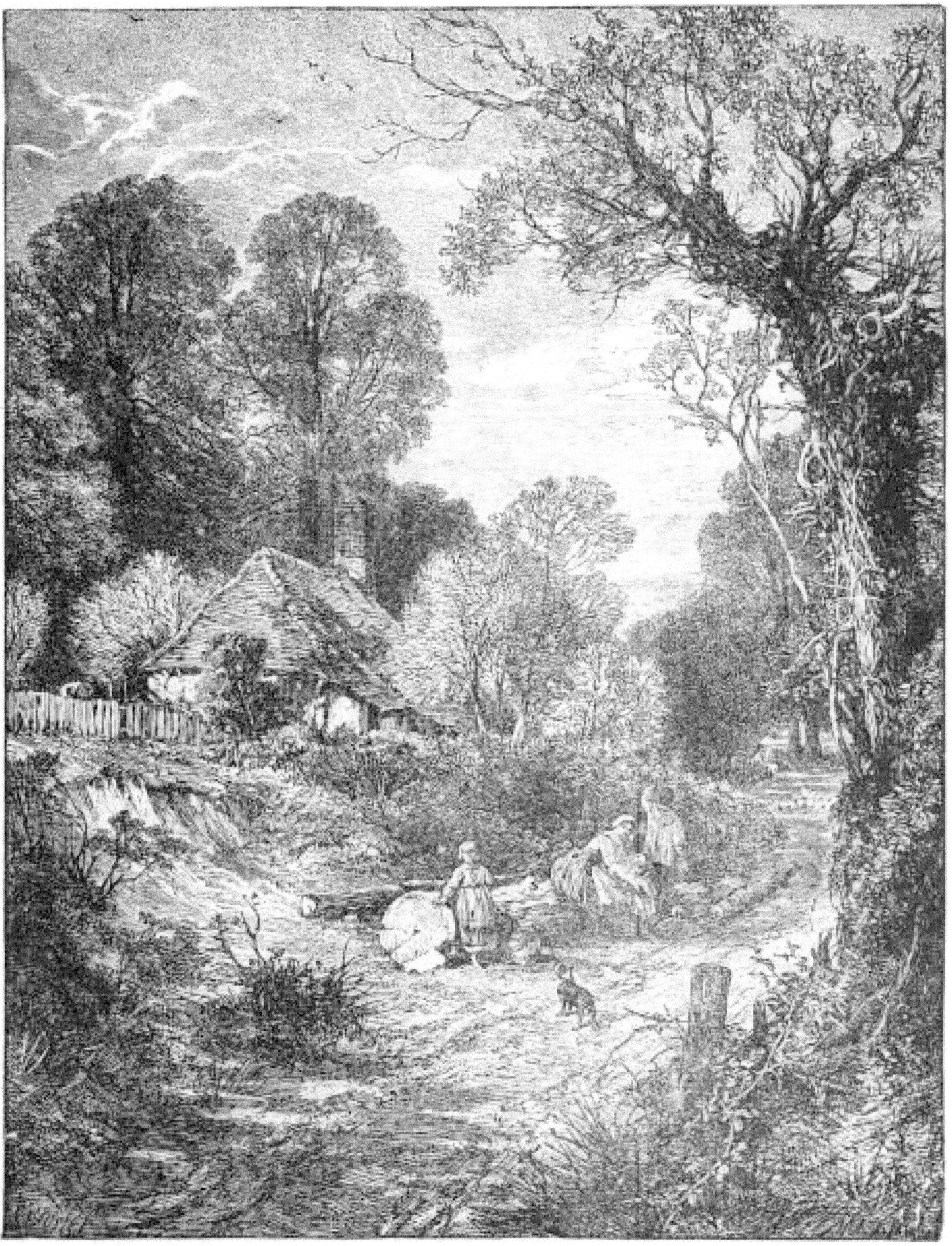

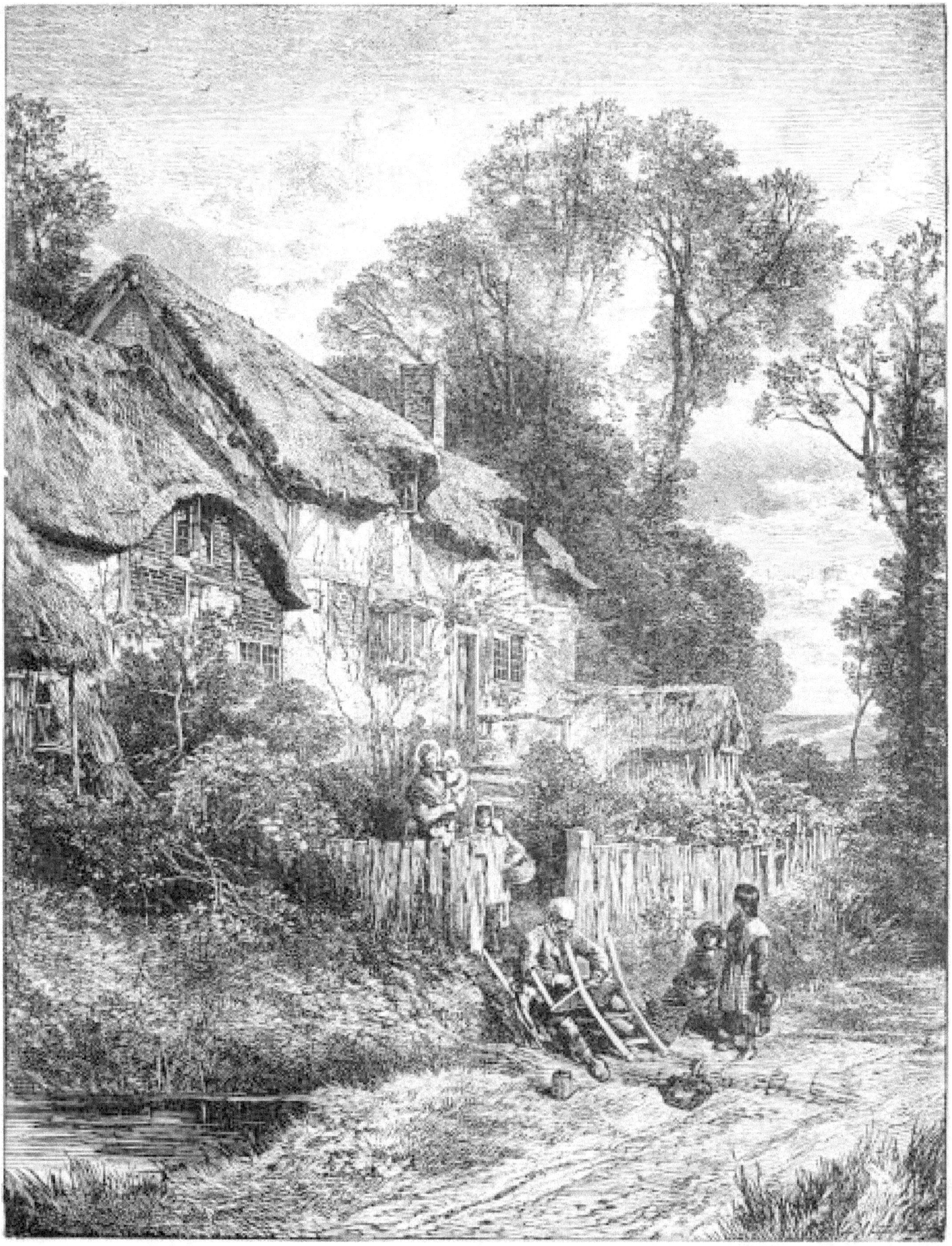

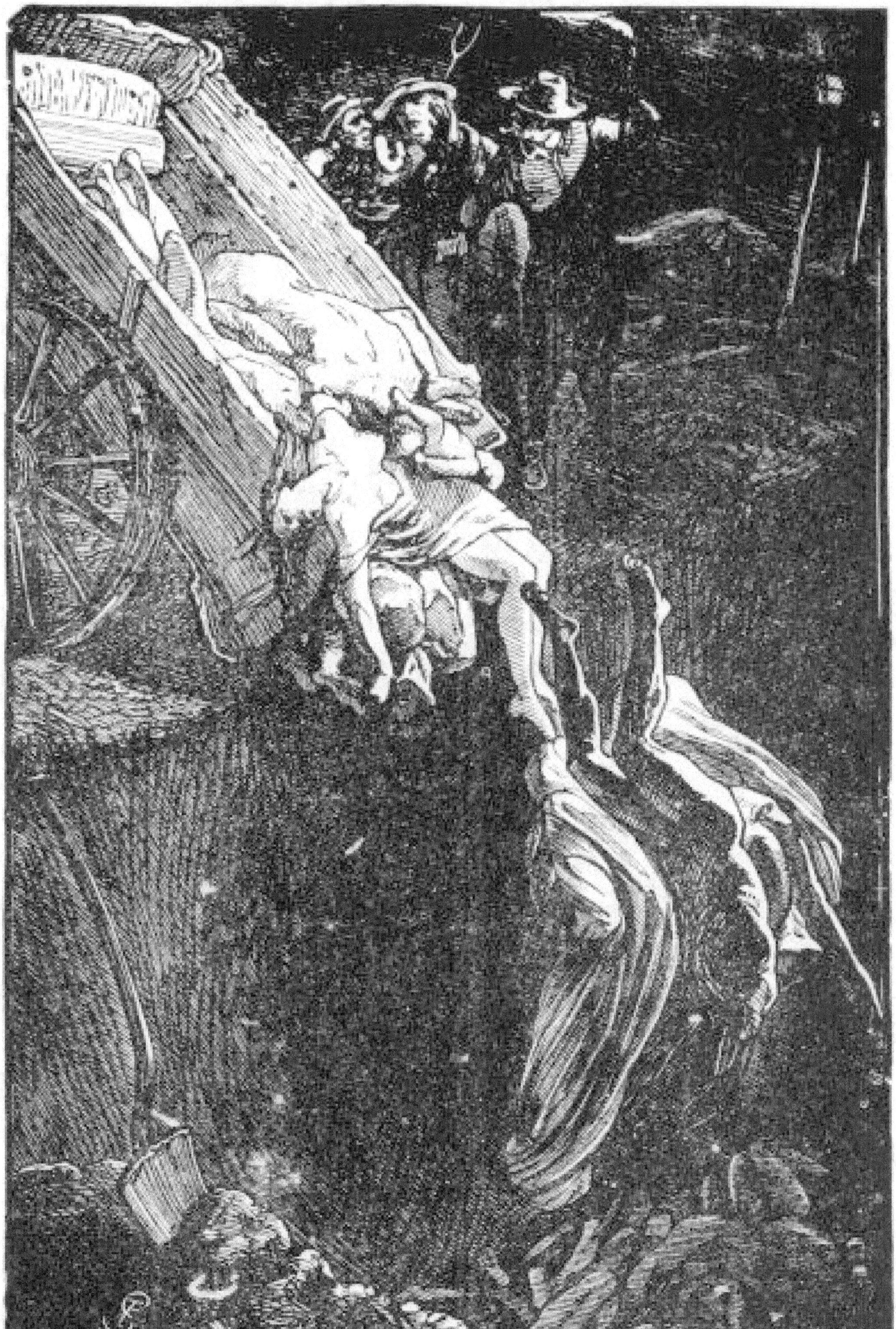

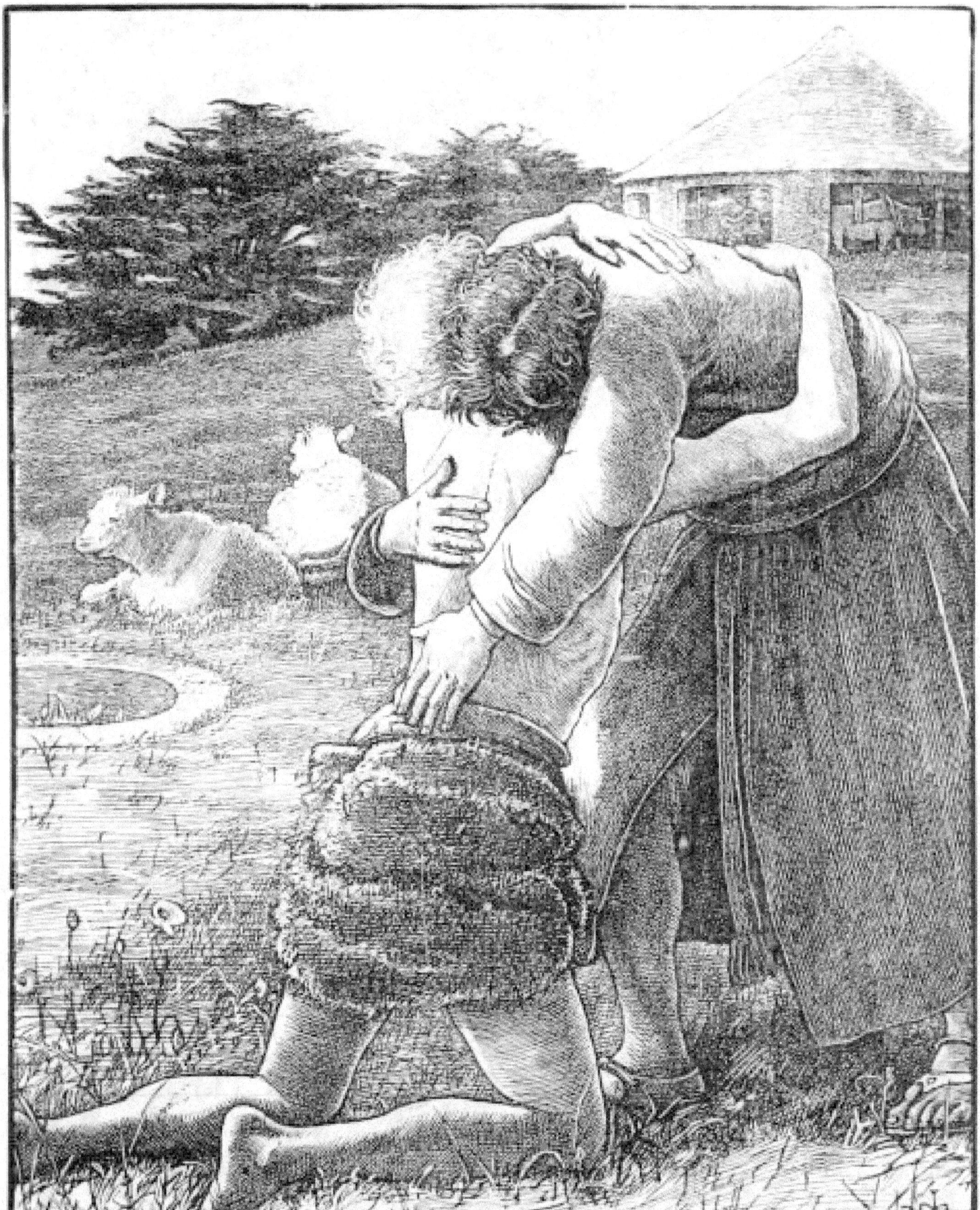

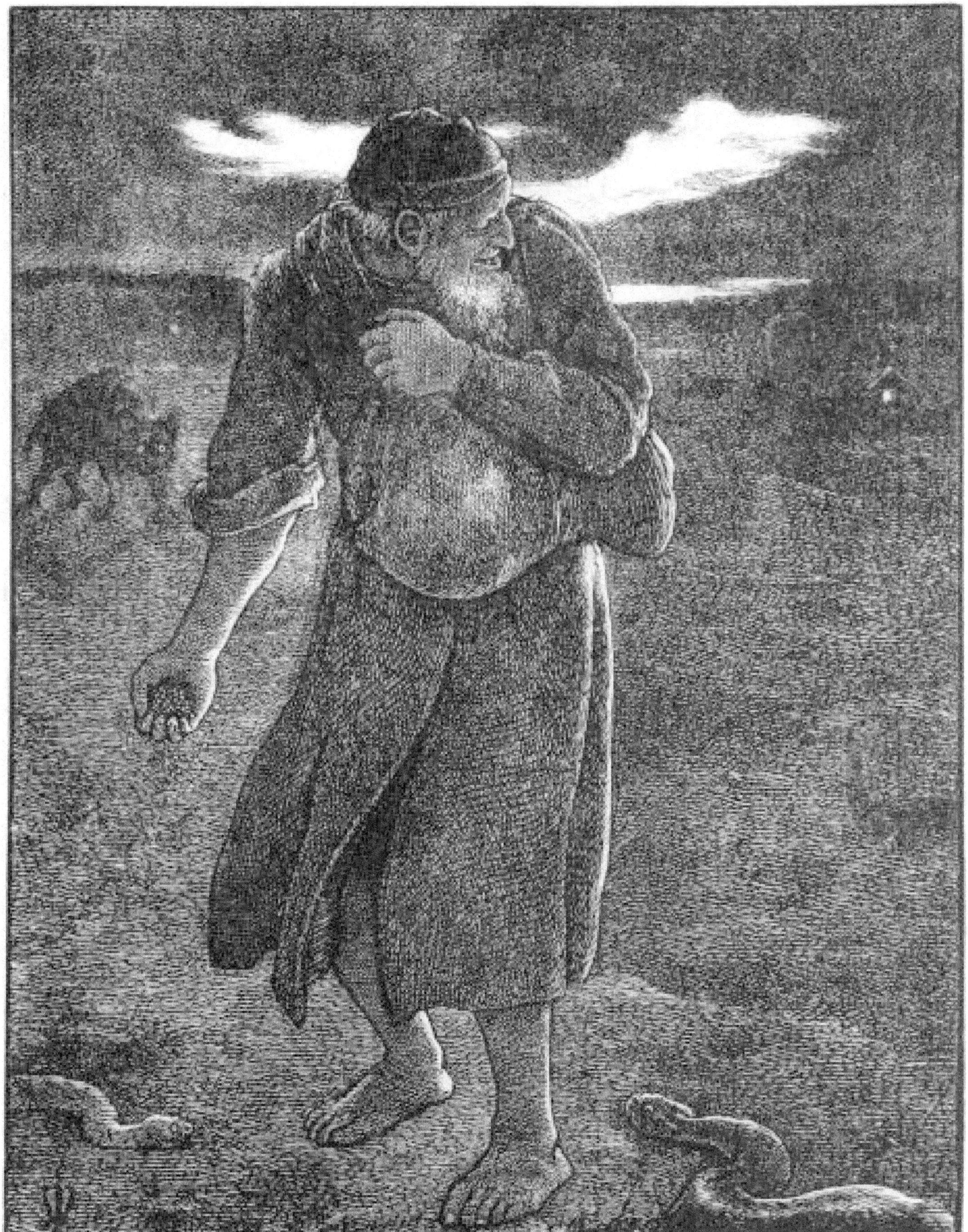

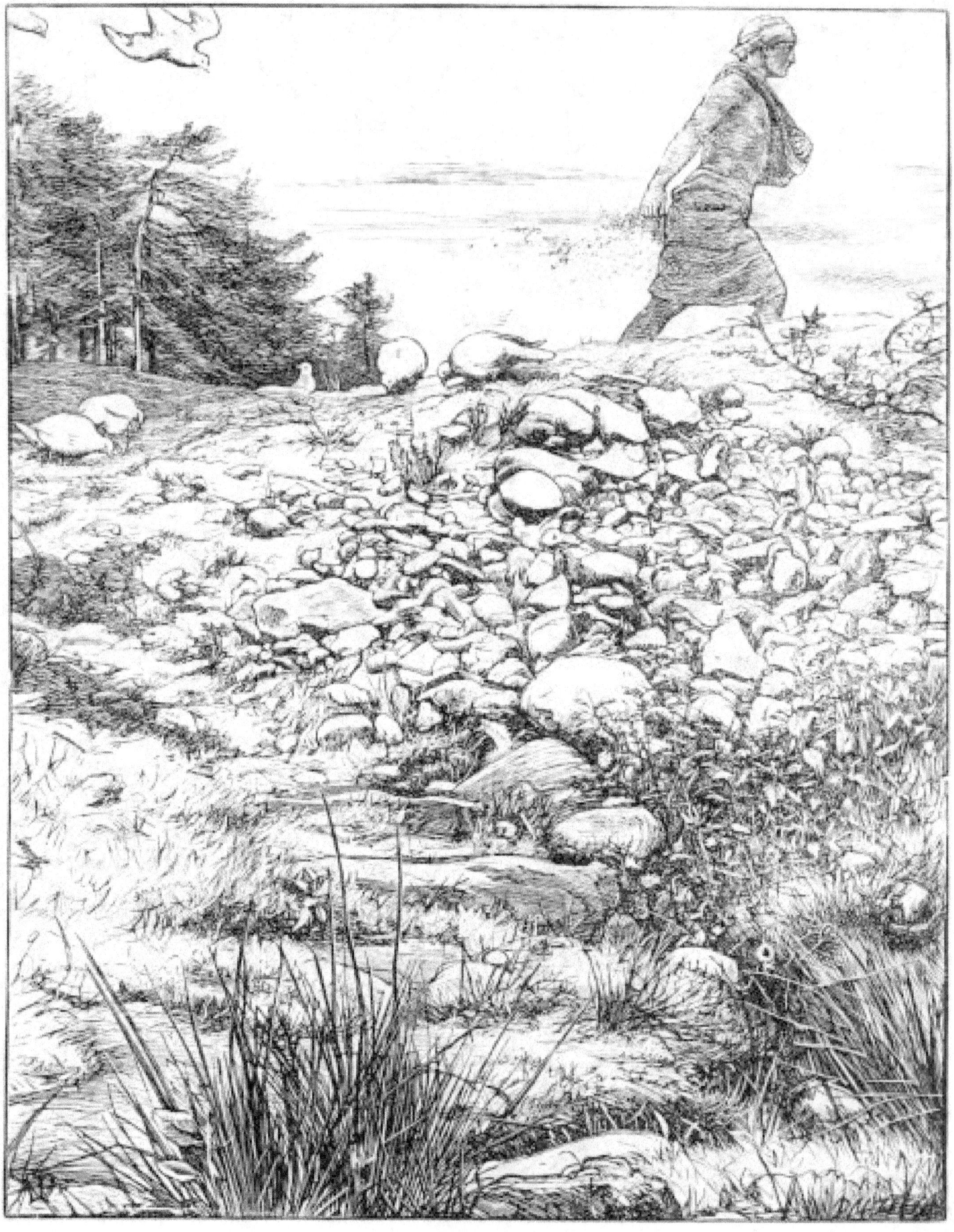

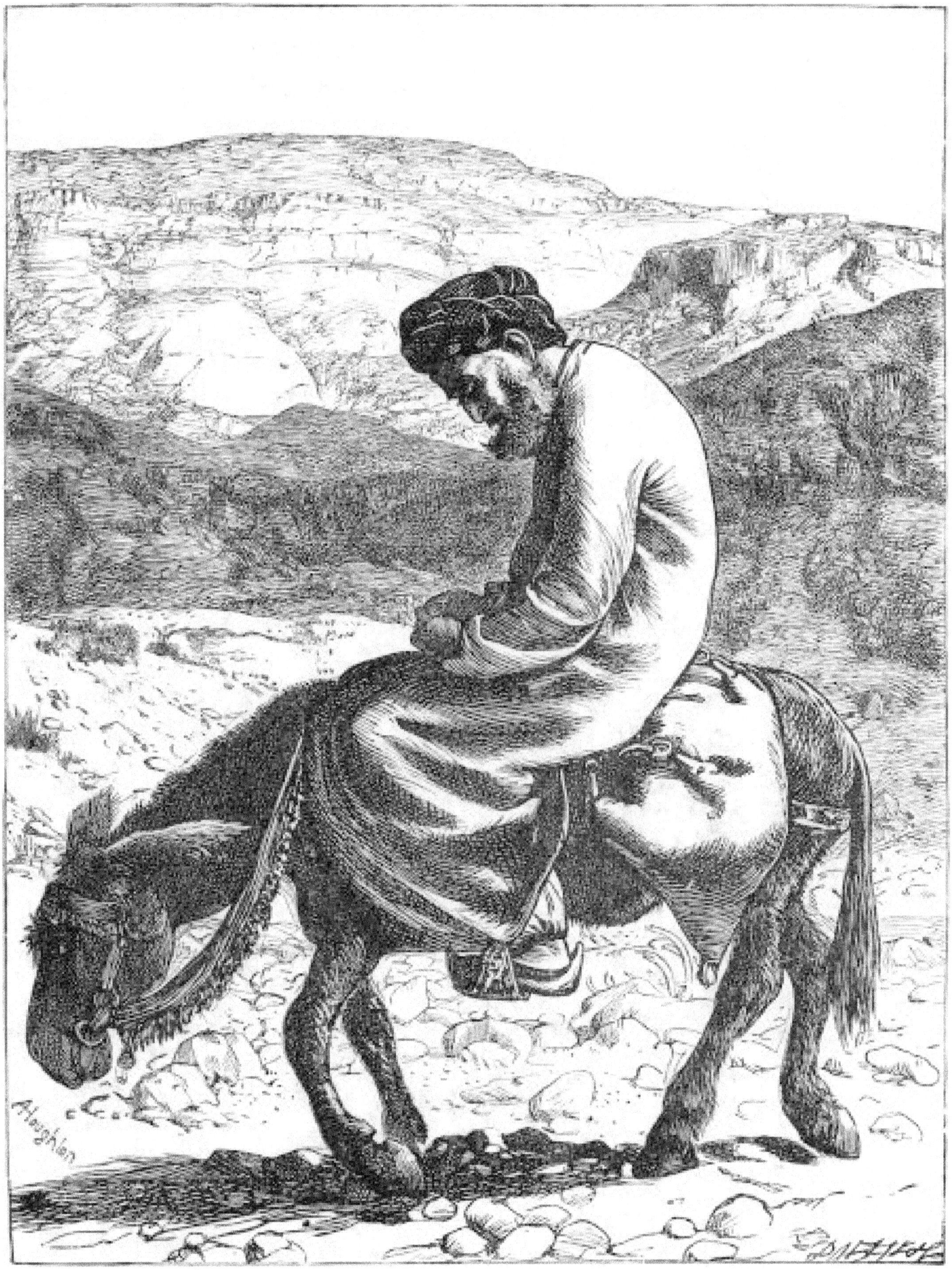

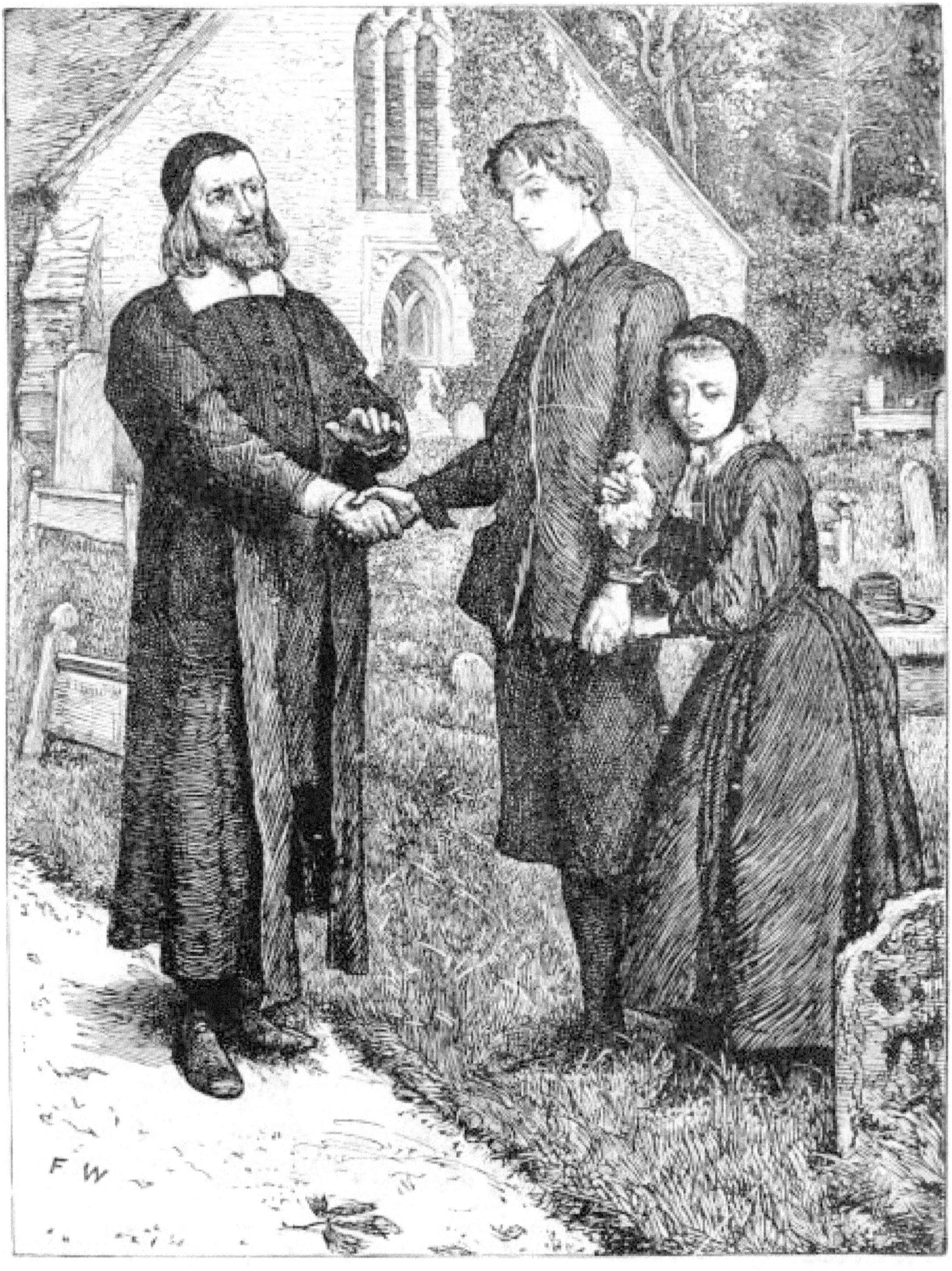
F W

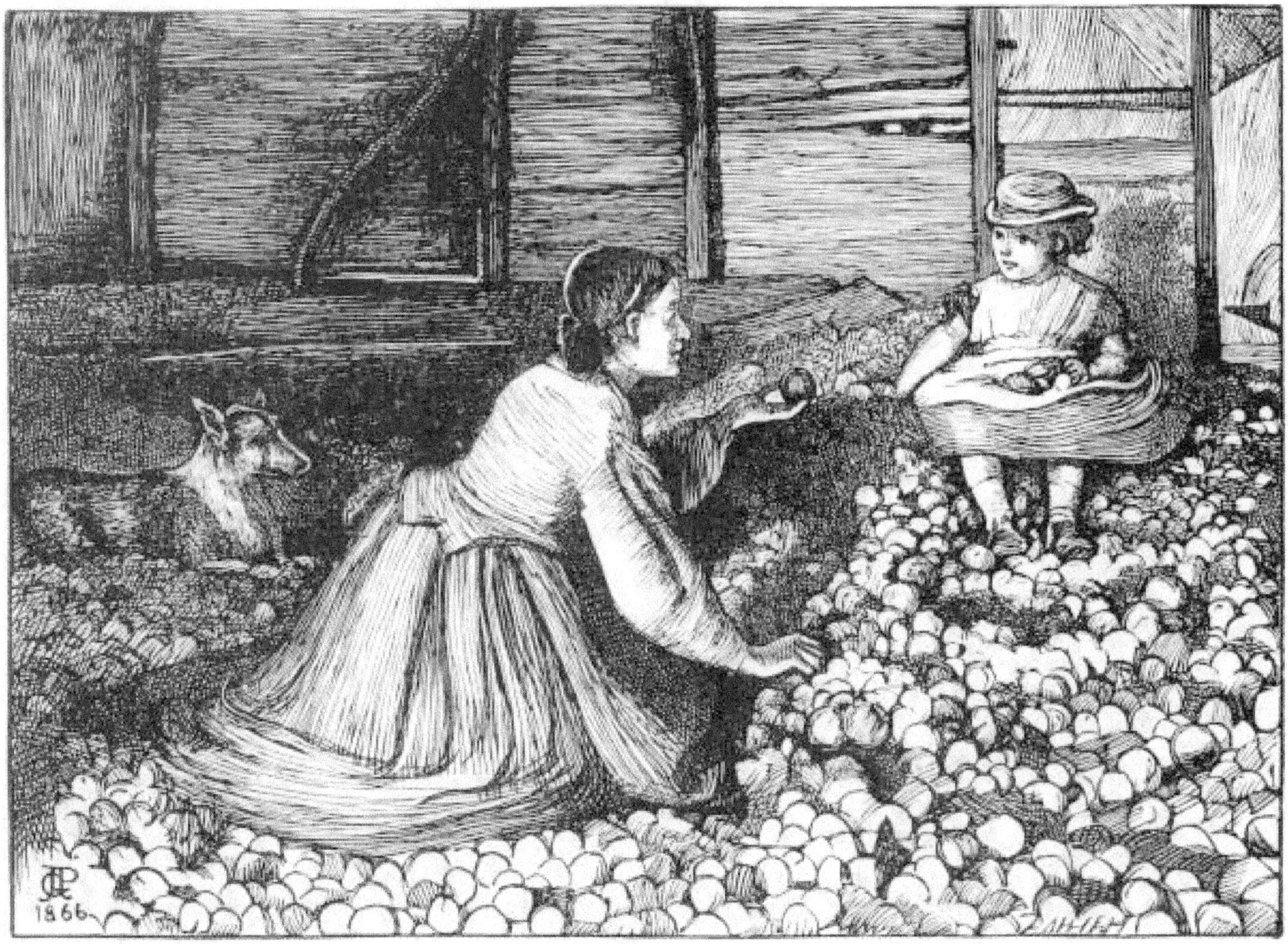
1866

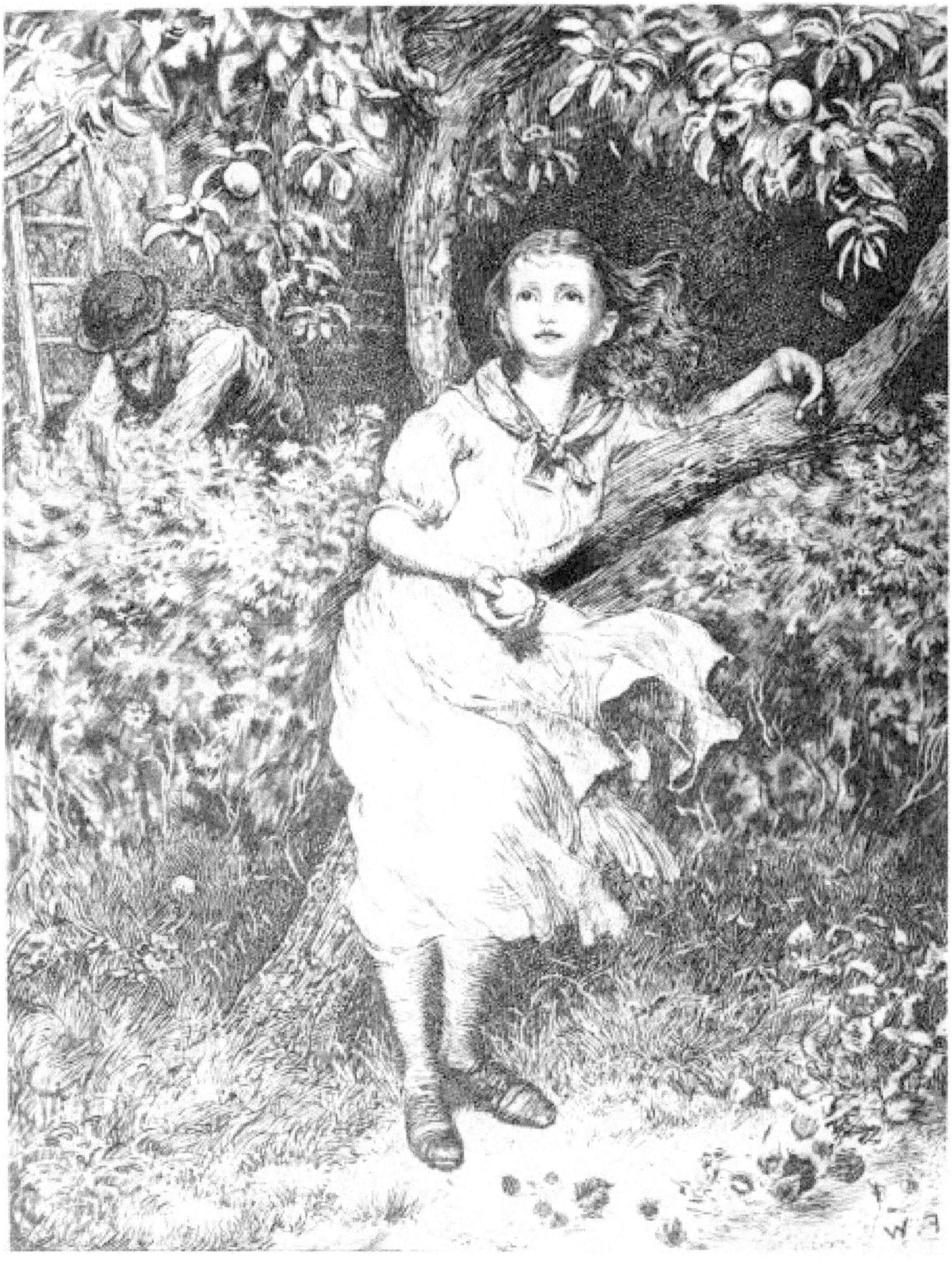

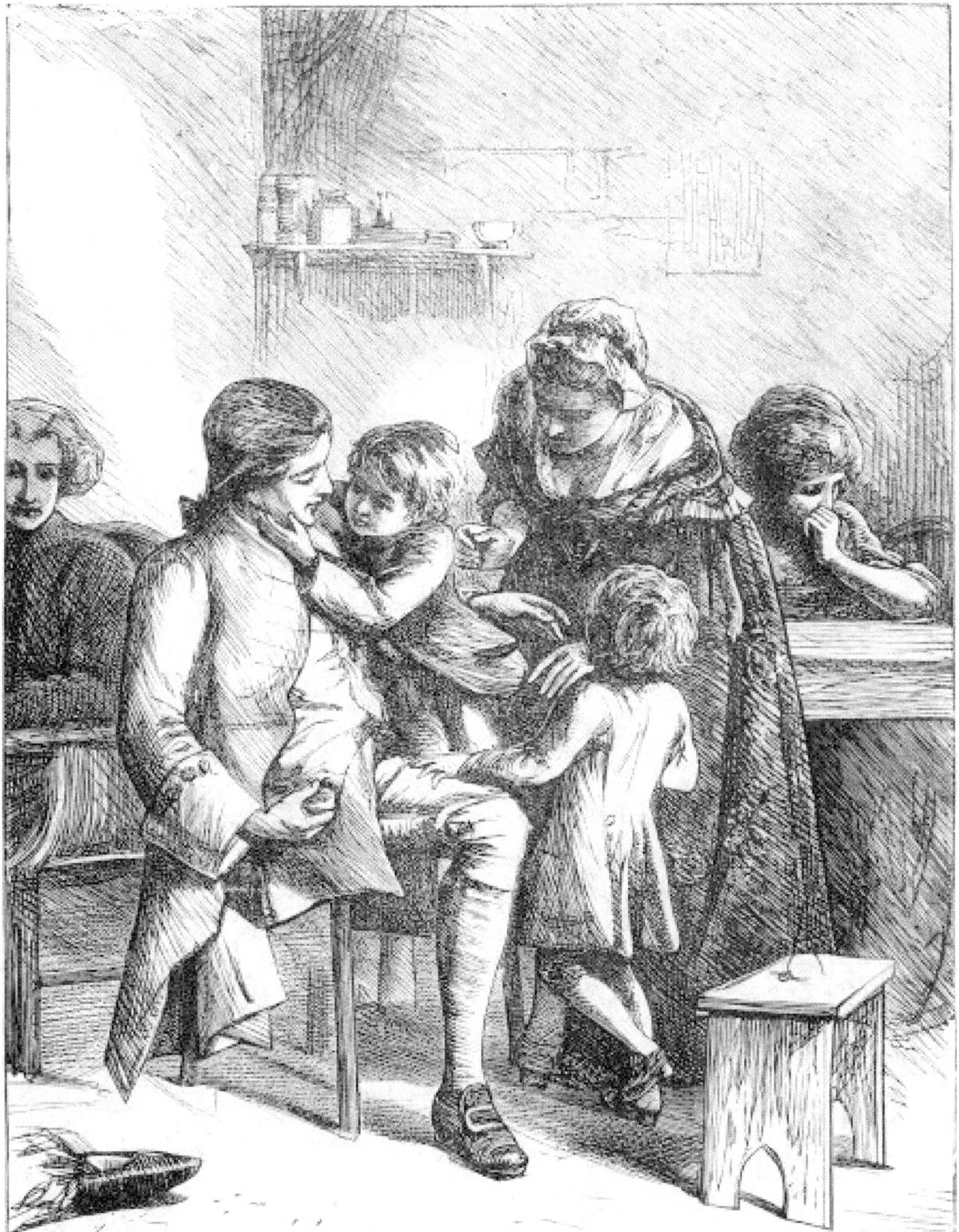

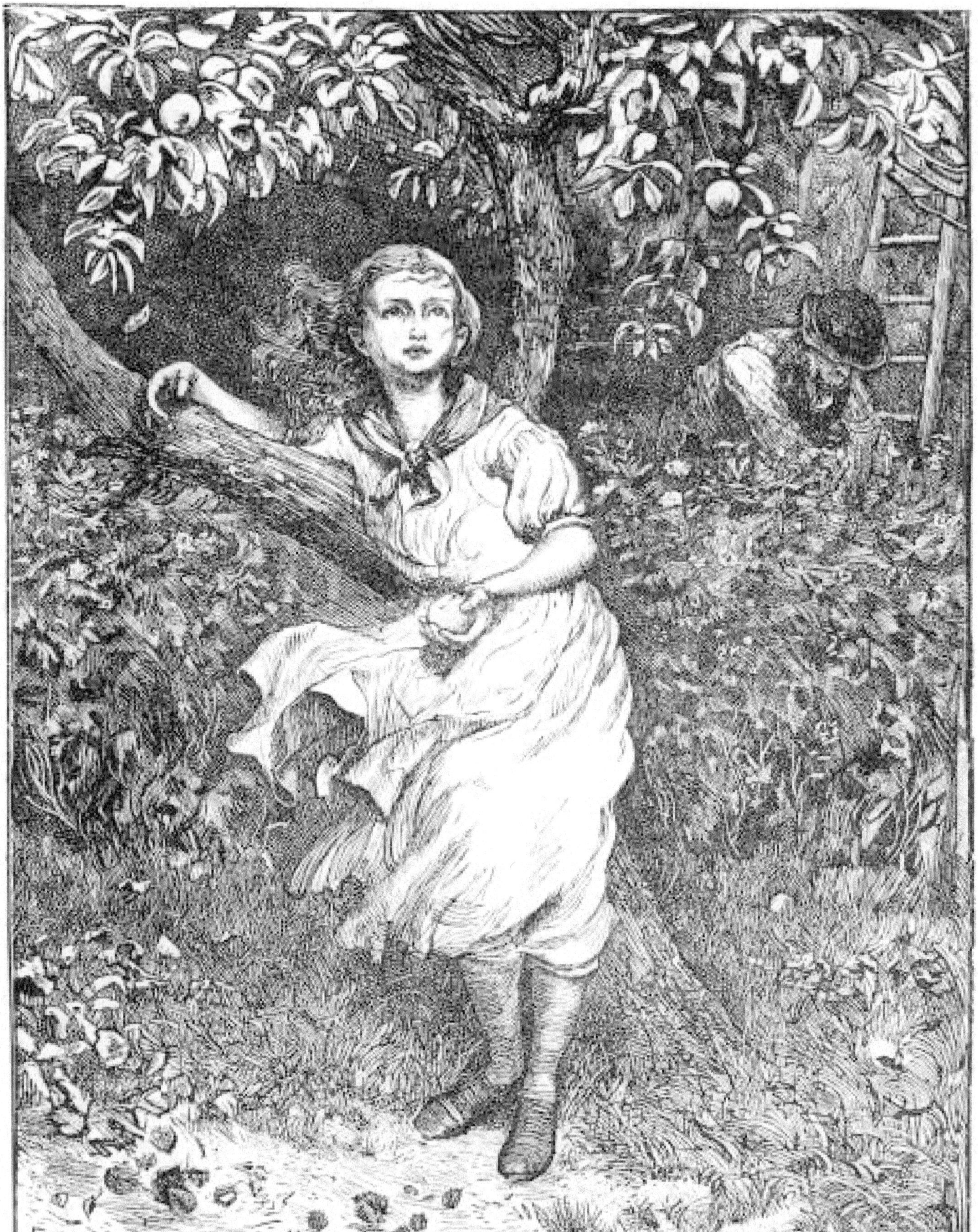
F. W

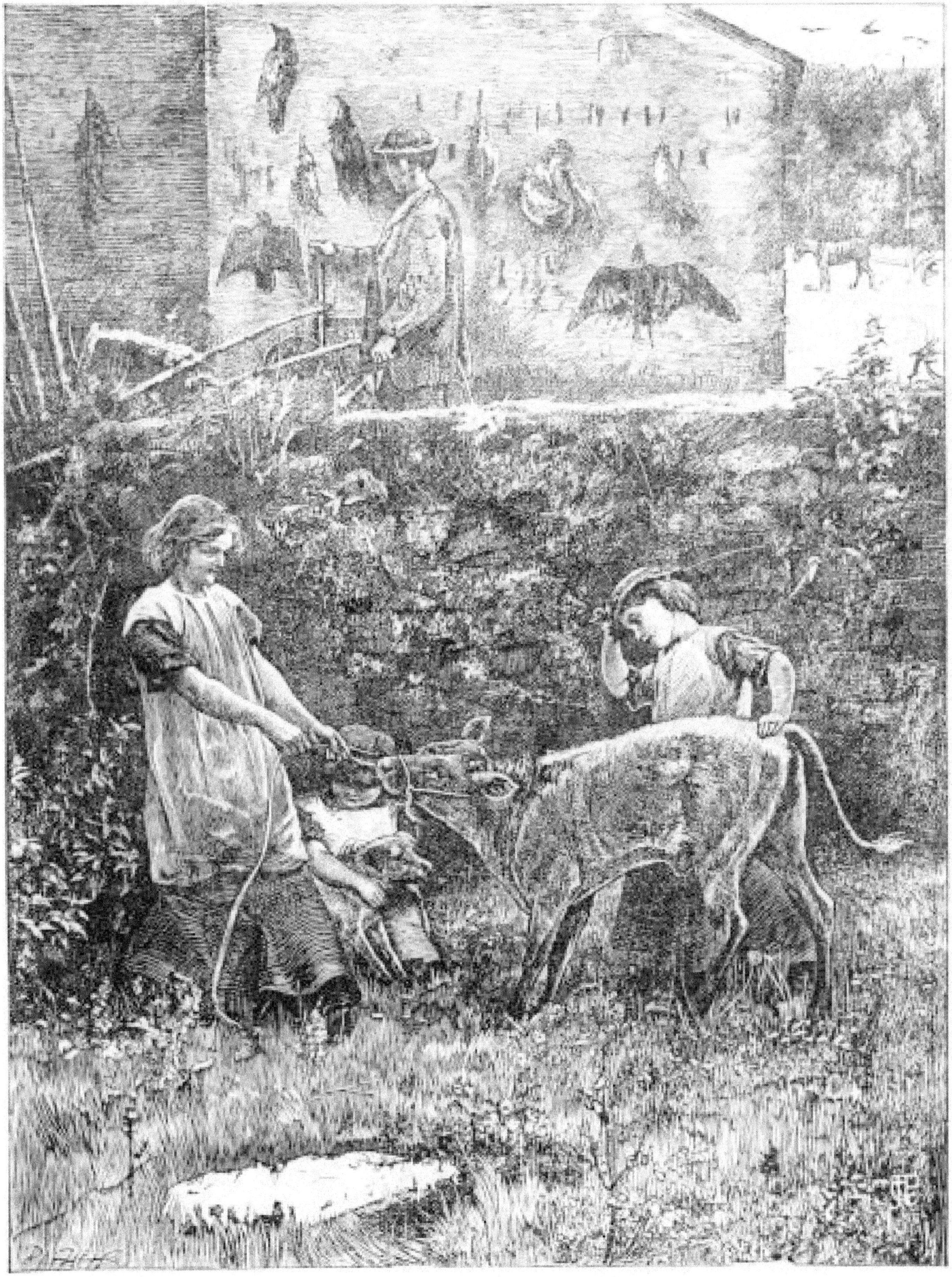

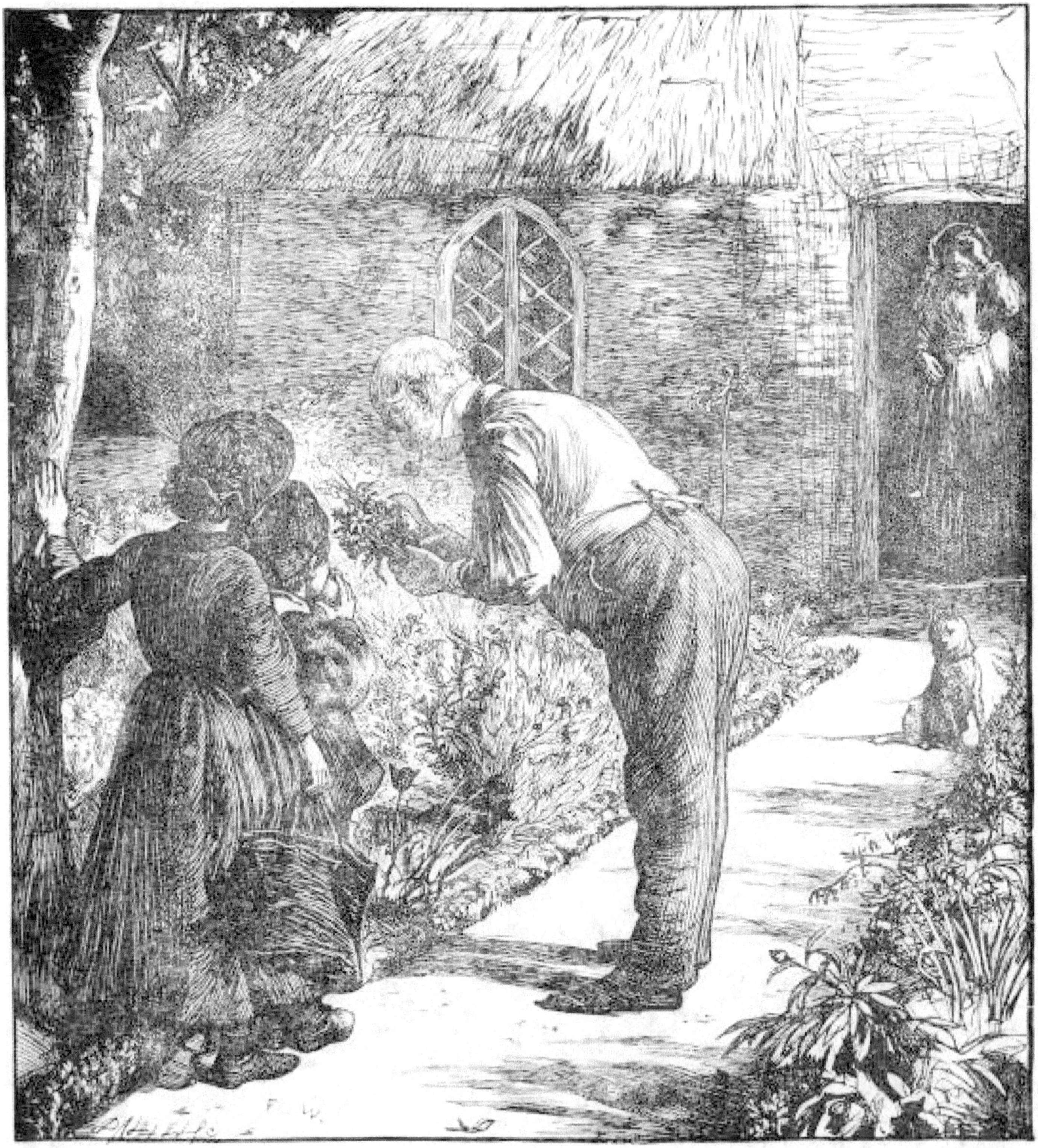

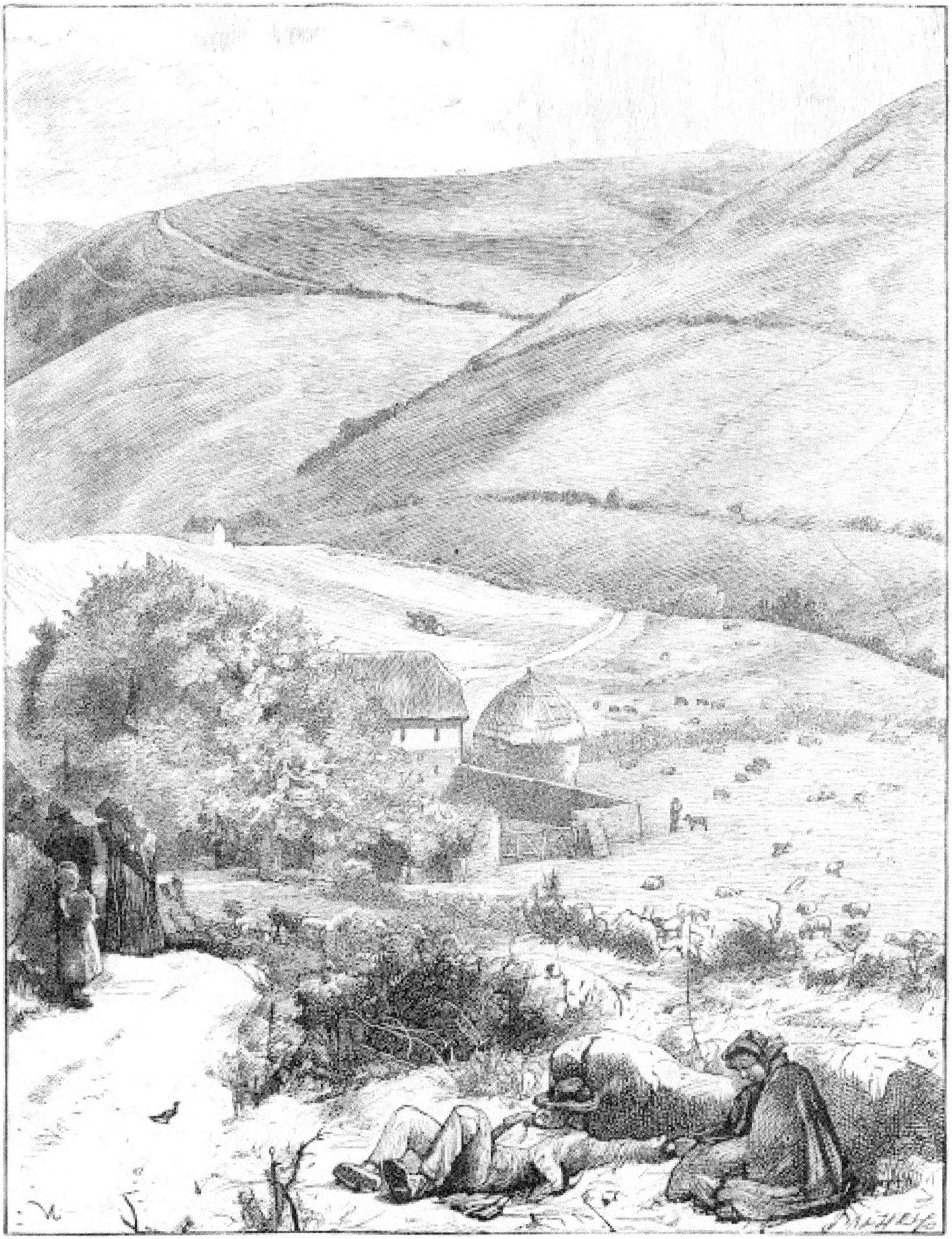

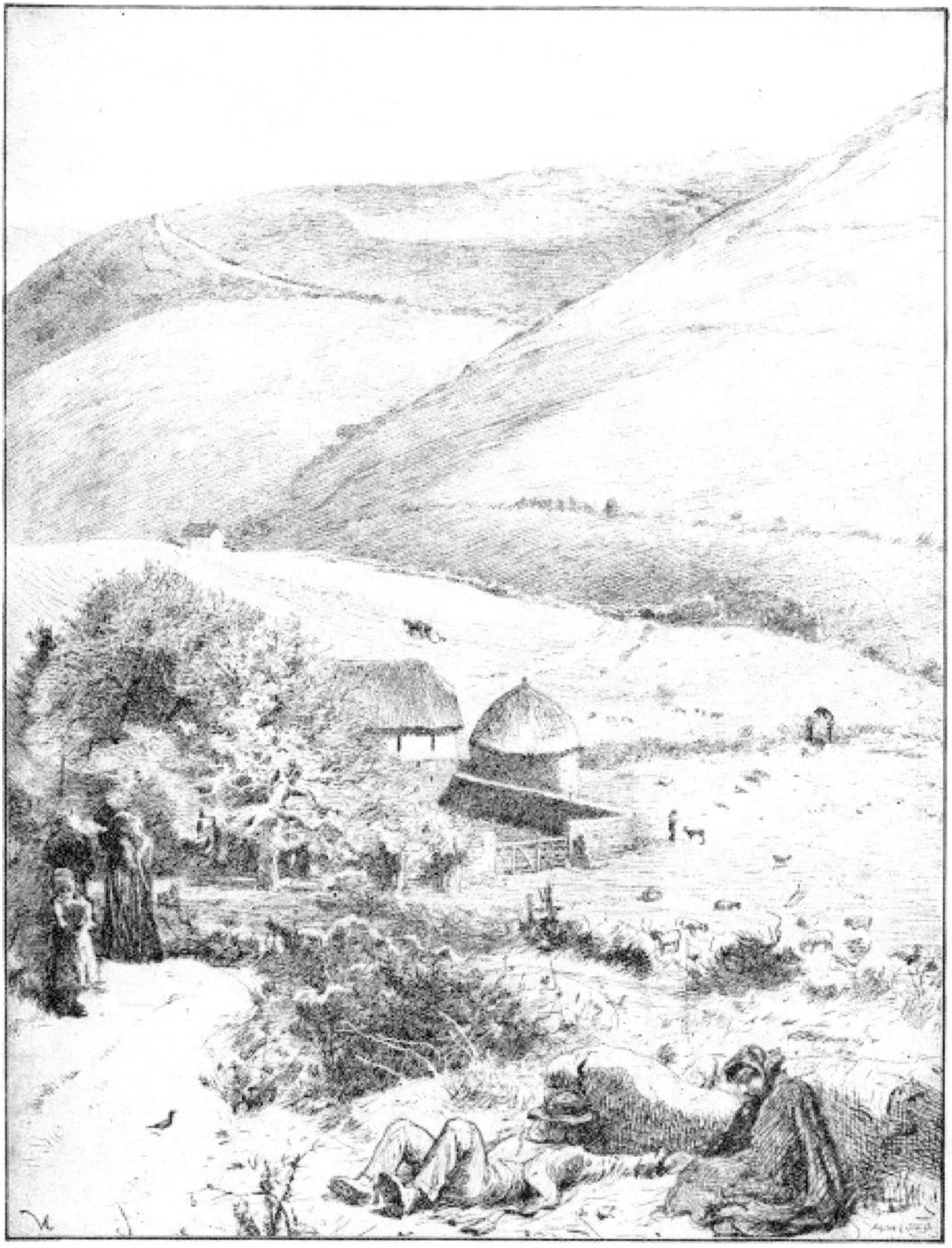

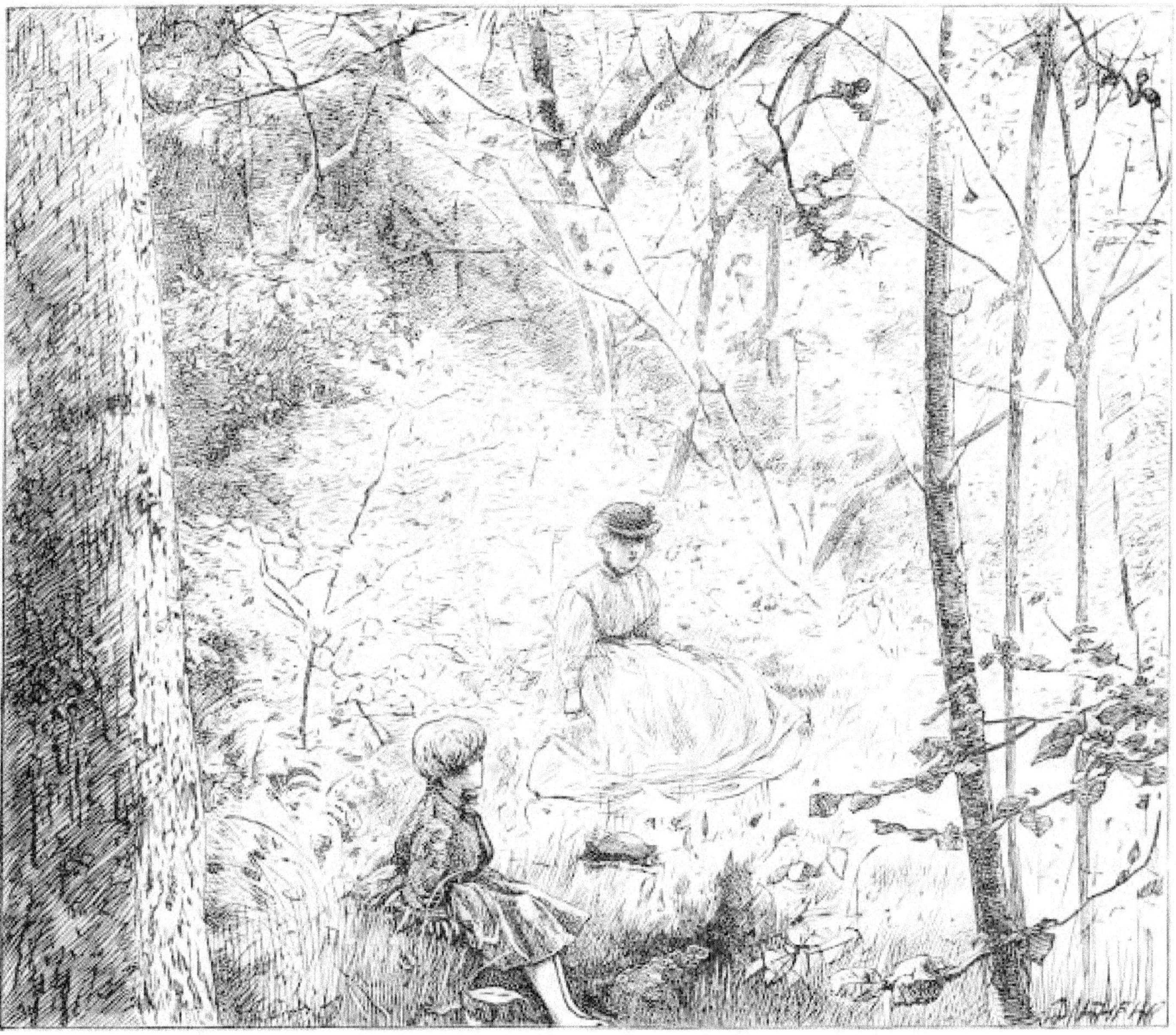

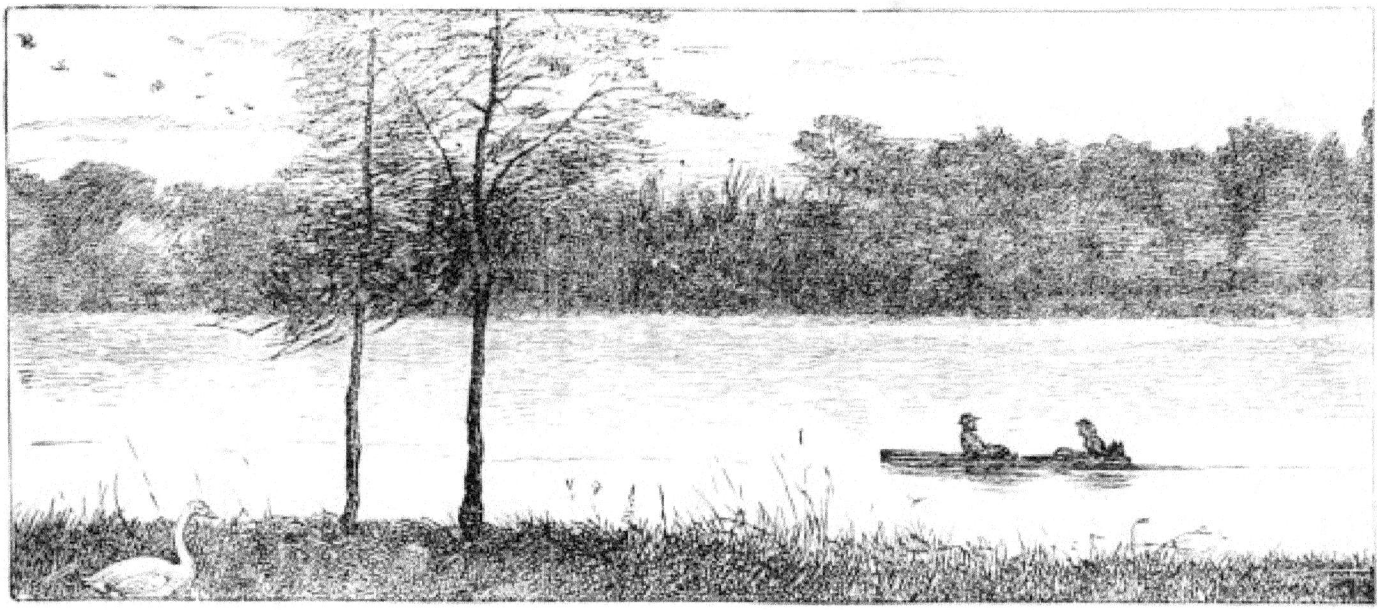

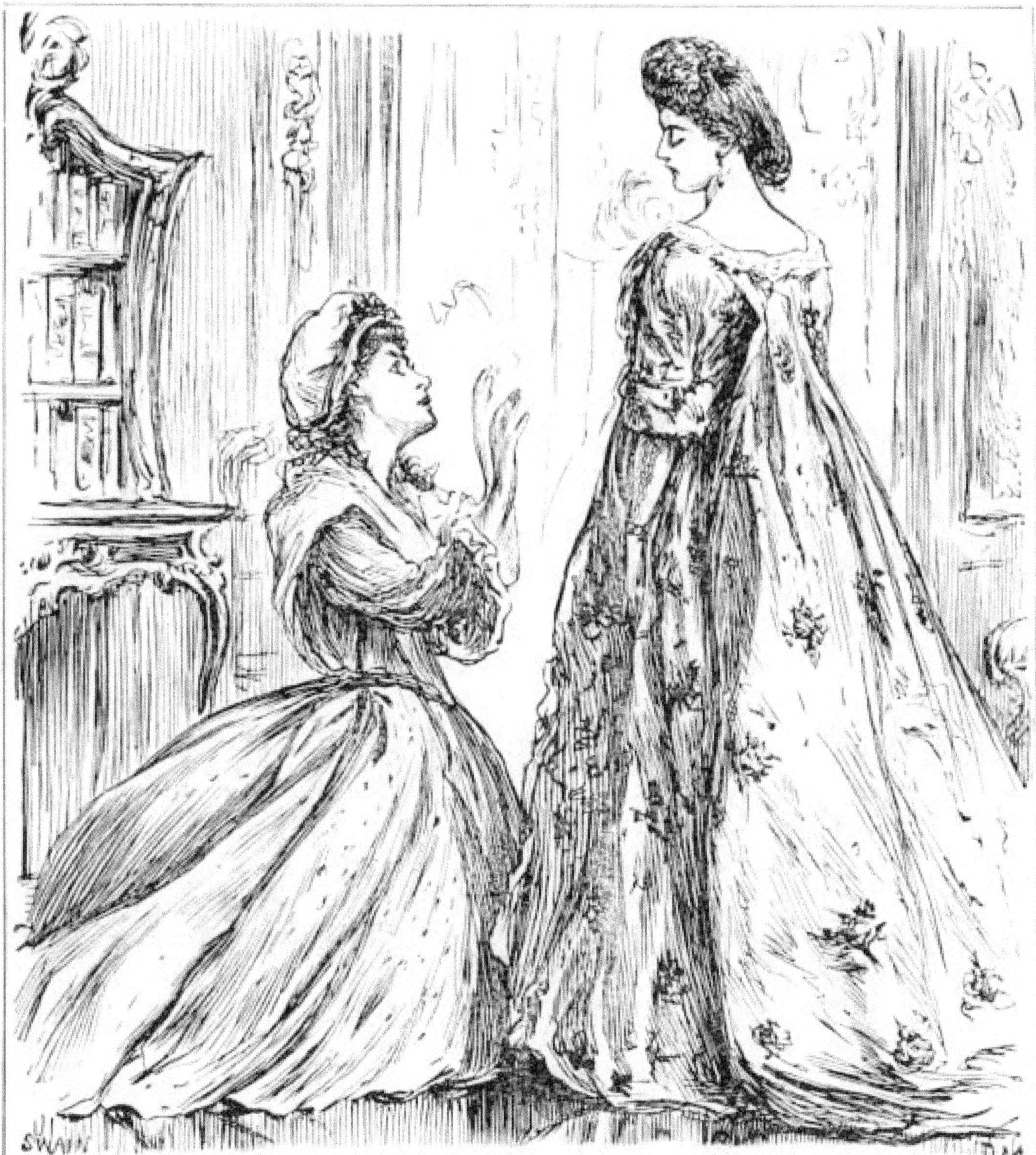
SWAIN
D.M

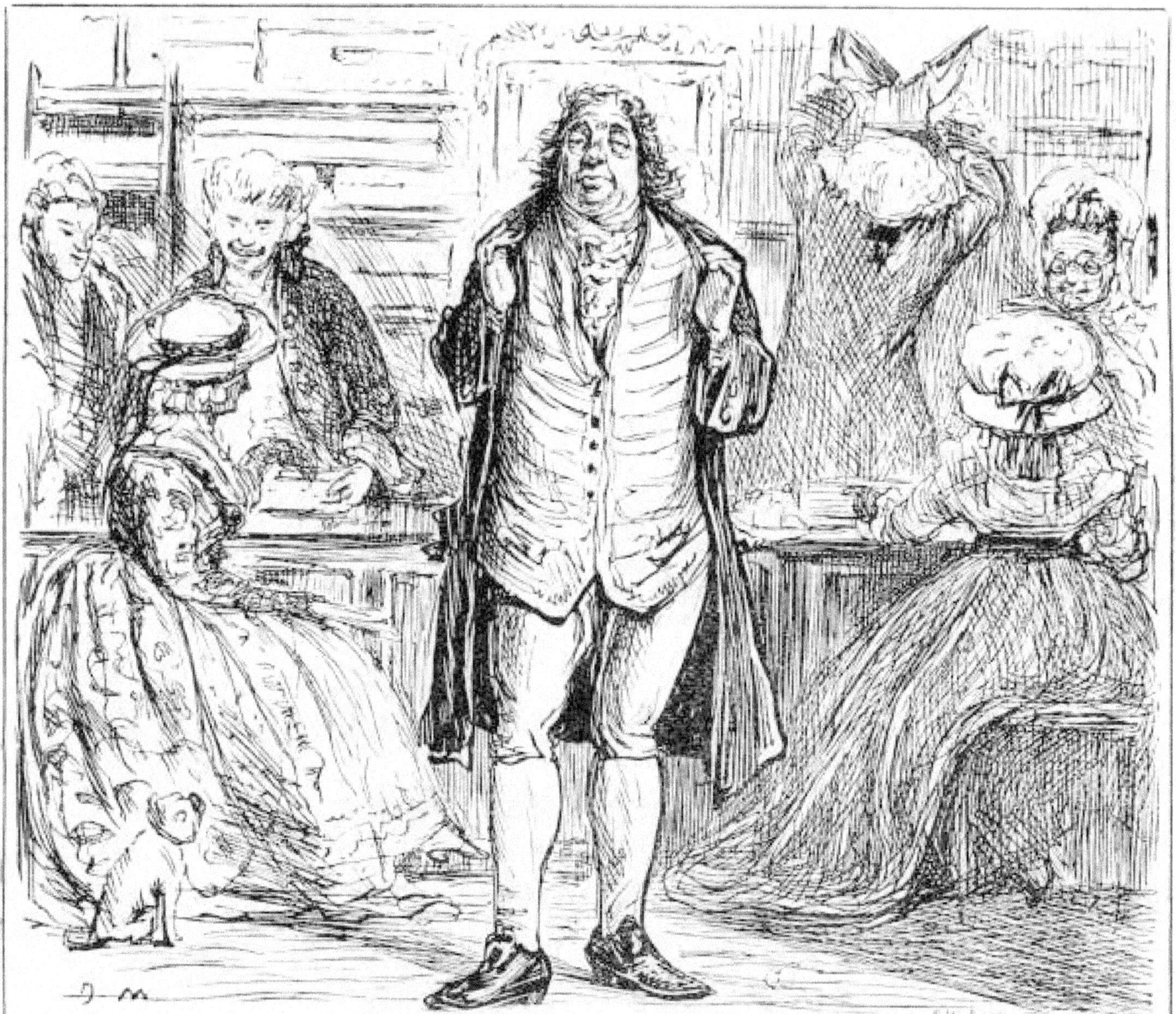

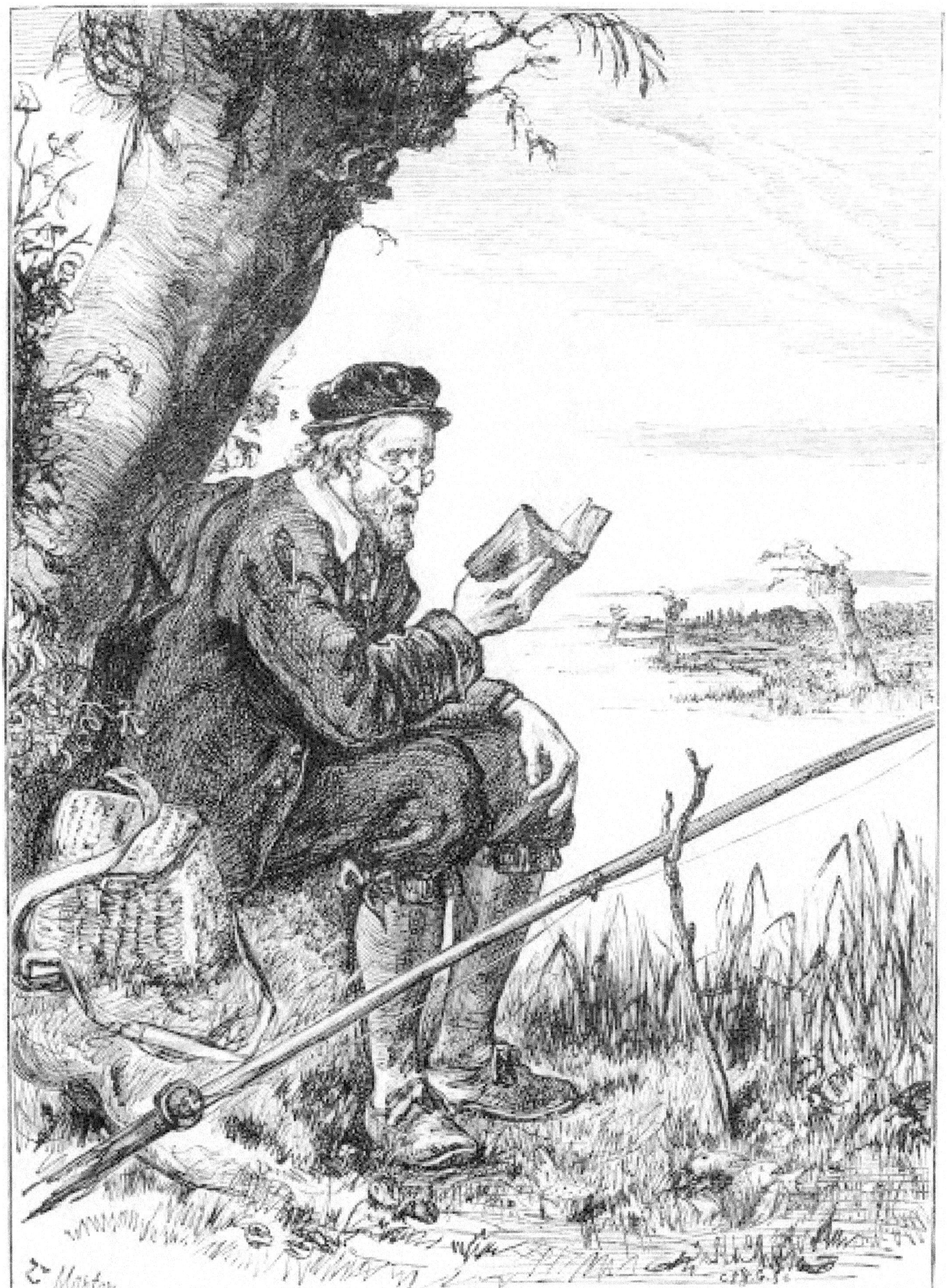

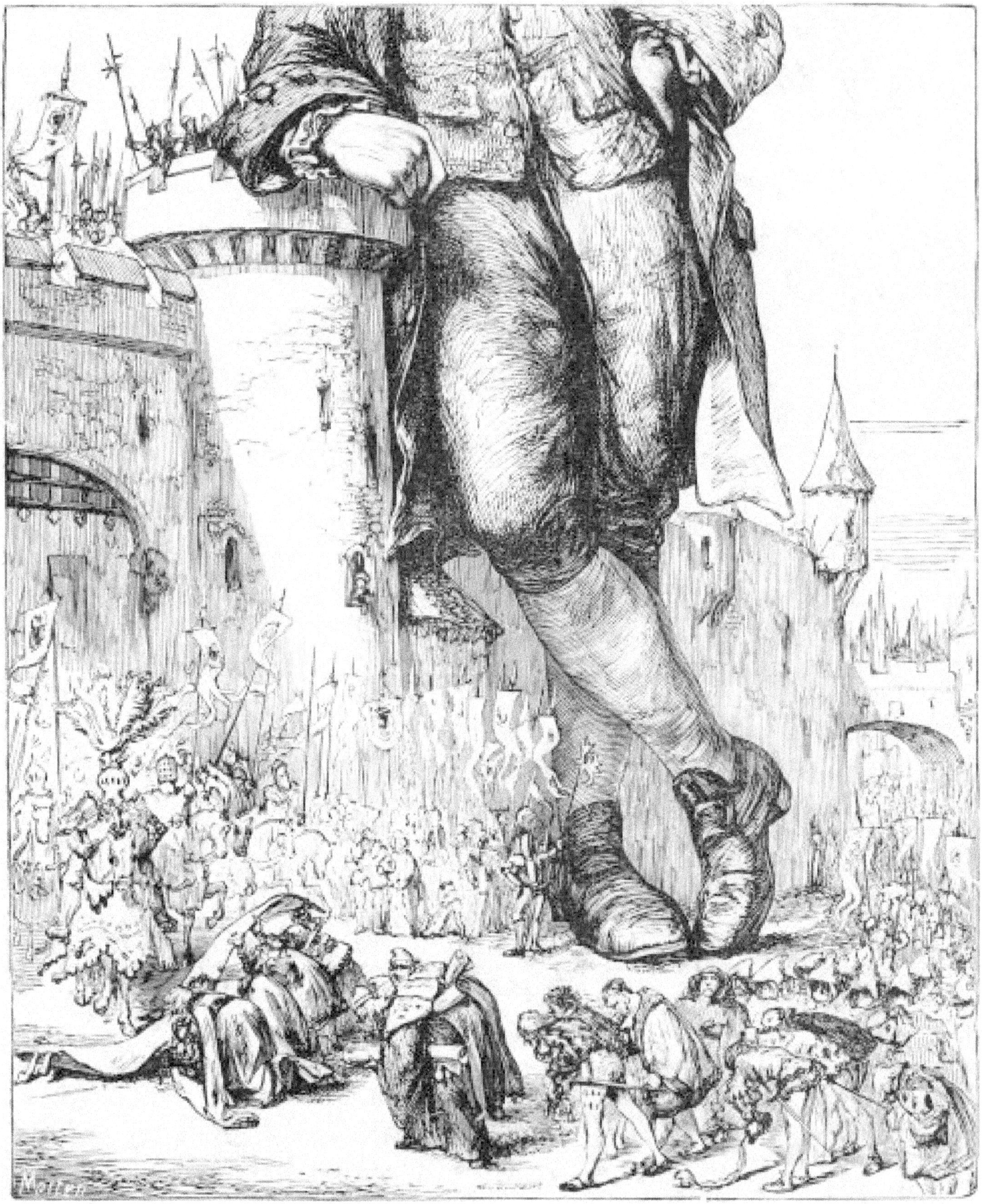

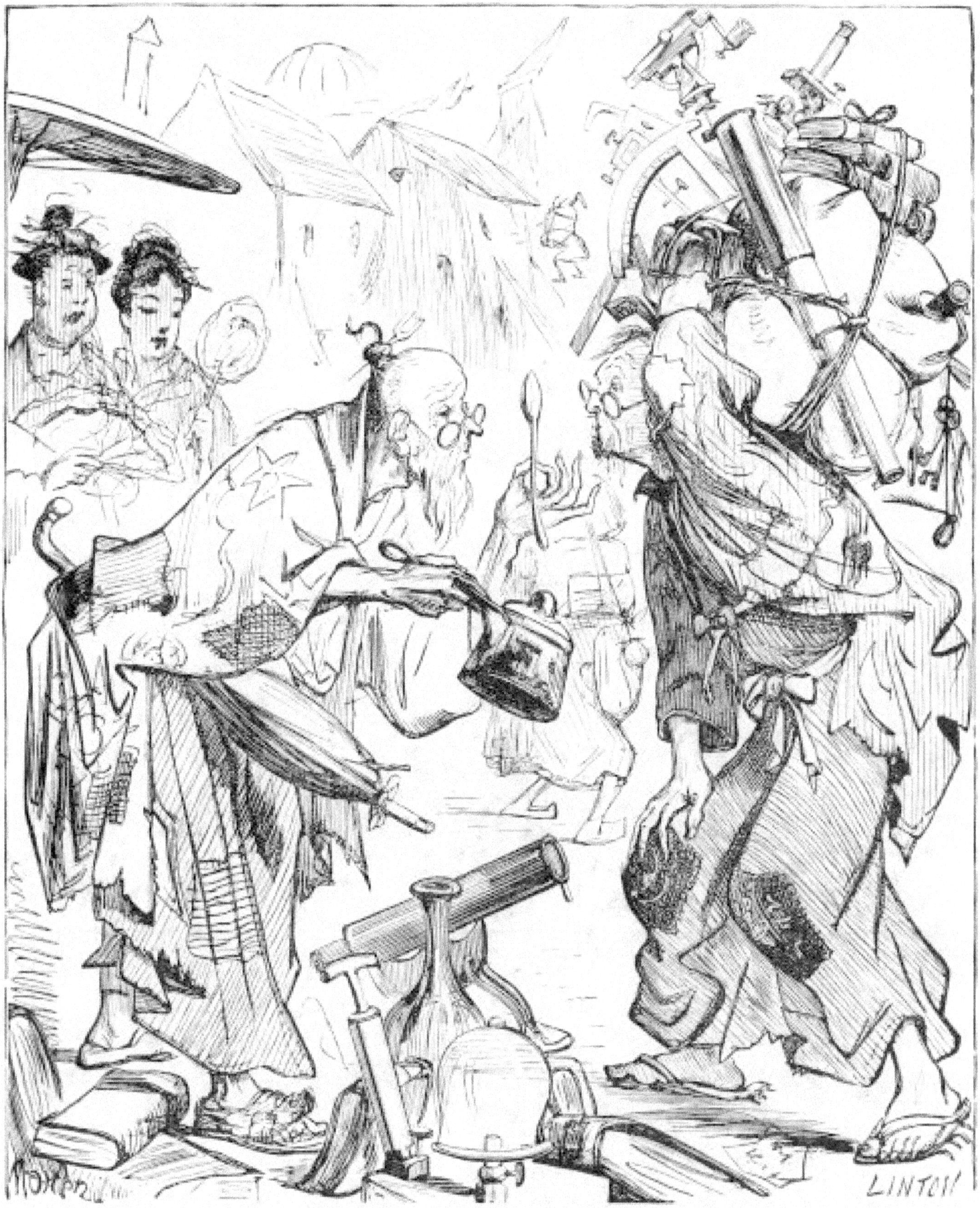

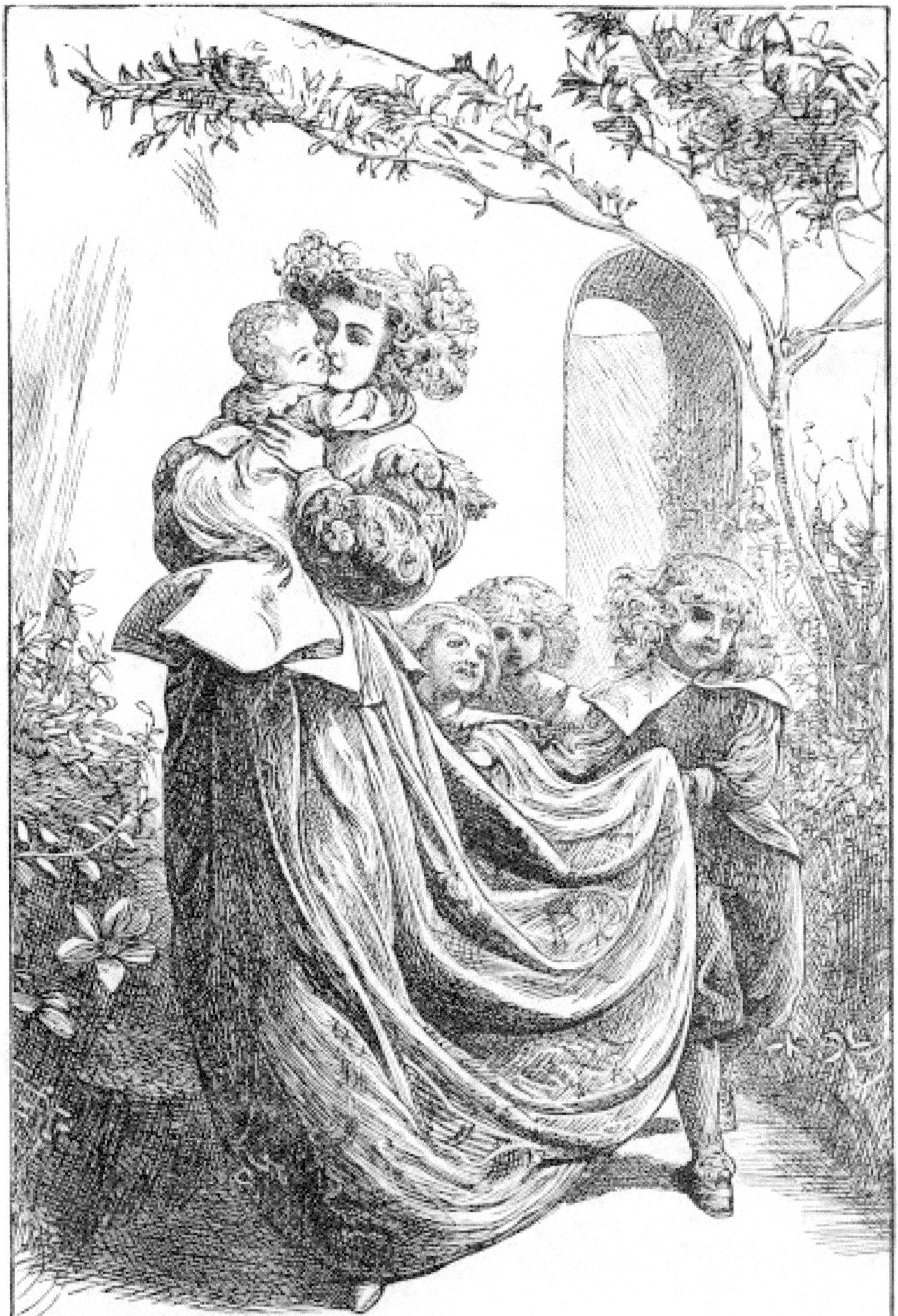

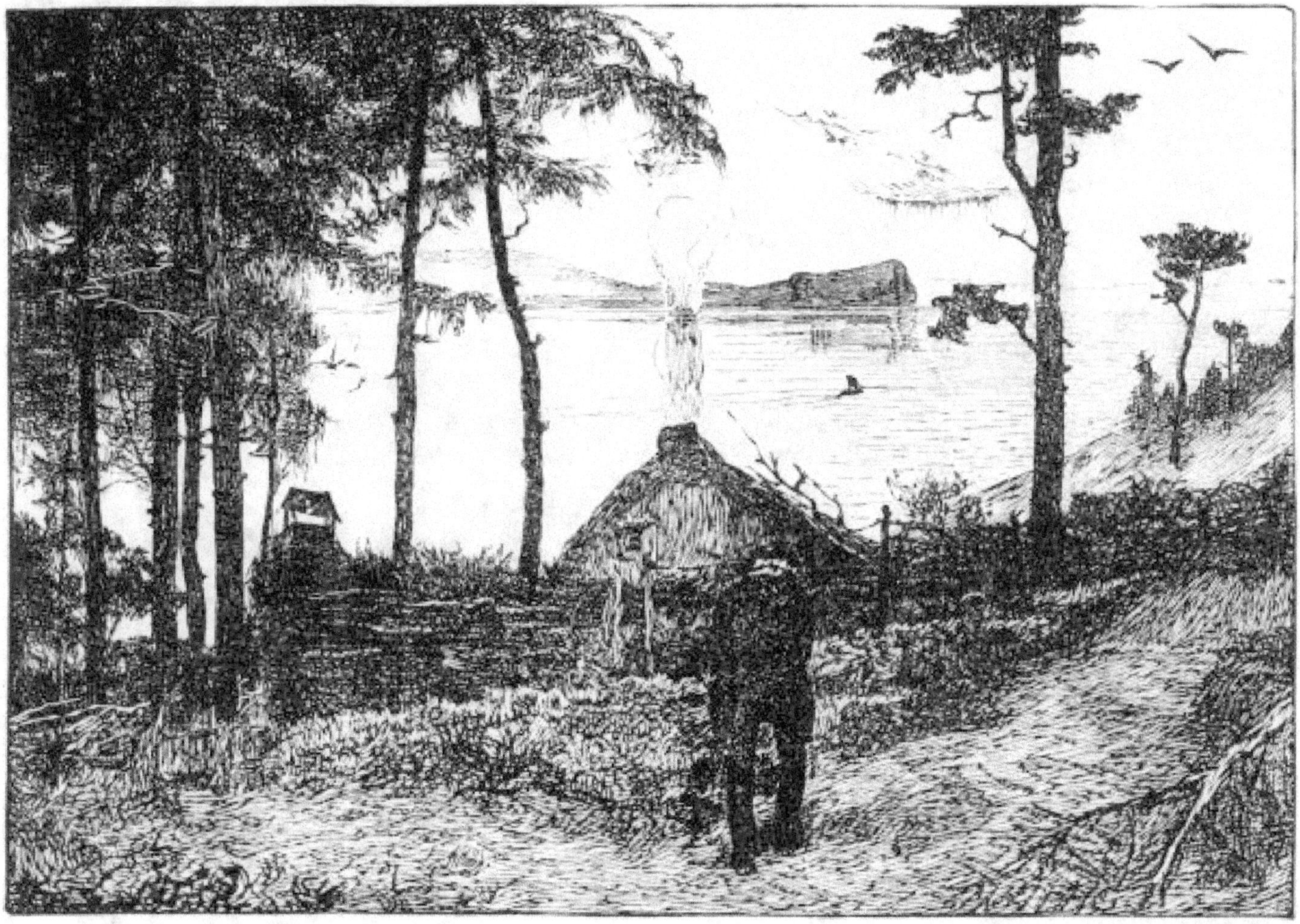

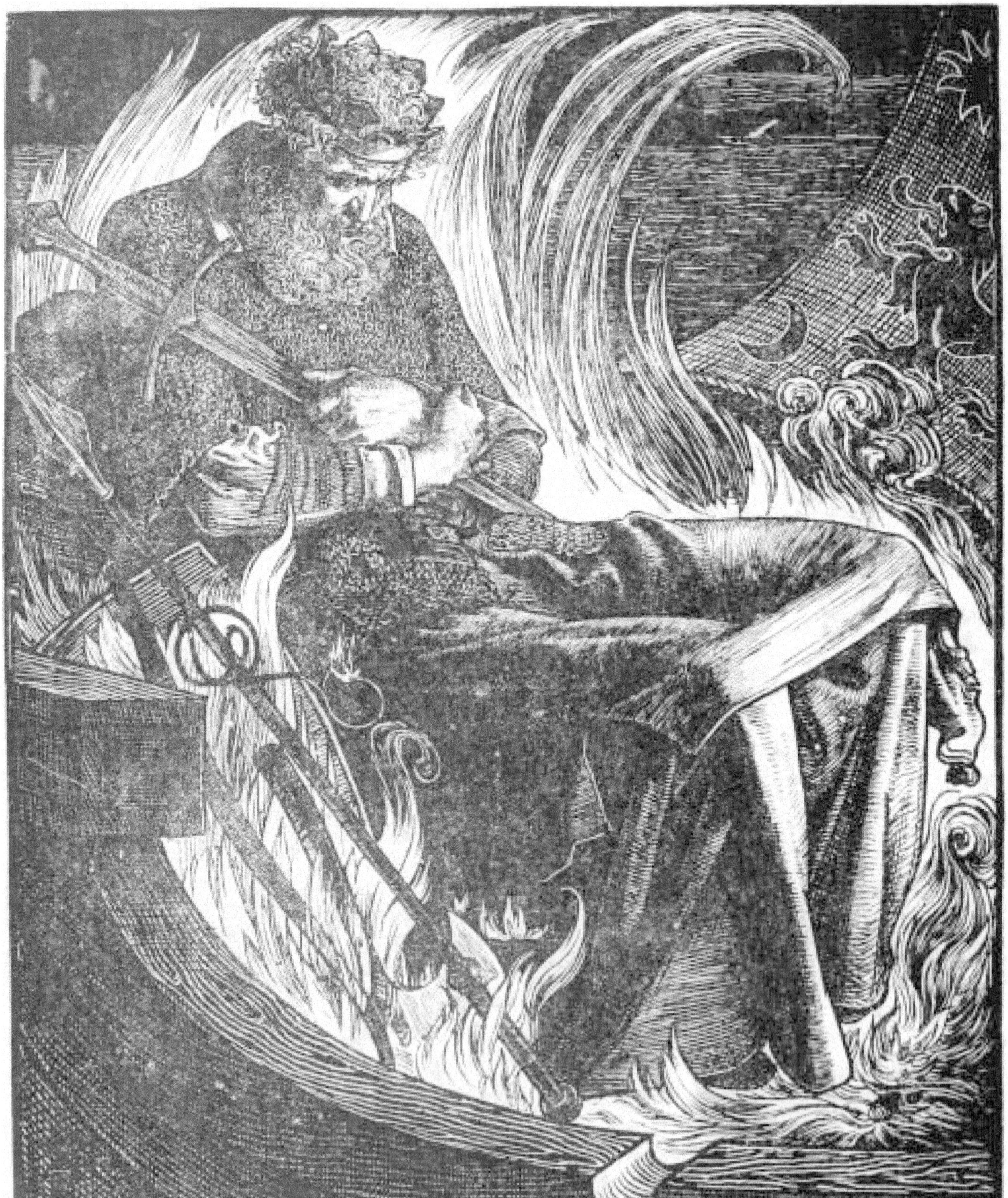

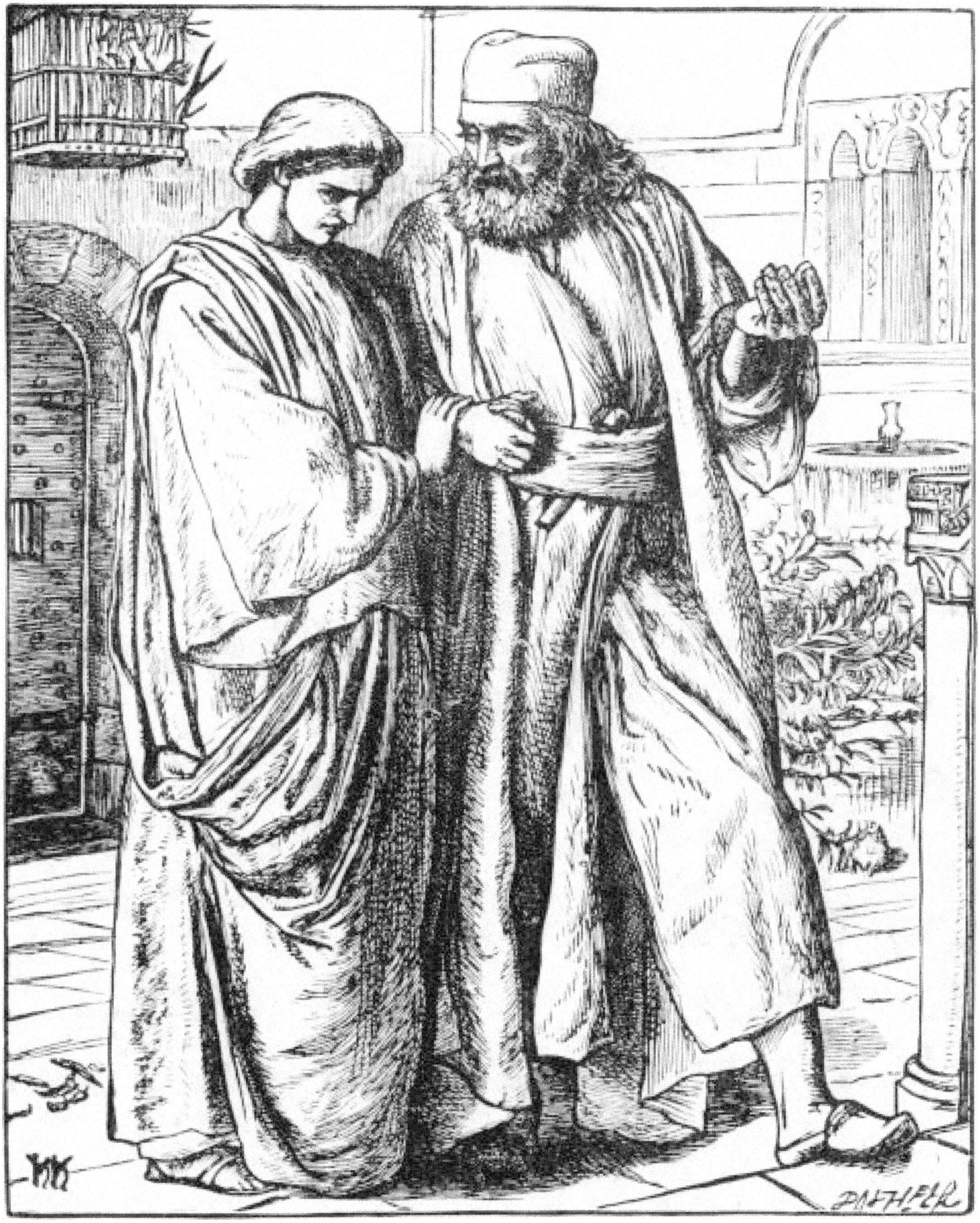
DALZIEL

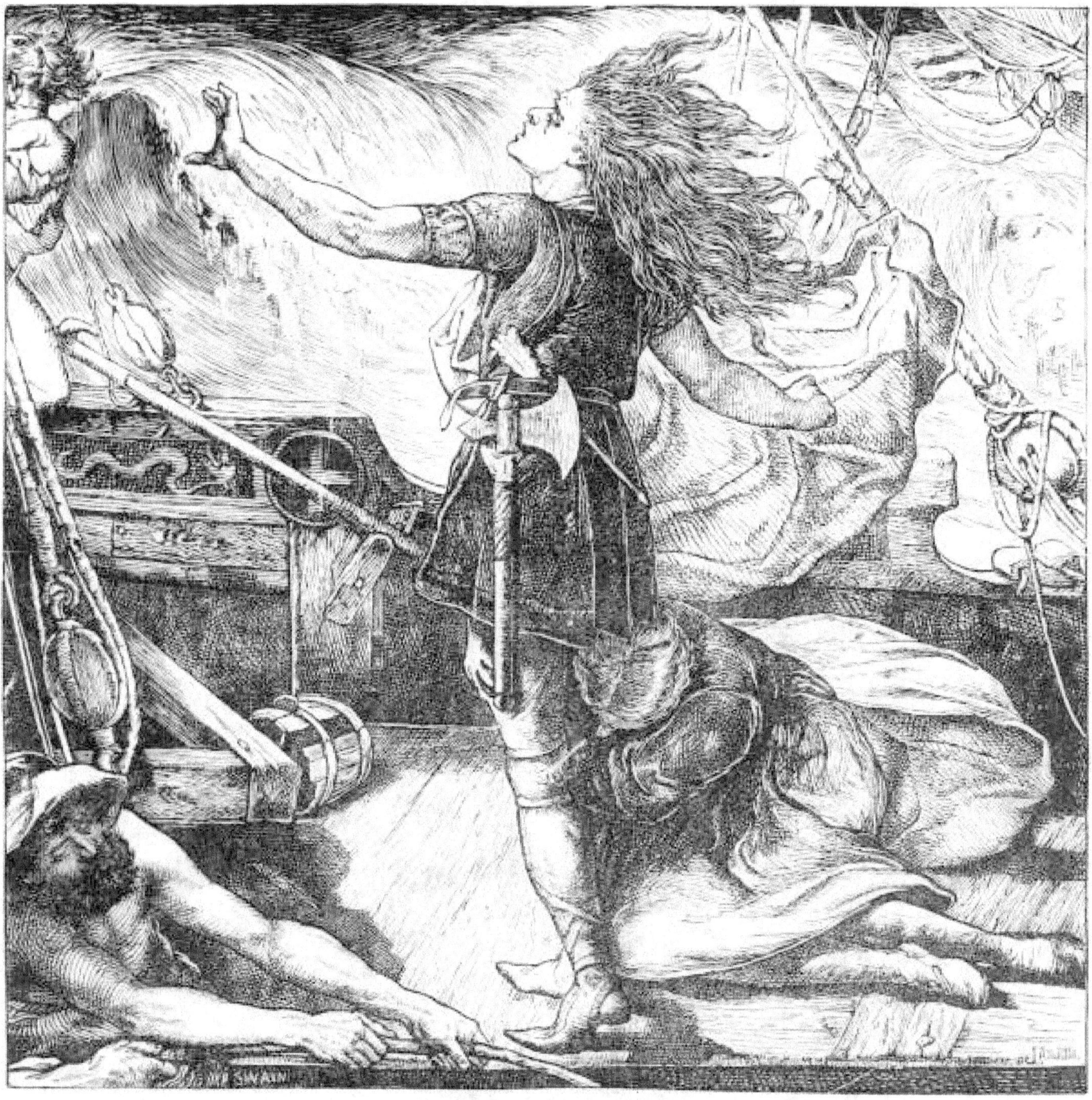
SWAIN

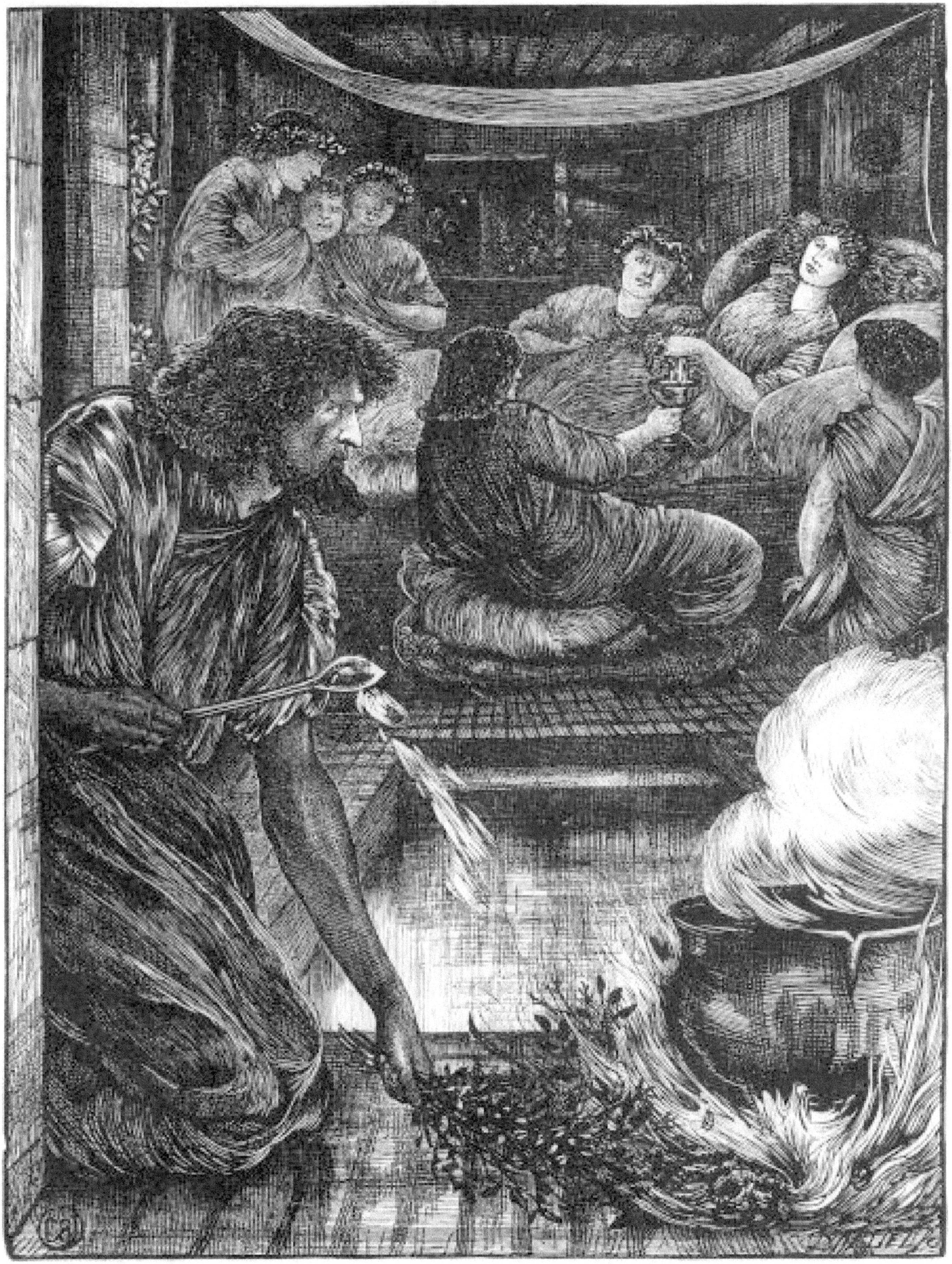

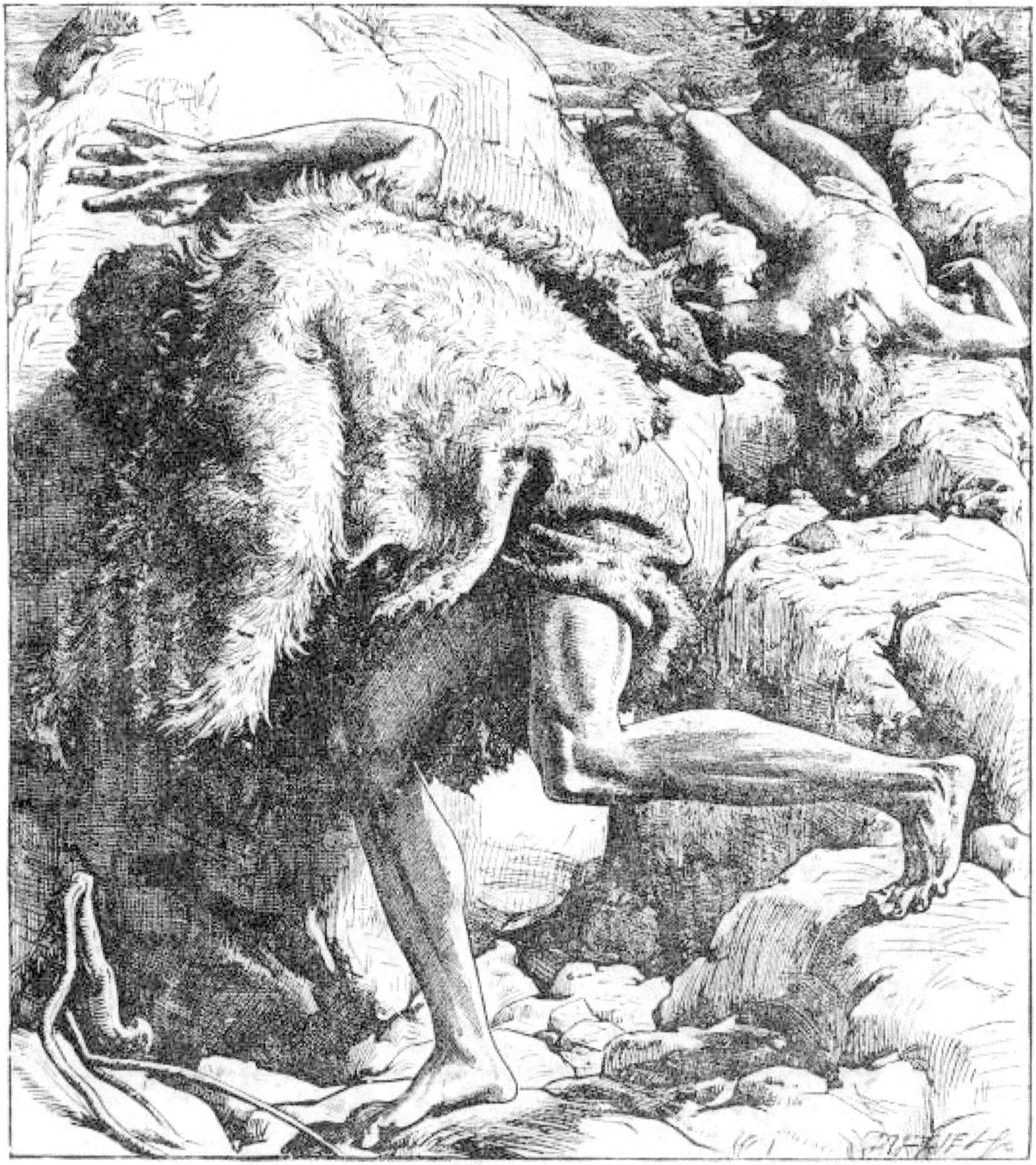

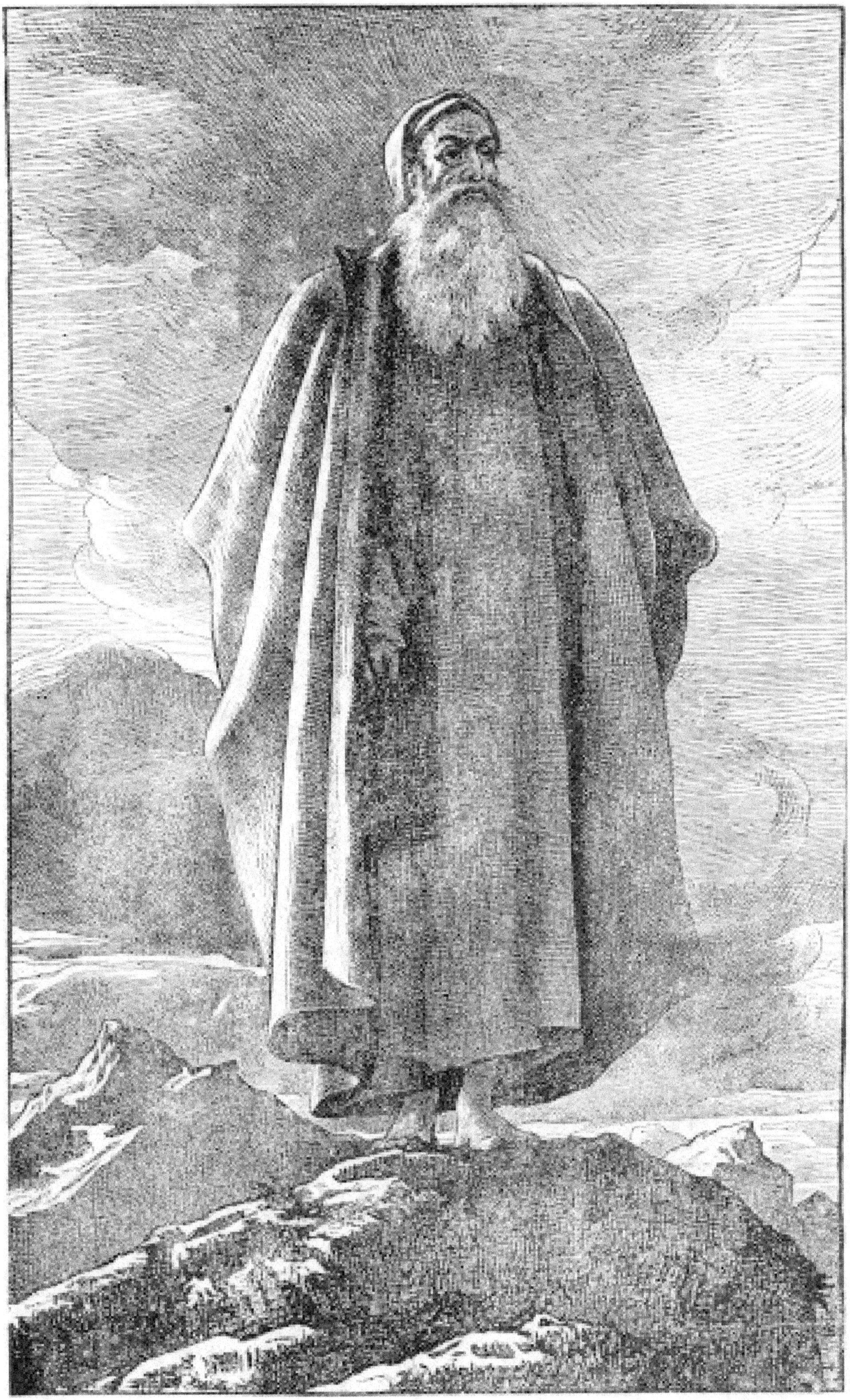

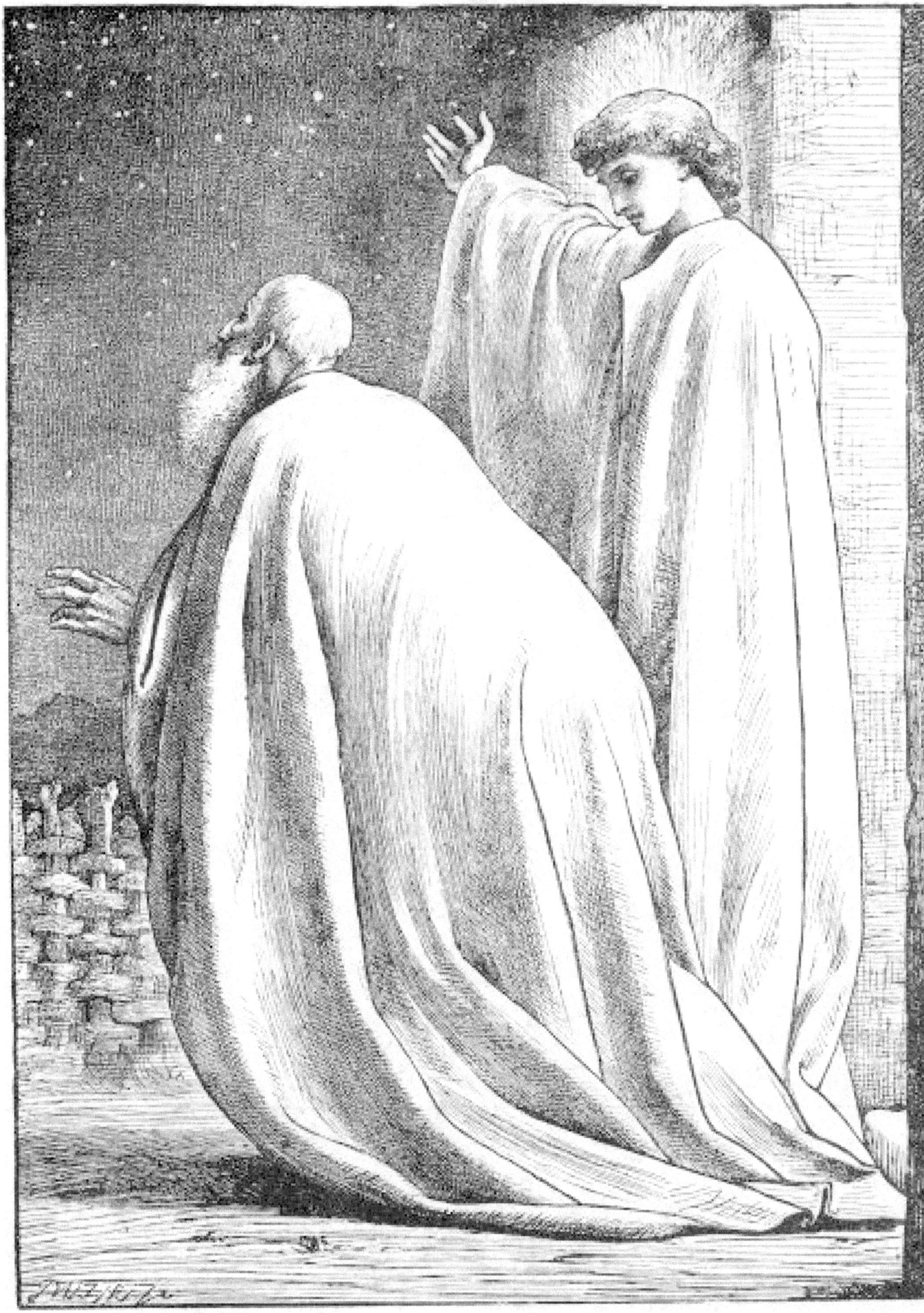

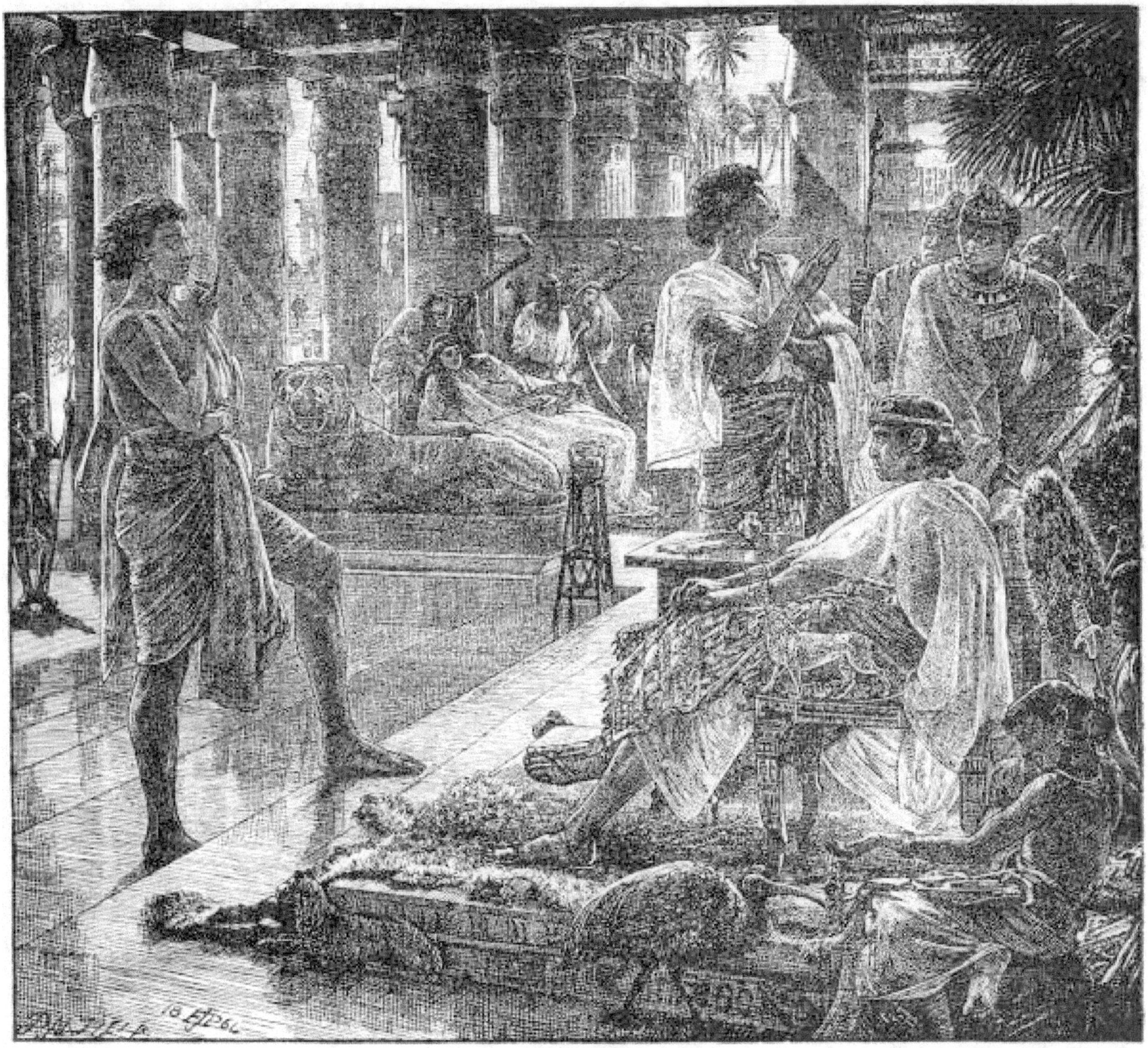

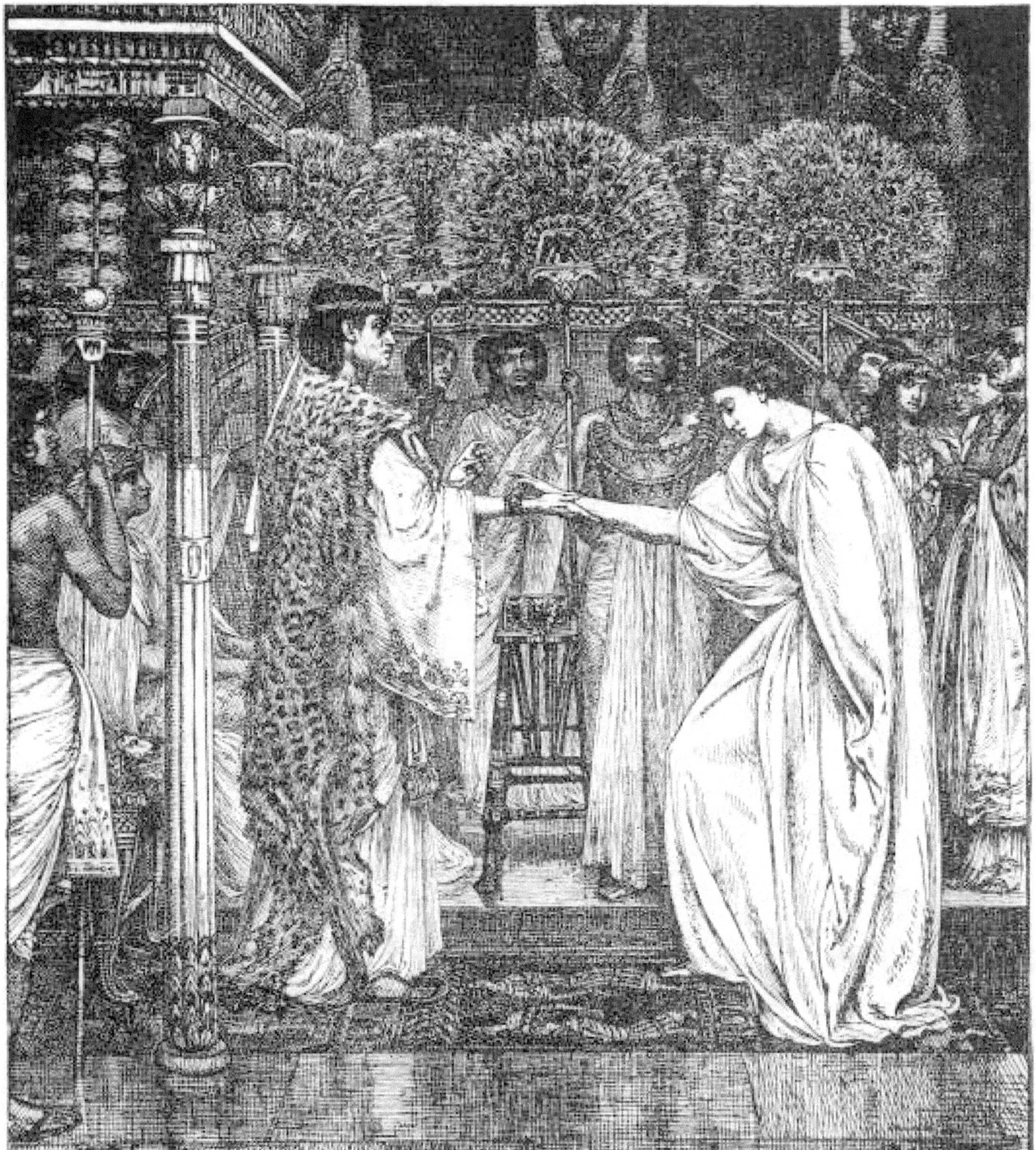

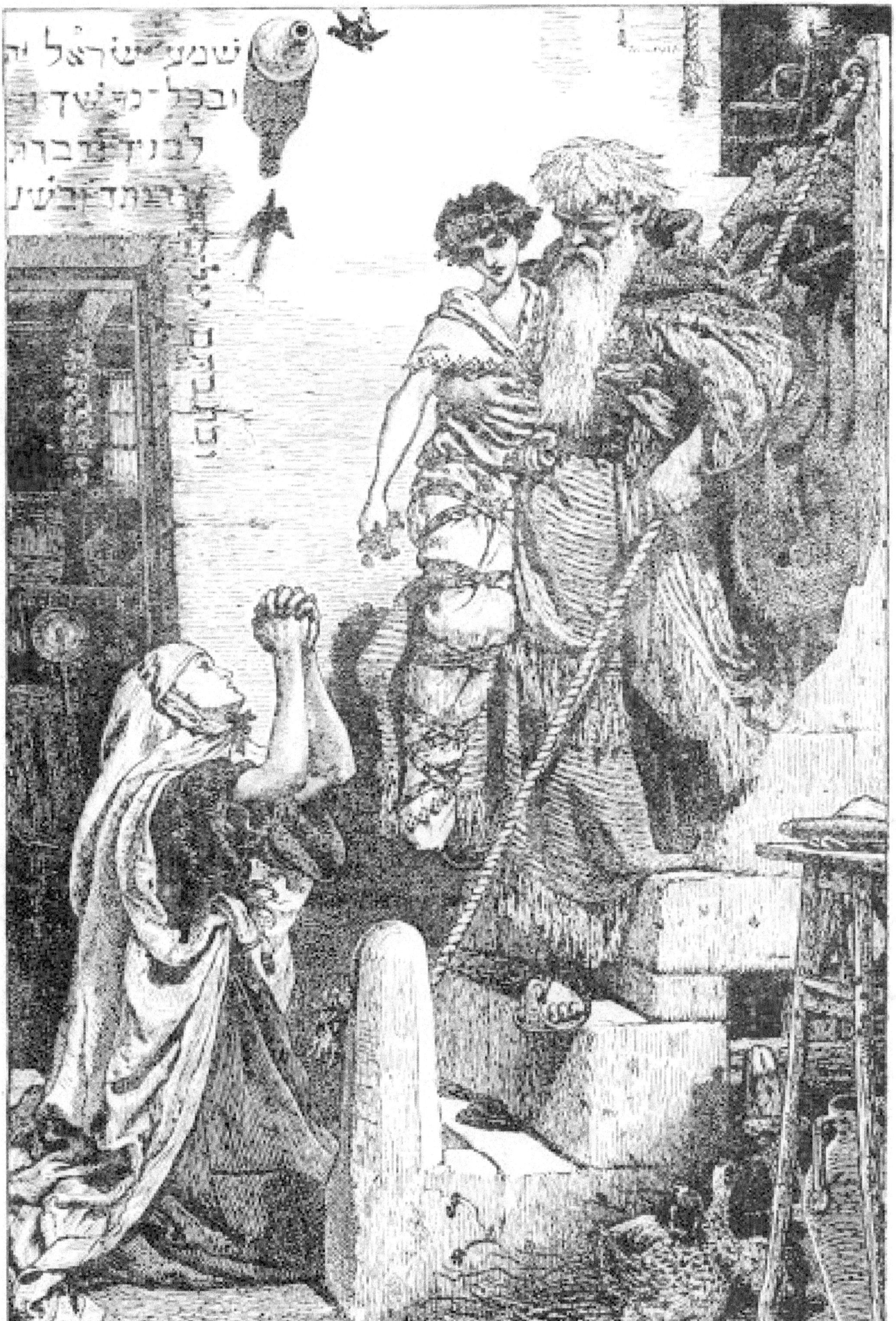
שמע ישראל

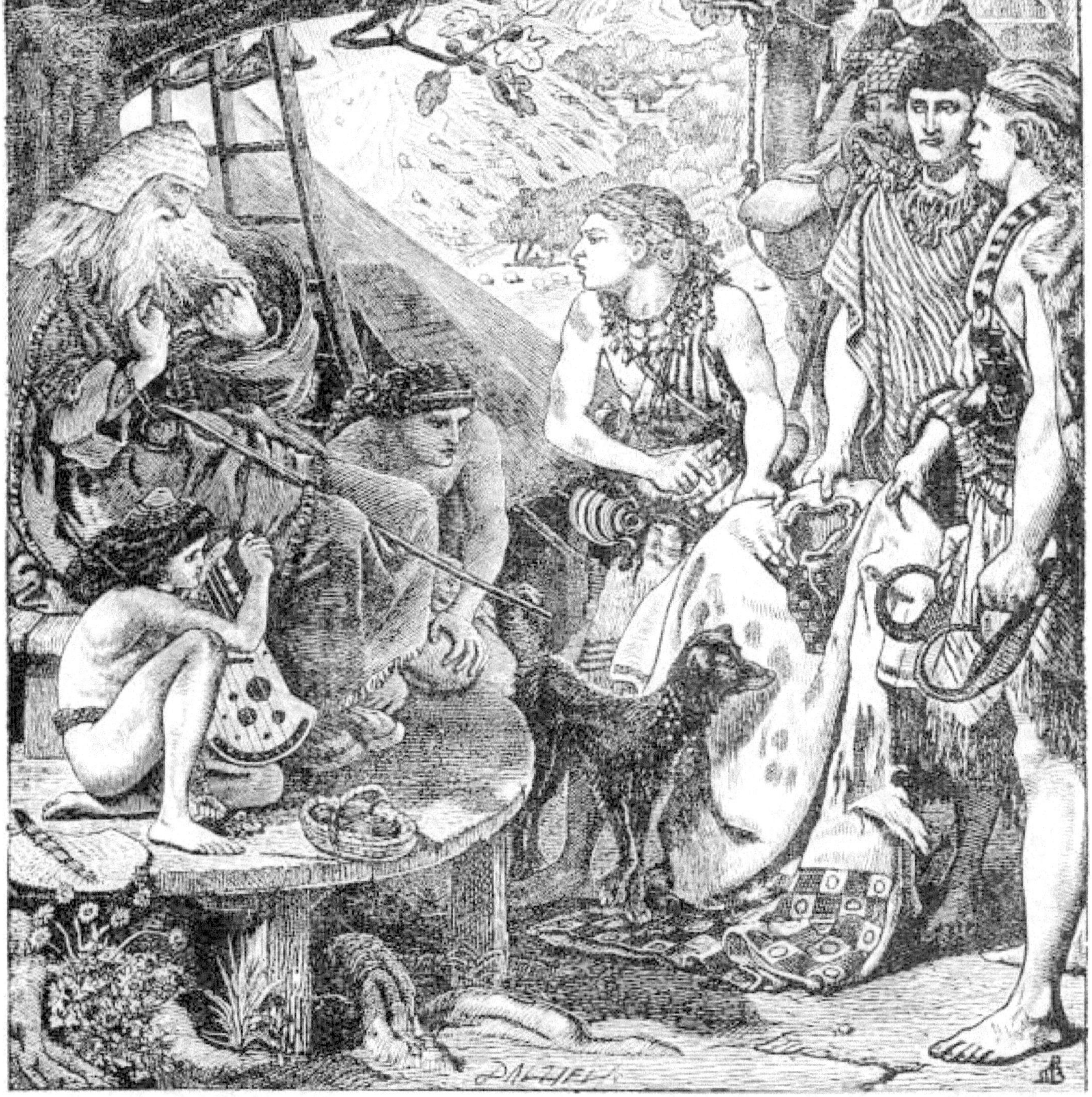
DALZIEL

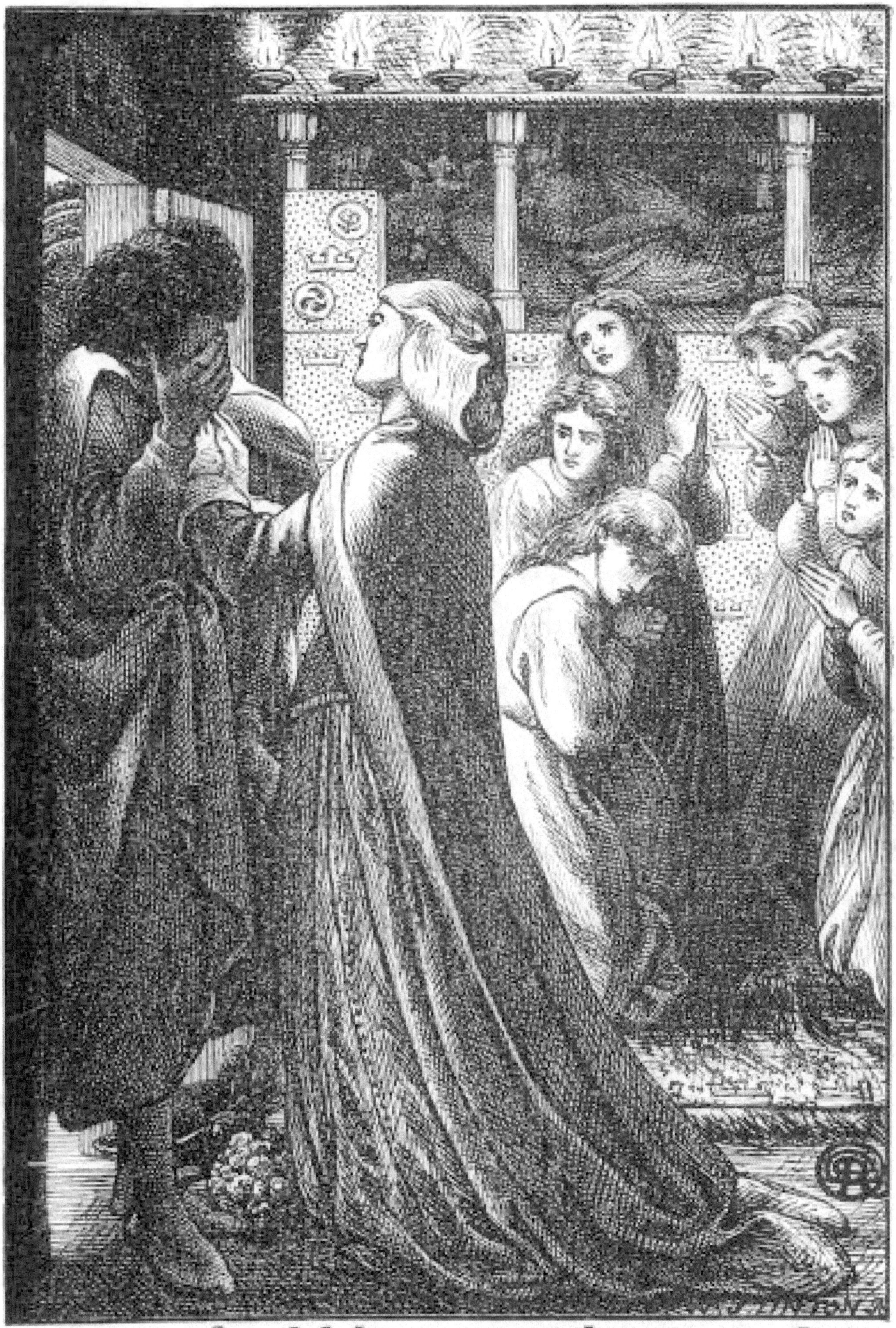

You should have wept her yesterday

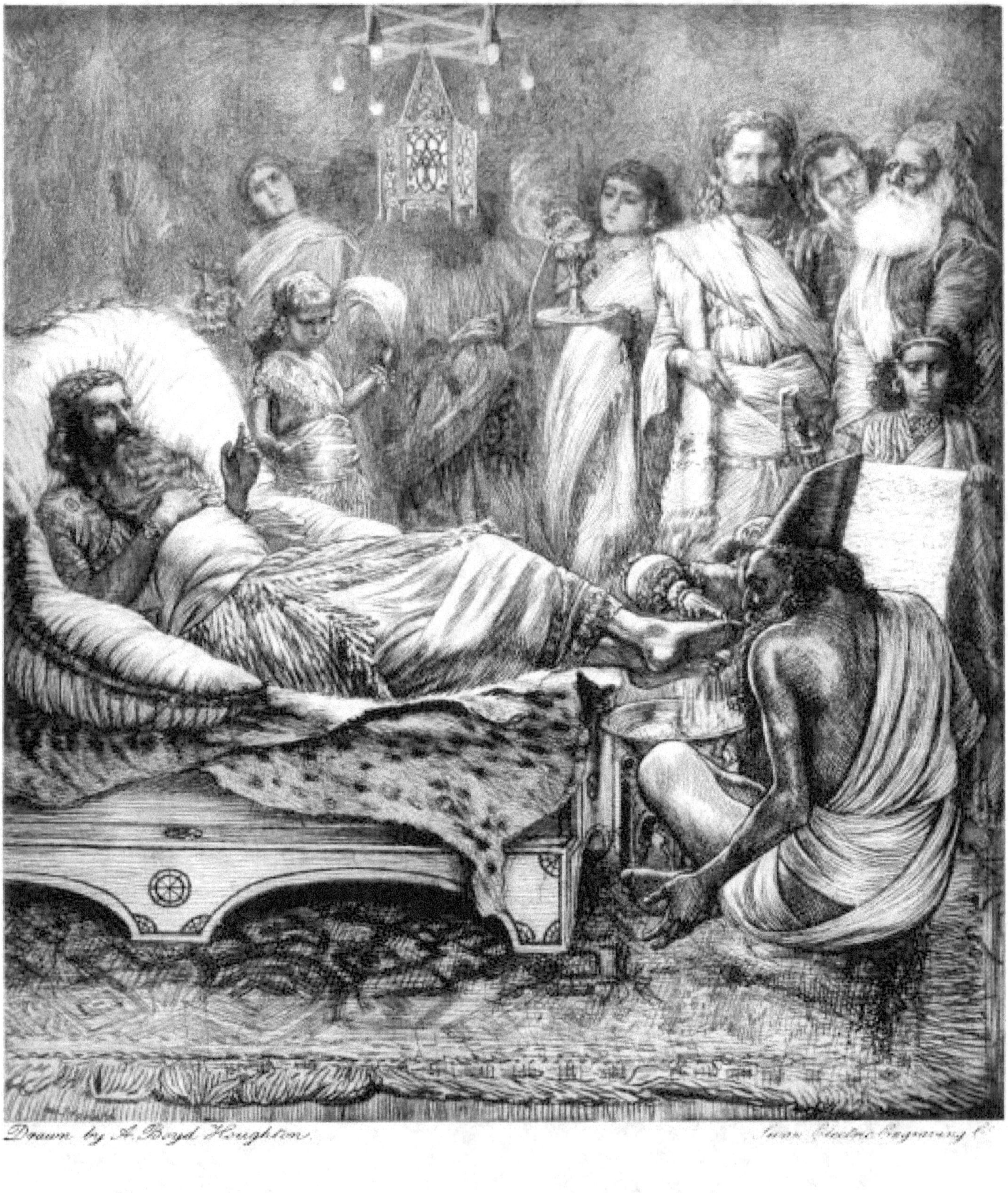

Drawn by A. Boyd Houghton. *Swain Electric Engraving Co.*

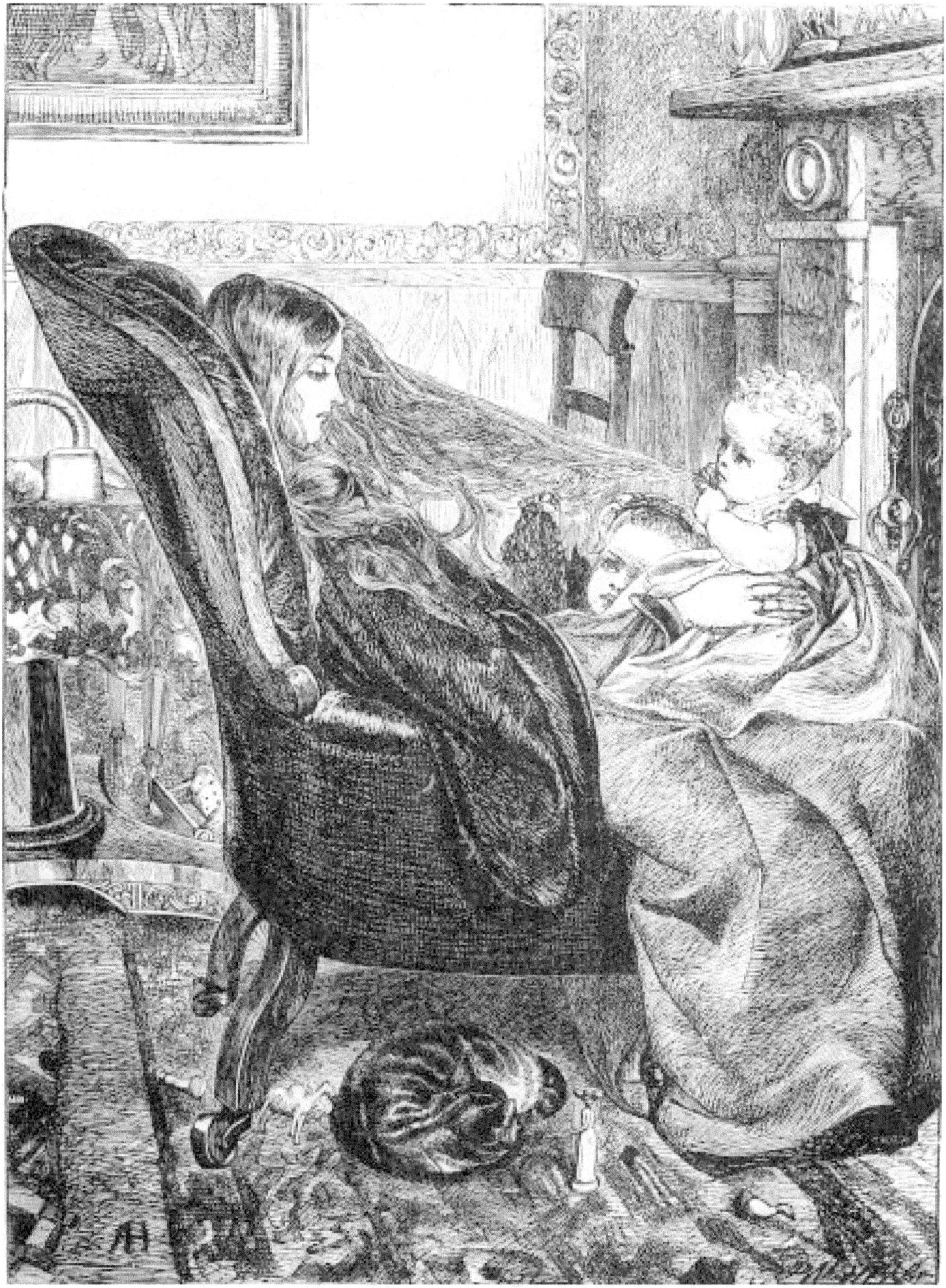

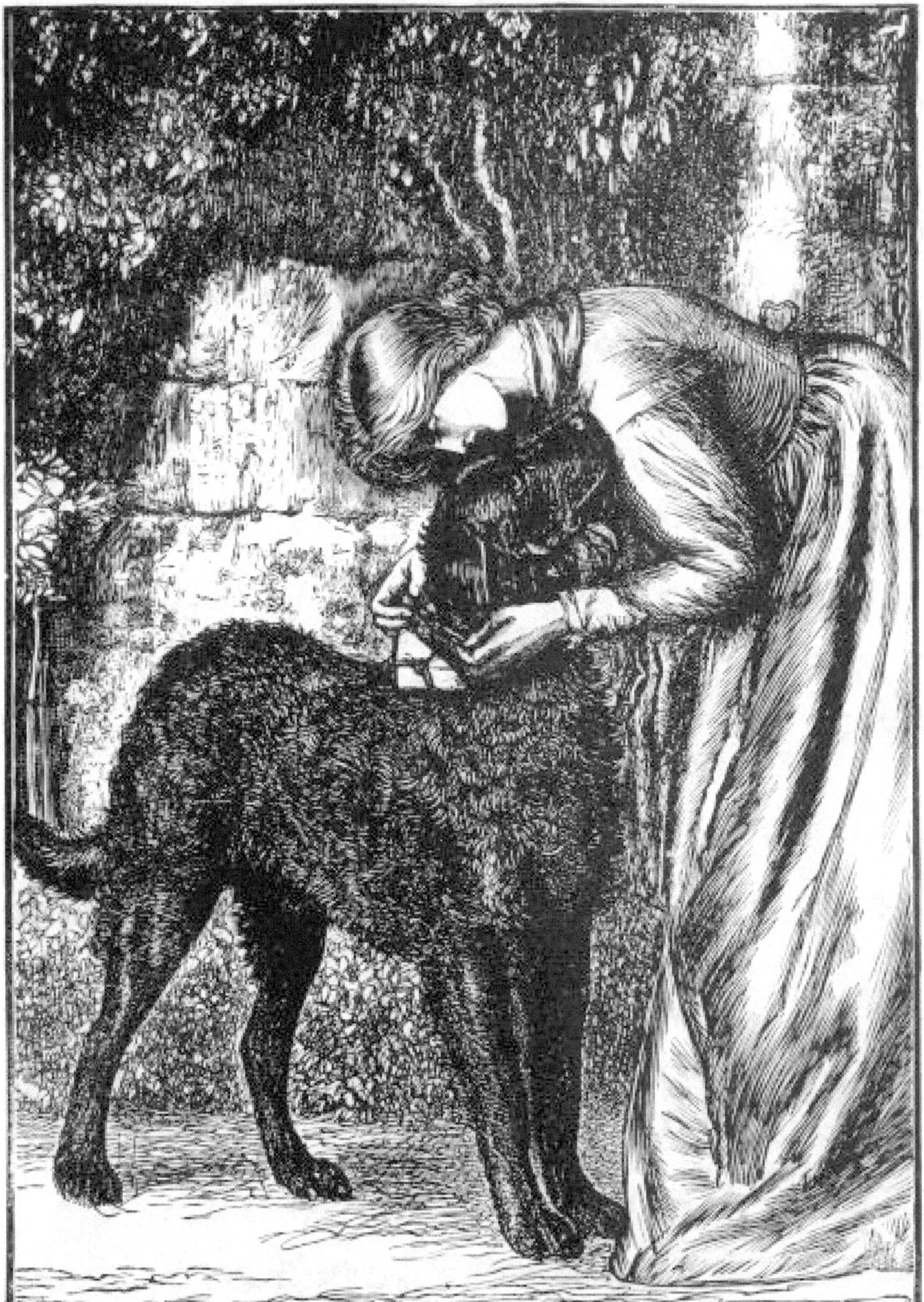

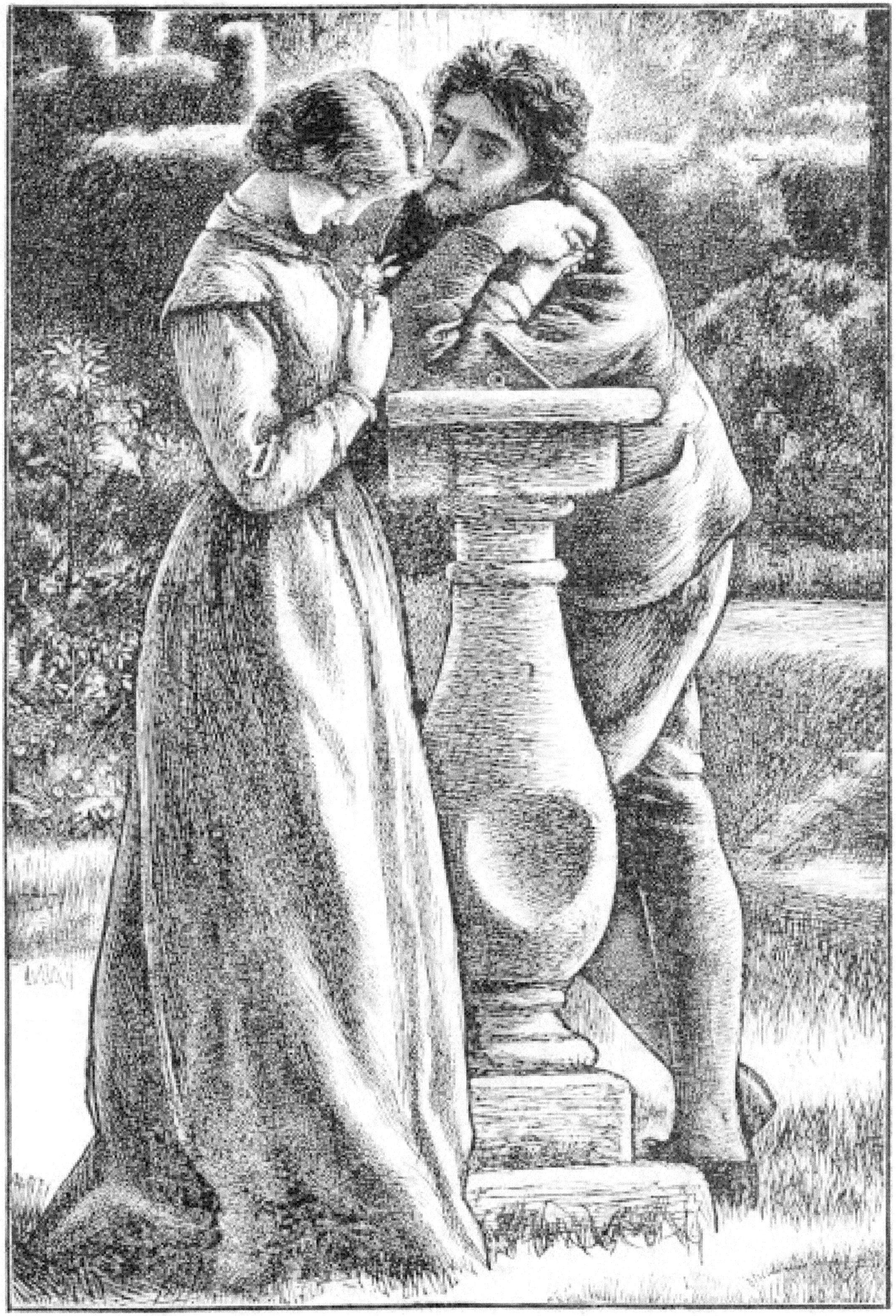

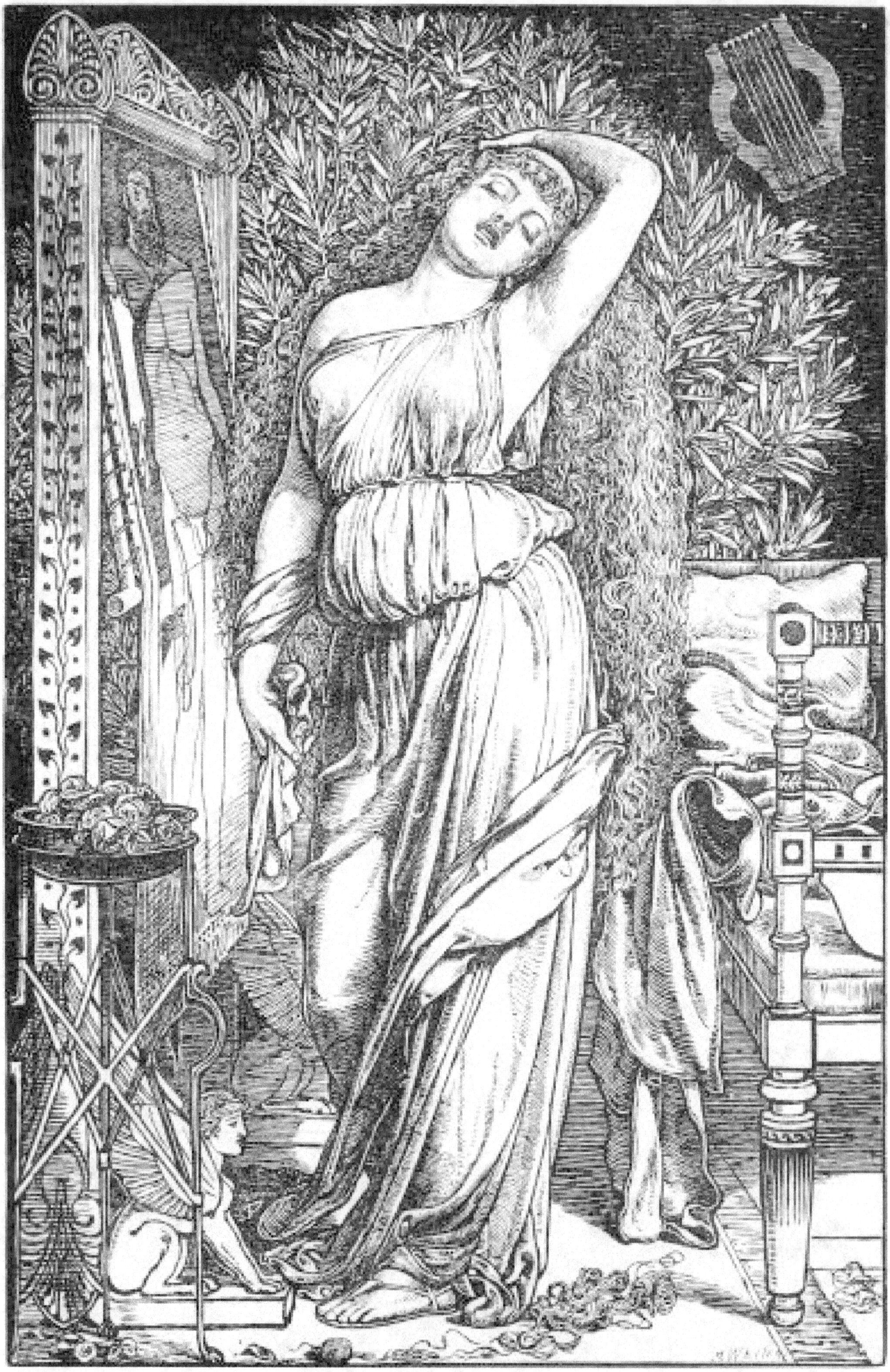

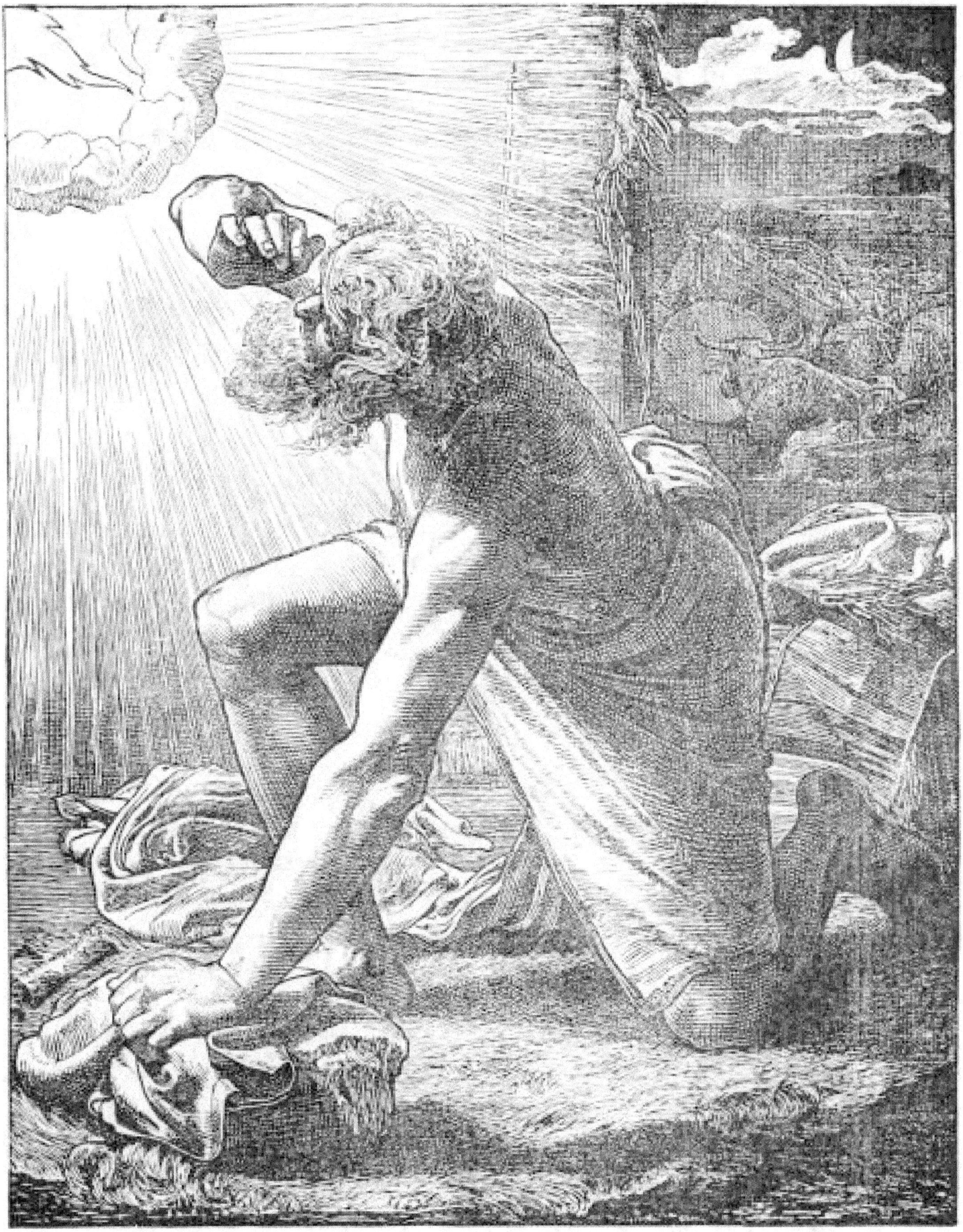

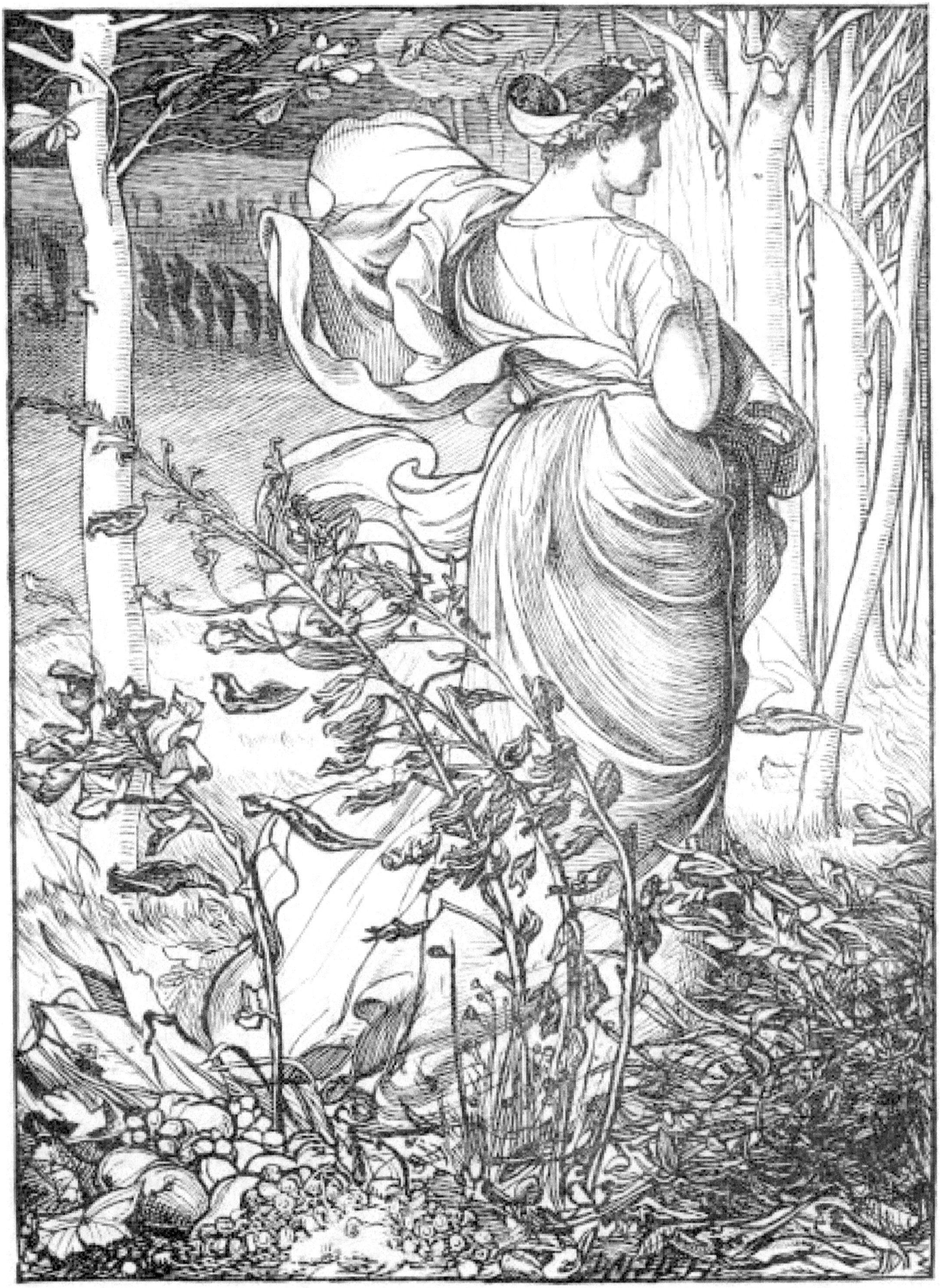

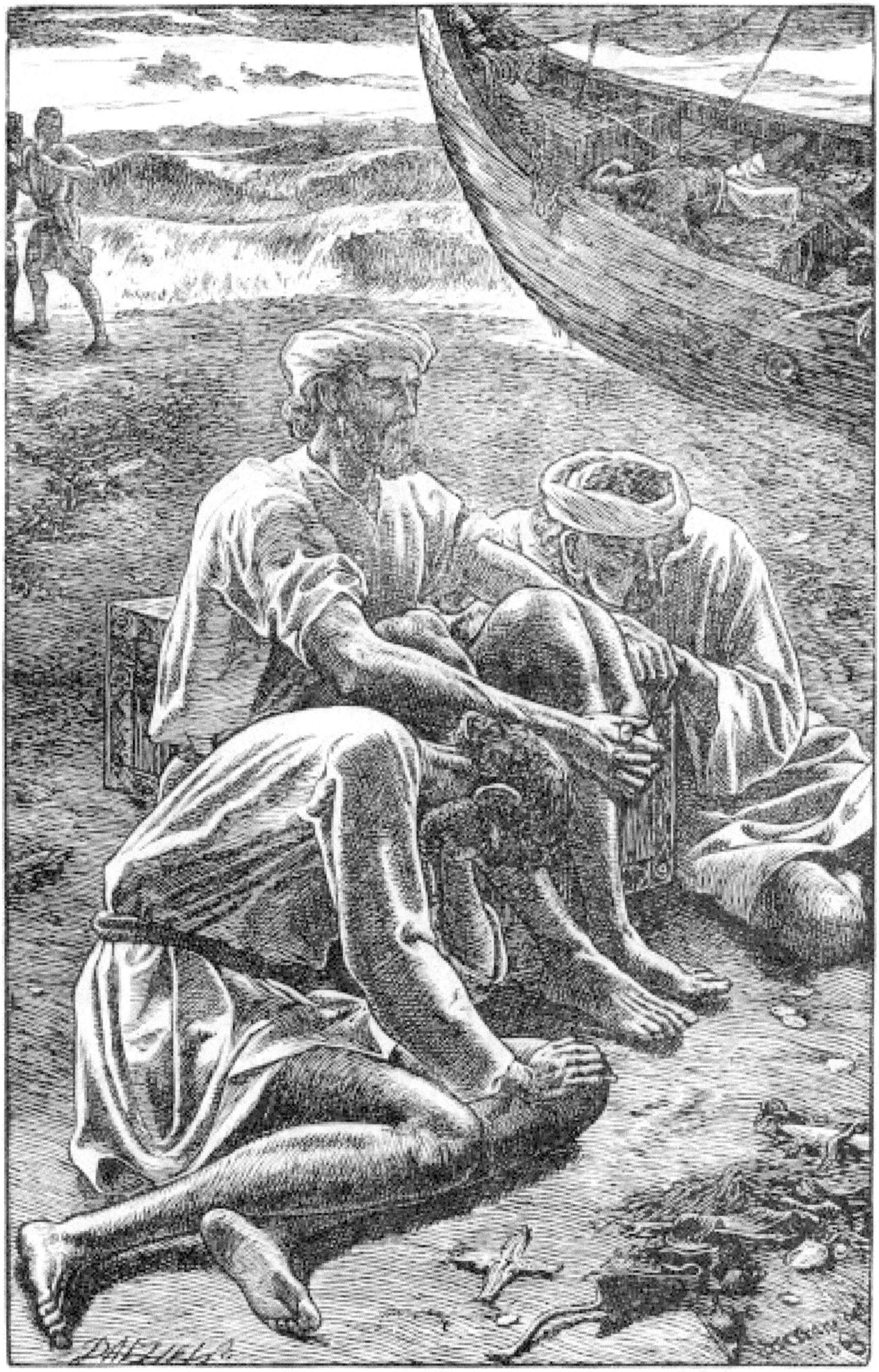
DALZIEL

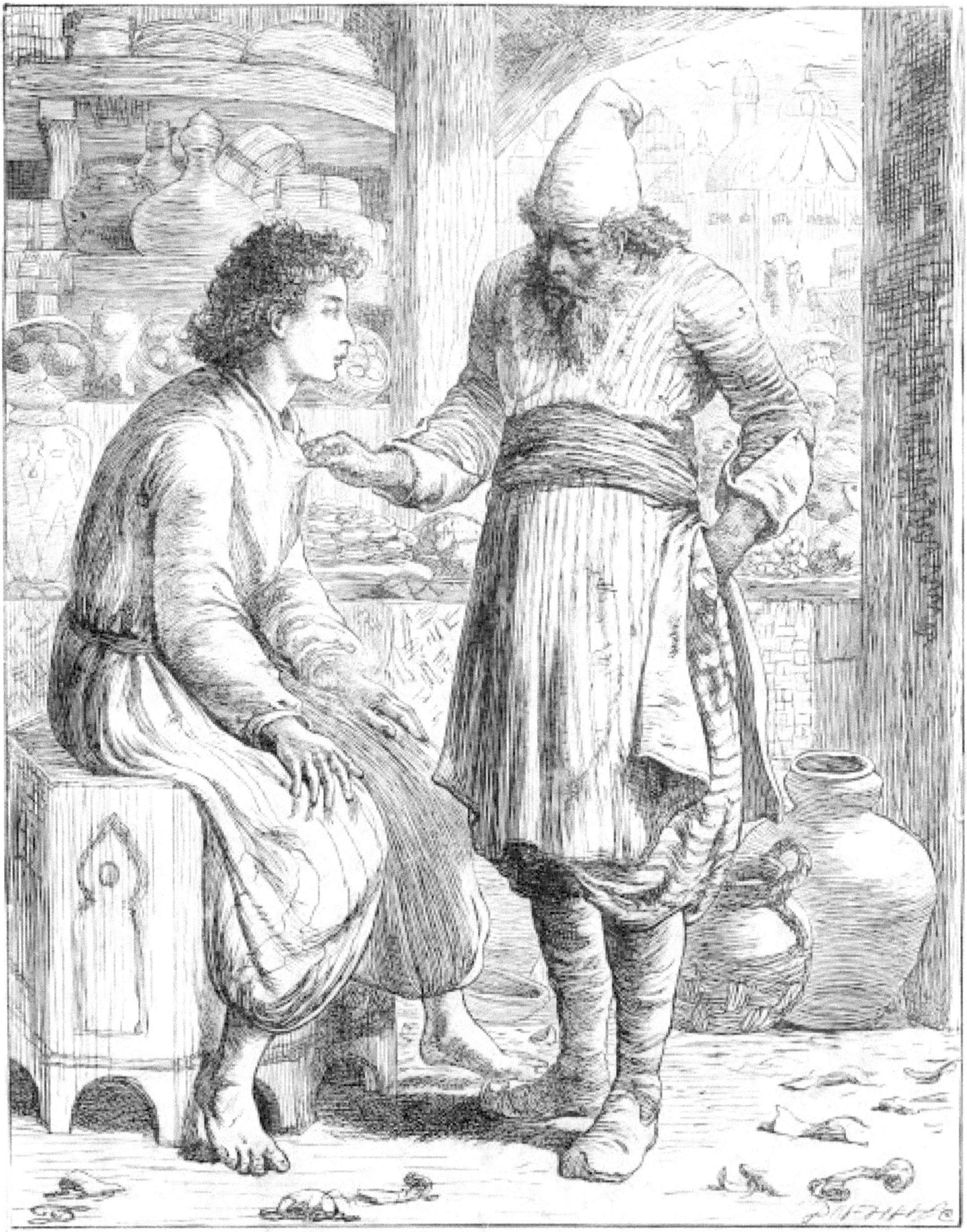

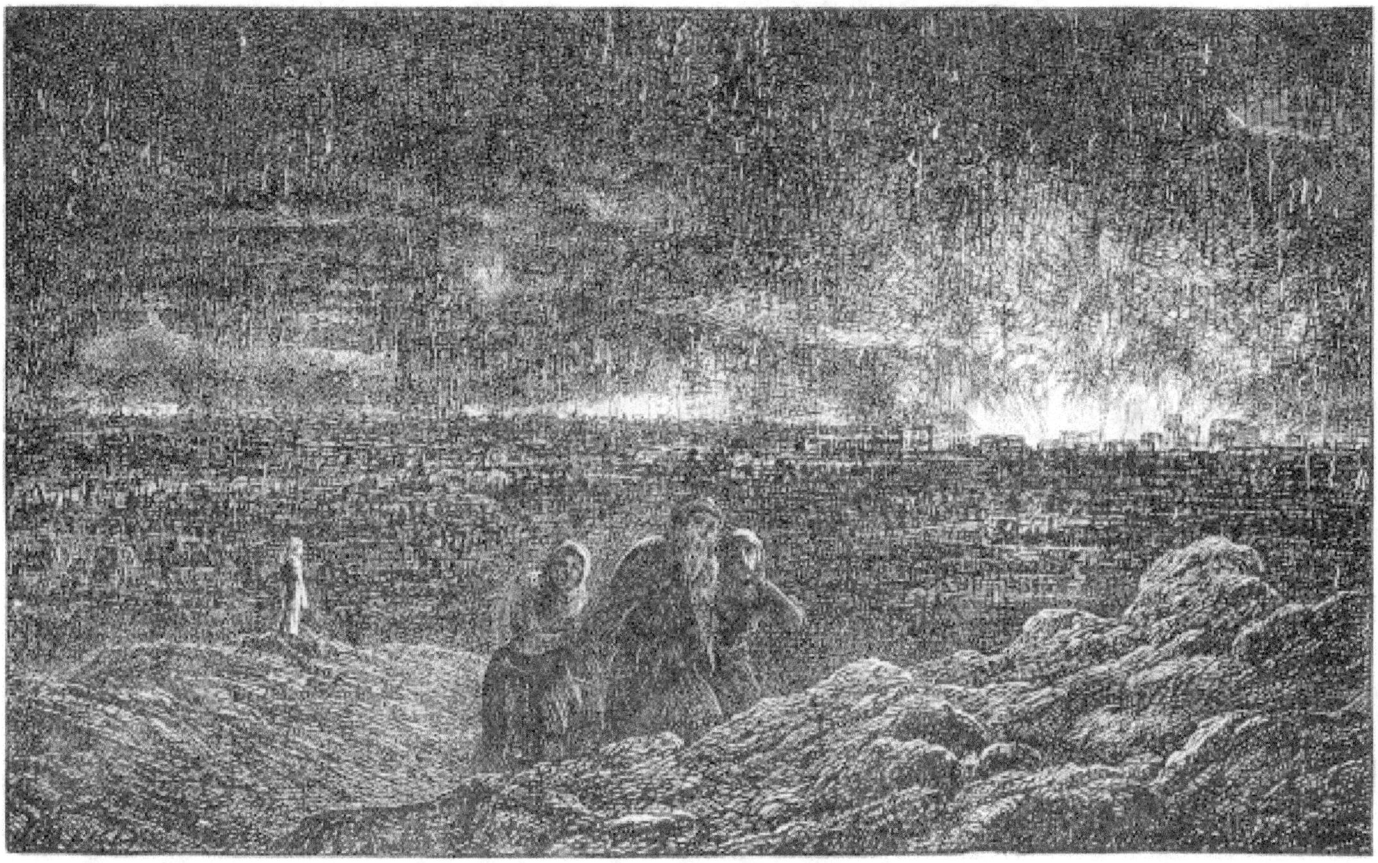

www.ingramcontent.com/pod-product-compliance
Lightning Source LLC
Chambersburg PA
CBHW081113180526
45170CB00008B/2828
* 9 7 8 1 5 4 6 5 7 1 5 1 3 *